Elgar Research Agendas outline the future of research in a given area. Leading scholars are given the space to explore their subject in provocative ways, and map out the potential directions of travel. They are relevant but also visionary.

Forward-looking and innovative, Elgar Research Agendas are an essential resource for PhD students, scholars and anybody who wants to be at the forefront of research.

Titles in the series include:

A Research Agenda for Management and Organization Studies
Edited by Barbara Czarniawska

A Research Agenda for Entrepreneurship and Context
Edited by Friederike Welter and William B. Gartner

A Research Agenda for Cities
Edited by John Rennie Short

A Research Agenda for Neoliberalism
Kean Birch

A Research Agenda for Human Resource Management
Edited by Paul Sparrow and Cary L. Cooper, CBE

A Research Agenda for Shrinking Cities
Justin B. Hollander

A Research Agenda for Women and Entrepreneurship
Edited by Patricia G. Greene and Candida G. Brush

A Research Agenda for Entrepreneurial Cognition and Intention
Edited by Malin Brännback and Alan L. Carsrud

A Research Agenda for Entrepreneurial Cognition and Intention

Edited by

MALIN BRÄNNBACK

Dean and Professor of International Business,
Åbo Akademi University, Finland

ALAN L. CARSRUD

Visiting Research Professor and Docent
Åbo Akademi University, Finland and
Visiting Research Professor, Paris
Business School, France

Elgar Research Agendas

Edward Elgar
PUBLISHING

Cheltenham, UK • Northampton, MA, USA

Published by
Edward Elgar Publishing Limited
The Lypiatts
15 Lansdown Road
Cheltenham
Glos GL50 2JA
UK

Edward Elgar Publishing, Inc.
William Pratt House
9 Dewey Court
Northampton
Massachusetts 01060
USA

A catalogue record for this book
is available from the British Library

Library of Congress Control Number: 2017950446

This book is available electronically in the **Elgar**online
Business subject collection
DOI 10.4337/9781784716813

MIX
Paper from
responsible sources
FSC® C013604

ISBN 978 1 78471 680 6 (cased)
ISBN 978 1 78471 681 3 (eBook)

Typeset by Servis Filmsetting Ltd, Stockport, Cheshire
Printed and bound by CPI Group (UK) Ltd, Croydon, CR0 4YY

Contents

List of contributors   vii

1   Where do we go from here? A research agenda for
    entrepreneurial cognitions   1
    Malin Brännback and Alan L. Carsrud

2   "Cruel intention" or "entrepreneurial intention": what did you expect?
    An overview of research on entrepreneurial intention—an
    interactive perspective   7
    *Adnane Maalaoui, Charles Perez, Gaël Bertrand, Myriam Razgallah and
    Rony Germon*

3   Who is the entrepreneur? The right question has been asked, in the
    wrong way   47
    Kelly G. Shaver and Alan L. Carsrud

4   A proposed model for the culture's mode of influence on the
    entrepreneurial process   62
    Francisco Liñán and Inmaculada Jaén

5   Theory of trying and "we-intentions": from individual to collective
    intentions in entrepreneurship and family business   84
    Malin Brännback, Alan L. Carsrud and Norris Krueger

6   Implementation intentions: the when, where, and how of
    entrepreneurial intentions' influence on behavior   105
    Leon Schjoedt

7   Revisiting entrepreneurial motivation and opportunity recognition   122
    Ronit Yitshaki and Fredric Kropp

8   On the use of configurational analysis in entrepreneurial research   142
    József Mezei and Shahrokh Nikou

9   Cognition to culture: a still-missing link in the development of an
    entrepreneurial resource   161
    Patricia G. Greene and Candida G. Brush

10 The co-development process of new venture ideas and
    entrepreneurs' learning   178
    Tadeu F. Nogueira and Gry A. Alsos

11   Entrepreneurial language through a linguistic lens:
     emerging opportunities   204
     Diana M. Hechavarría and Amy Ingram

Index   215

Contributors

Gry A. Alsos is Professor of Innovation and Entrepreneurship at Nord University Business School, Norway, where she also acts as Program Director of the PhD program. Her research interests include entrepreneurial behavior and new venture start-up processes, entrepreneurship policy, as well as family and gender perspectives to entrepreneurship. She is particularly interested in how different types of entrepreneurs develop their ventures and how they acquire and utilize knowledge and other resources in these processes. She is Field Editor of Entrepreneurship in the *Scandinavian Journal of Management* and is on the editorial board of *Entrepreneurship Theory and Practice*.

Gaël Bertrand received his PhD from the University of Montpellier, France, in 2010. He is currently Associate Professor at the Paris School of Business. His research interests are entrepreneurship and outcomes of newly founded firms and, more generally, SME success and survival.

Malin Brännback is Professor of International Business and also the Dean at Åbo Akademi University, Finland, where she received her doctoral degree in Management Science in 1996. She has also held a BSc in Pharmacy from Åbo Akademi University since 1986. She has been visiting Professor in Entrepreneurship at Stockholm Business School, Sweden, from 2012 to 2014. She has published widely on entrepreneurship, biotechnology business, and knowledge management. She has co-authored several books with Alan L. Carsrud, including: *Understanding the Entrepreneurial Mind – Opening the Black Box* (2009) Springer Verlag; *Handbook of Research Methods and Applications in Entrepreneurship and Small Businesses* (2014) Edward Elgar; *Revisiting the Entrepreneurial Mind – Inside the Black Box* (2017) Springer Verlag. She is on the review board of the *Journal of Small Business Management*. Her current research interests are in entrepreneurial intentionality, entrepreneurial cognition and entrepreneurial growth and performance in technology entrepreneurship, as well as social media use.

Candida G. Brush is the Vice Provost of Global Entrepreneurial Leadership and a Full Professor at Babson College, MA, USA, and is holder of the Franklin W. Olin Chair in Entrepreneurship. She is well known for her pioneering research in women's entrepreneurship. She is a Visiting Adjunct Professor to the Bodø Graduate School, Nord University, Norway. Professor Brush is a founding member of the Diana Project International and holds an honorary doctorate from Jönköping University, Sweden, for her contributions to entrepreneurship research. Her research investigates nascent entrepreneurial ventures, women's entrepreneurship and financing of growth-oriented ventures. She is an active angel investor and serves on the boards of several companies.

Alan L. Carsrud is Visiting Research Professor and Docent at Åbo Akademi University, Finland and Visiting Research Professor, Paris Business School, France. His prior academic positions include the Loretta Rogers Chair in Entrepreneurship at the Ted Rogers School of Management at Ryerson University in Toronto, ON, Canada; Clinical Professor of Entrepreneurship, Professor of Industrial & Systems Engineering, Professor of Hospitality Management, and Executive Director of the Eugenio Pino & Family Global Entrepreneurship Center at Florida International University, FL, USA; Senior Lecturer and Academic Coordinator of the Price Center at the Anderson School at University of California Los Angeles (UCLA) and Senior Lecturer in Electrical Engineering at UCLA, CA, USA. He has also been on the graduate faculties of the Australian Graduate School of Management, Bond University (QLD, Australia); Anahuac University (Mexico); Nanyang Technological University (Singapore); University of Southern California (CA, USA); Pepperdine University (CA, USA) and The University of Texas at Austin (TX, USA). He is a Fellow of the Family Firm Institute. He is Associate Editor of the *Journal of Small Business Management*, and co-founded *Entrepreneurship and Regional Development.* He founded the UCLA Venture Development and Global Access Programs, which help create new, technology-based ventures in Australia, Chile, Finland, France, Italy, Mexico and the USA. In addition, he created the Family and Closely-Held Business Program at UCLA. He has published over 200 articles and chapters on entrepreneurship, family business, and psychology, and has co-authored with Dr. Malin Brännback several books on entrepreneurship and family business.

Rony Germon received his PhD from the University of Technology of Troyes, France, in 2013. He is currently Associate Professor at the Paris School of Business. His research interests include crowdfunding, big data, digital transformation, and entrepreneurship.

Patricia G. Greene is the Paul T. Babson Chair in Entrepreneurial Studies at Babson College. Dr. Greene served as the founding National Academic Director of Goldman Sachs *10,000 Small Businesses* and currently serves as the Global Academic Director of the *10,000 Women* program. Greene is a founding member of the Diana Project, a research group dedicated to studying women business owners and their businesses. She is a former federal appointee to the national advisory board for the Small Business Administration's Small Business Development Centers. Her latest entrepreneurial endeavor is as a co-owner of Artworks, a specialty store in Gettysburg, PA, USA.

Diana M. Hechavarría is an Assistant Professor of Entrepreneurship in the Muma College of Business at the University of South Florida, FL, USA. Hechavarría investigates the various dynamics confronted by founders during the start-up process. Her research interests tend to focus on how various social processes and institutional factors influence individuals differentially when aiming to establish a new firm. Hechavarría's research has been published in journals such as *Entrepreneurship Theory & Practice*; *Small Business Economics*; *International Journal of Gender and Entrepreneurship*; *Journal of Business and Entrepreneurship*; *International Journal of Entrepreneurial Behavior & Research*; *International Journal of Entrepreneurship and Innovation*; and *International Entrepreneurship and Management Journal*. Hechavarría has a PhD in Business Administration from University of Cincinnati (OH, USA), an MA in Liberal Studies from Florida International University (FL, USA), and a BA in Sociology from University of Florida (FL, USA).

Amy Ingram is an Assistant Professor of Strategy and Entrepreneurship at Clemson University, SC, USA. She received her doctorate from the University of Cincinnati, OH, USA, in 2011. Her research focuses on the intersection of non-market strategy, entrepreneurship, paradox, linguistics, and gender.

Inmaculada Jaén has a PhD in Economics (2014) from the University of Seville, Spain, with international mention. Inmaculada is an Assistant Professor of Economics at the Department of Applied Economics, University of Seville, and a member of the research group "SMEs and Economic Development". She has participated in several research projects, funded by the regional and national administrations. Dr. Jaén is taking part in the ELITE project (Ref.: ECO2016-75655-P) financed by the Ministry of Economy and Competitiveness in Spain. Dr. Jaén has published a number of contributions in academic journals and edited books.

Fredric Kropp is a Professor Emeritus at the Middlebury Institute of International Studies at Monterey, CA, USA, and is a Professor of Entrepreneurship, Innovation and Creativity at the Entrepreneurship, Commercialisation and Innovation Centre at the University of Adelaide, SA, Australia. Over the last decade his research has focused on the motivation of social entrepreneurs, including entrepreneurial passion, identities and compassion, and necessity-based entrepreneurs. Prior to entering academia, Fredric worked for consulting firms that specialized in strategic design, policy analysis, and forecasting, and also as committee staff for the Washington State Senate Energy Committee. He enjoys living in Monterey and traveling.

Norris Krueger received his doctorate from Ohio State University in 1989. A mentee of the late Al Shapiro, he often describes himself as a recovering entrepreneur turned entrepreneurship scholar and educator. Today his interests have turned to social entrepreneurship, in particular building entrepreneurial communities. He continues to balance his entrepreneurial bent with highly cited cutting edge academic work in entrepreneurial cognition to grow entrepreneurial mindsets and growing entrepreneurial ecosystems. Currently, he works in entrepreneurial economic development through his consulting firm, Entrepreneurship Northwest, located in Boise, ID, USA. He formerly served on the faculty of Boise State University, but now maintains his academic research in entrepreneurship through multiple outlets, including as a Research Fellow with the Center for Global Business Research, School of Advanced Studies, AZ, USA.

Francisco Liñán is Professor of Entrepreneurship and Innovation at Anglia Ruskin University, UK, and the University of Seville, Spain. Professor Liñáns research interests include entrepreneurship, entrepreneurial intentions and entrepreneurship education, leading to several publications in well-known academic journals. He has participated in projects funded by the Spanish National Government, EU and OECD, and is the Main Researcher in the ELITE Project (Ref.: ECO2016-75655-P). Professor Liñán is Regional Editor at the *Journal of Organizational Change Management* and is an editorial board member at the *International Entrepreneurship and Management Journal, Journal of Global Entrepreneurship Research* and the *International Journal of Management Science and Information Technology.*

Adnane Maalaoui is Head of the Chair for Entrepreneurship and Diversity at the Paris School of Business. His research mainly focuses on issues of entrepreneurship, and in particular disadvantaged entrepreneurs (elderly, immigrant, disabled entrepreneurs, etc.). He works on topics such as entrepreneurial intention and the cognitive approach to entrepreneurship. He mainly applies questions to cases of diversity and social entrepreneurship. Maalaoui is the author of over 20 articles published in academic journals, and has also authored articles published in professional journals and edited books. Maalaoui is the author of a series of French speaking MOOCs on entrepreneurship.

József Mezei is currently a Research Fellow at the School of Business and Management at Lappeenranta University of Technology, Finland. He obtained his DSc in 2011 from Åbo Akademi University, Finland. His recent work has focused on decision making under uncertainty, analytics, soft computing, and fuzzy logic. He has over 60 papers in conference proceedings and journals, including *Information Systems Journal*; *International Journal of Approximate Reasoning*; *Decision Support Systems*; and *IEEE Transactions on Fuzzy Systems.*

Shahrokh Nikou is a Docent of Business Administration, especially in Information Systems at the Åbo Akademi University, Finland. Nikou is currently a Senior Lecturer and Researcher at the Åbo Akademi University. He has also studied at the Royal Institute of Technology (KTH) in Sweden and the University of Technology (TU DEflt) in the Netherlands. Nikou received his PhD (Econ) from the Department of Information Technologies, Åbo Akademi University, Finland, in 2012. He is a member of the editorial board of *Electronic Markets*; *International Journal of Electronic Business Research* (IJEBR); and *International Journal of Web Engineering and Technology* (IJWET), and has been a member of program committees in several IEEEs and international conferences. His current research interests include Information Systems theories, digital economy, and entrepreneurship. Nikou has over 40 articles in journals and conference proceedings.

Tadeu F. Nogueira is a PhD candidate at Nord University, Norway. His research focuses on entrepreneurial learning, entrepreneurial opportunities, new venture creation, and technology-based entrepreneurship. He is especially interested in research questions that explore the opportunity development process from a learning perspective. Nogueira has published research on the ethical dimension of innovation, business ethics, and corporate responsibility. He holds an MSc in Economics and Business Administration, with specialization in innovation and entrepreneurship, from Aalborg University, Denmark. He also holds a bachelor's degree in Business Administration from Santo Andre Foundation University, Brazil.

Charles Perez received his PhD from the University of Technology of Troyes, France, in 2014. He is currently Associate Professor at Paris School of Business. His research interests include social network analysis, big data, data mining, and entrepreneurship.

Myriam Razgallah is currently a second year PhD student in the University of Carthage, Tunisia, and the University of Grenoble, France, under the co-supervision of Olfa Zeribi (Pr, University of Carthage) and Alain Fayolle (Pr, EM Lyon). Her doctoral researches focus on resource acquisition process in social entrepreneurship. Her major research interests include entrepreneurship, entrepreneurial process, and entrepreneurial intentions.

Leon Schjoedt is a Professor of Entrepreneurship and Management at Mahasarakham University, Thailand. His research focuses on entrepreneurial behavior. He has published more than 40 articles and book chapters. Schjoedt's work has appeared in journals, including *Entrepreneurship Theory and Practice*; *International Journal of Entrepreneurial Behaviour & Research*; and *Small Business Economics*, and has been featured in the *Wall Street Journal*. Schjoedt serves on the editorial review boards of several journals, including *Entrepreneurship Theory & Practice*; *Journal of Business Venturing*; and *Journal of Small Business Management*, and he serves as an Associate Editor of *Small Business Economics.*

Kelly G. Shaver is Professor of Entrepreneurial Studies at the College of Charleston, SC, USA. He is a Fellow of the American Psychological Society, a Justin Longenecker Fellow of the United States Association for Small Business and Entrepreneurship, and past Chair of the Entrepreneurship Division of the Academy of Management. Shaver's previous appointments include the College of William & Mary, the Entrepreneurship and Small Business Research Institute in Stockholm, and the National Science Foundation. He has won a teaching award from the Entrepreneurship Division of the Academy of Management, a Best Paper Award from the National Federation of Independent Businesses, and the Distinguished Research Award from College of Charleston School of Business. His internationally recognized entrepreneurship research has been supported by the Ewing Marion Kauffman Foundation and the National Science Foundation. He has served as Editor of *Entrepreneurship Theory and Practice* and is currently an Associate Editor of the *Journal of Small Business Management*. He is the founder of MindCette, LLC, an entrepreneurship testing and consulting company.

Ronit Yitshaki is an Assistant Professor at the Department of Economics and Business Administration at Ariel University, Israel. Her research interests include start-ups' accelerations processes, social entrepreneurship, entrepreneurial motivations and opportunity recognition, entrepreneurial identities, and psychology of entrepreneurship.

1   Where do we go from here? A research agenda for entrepreneurial cognitions

Malin Brännback and Alan L. Carsrud

Focus of this volume

In this edited book of eleven chapters, we examine a variety of approaches that may be useful in advancing our understanding of the cognitions that drive entrepreneurial activity. Although we pay special attention to entrepreneurial intentions because it is perhaps the widely researched cognitions, our focus is far broader. In our previous books on this general topic (Carsrud & Brännback, 2009; Brännback & Carsrud, 2017) we examined a variety of key areas in the psychology of the entrepreneur and subsequently how that research changed over the course of some nine years. We have also suggested that serious research methods issues limit our understanding of entrepreneurial processes (Carsrud & Brännback, 2014). In this volume, we move beyond what has been done to take a more forward-looking approach. We do this by examining areas we feel still have been under-researched, ignored, or are often not thought of as having an impact on the thinking and cognitions of entrepreneurs. We are most appreciative of the publisher, Edward Edgar, for their willingness to allow us to take a more forward-looking approach.

Rationale behind the volume

We were partially driven to this tactic after realizing that most of our fellow researchers and educators in entrepreneurship think they are doing the right thing in the right way. Yet when one asks real entrepreneurs and business owners how they perceive research in the field, few think the published research addresses issues important to them. This is not just cognitive research but most of what we publish in our field. Perhaps we need to not only better understand what our "customer" wants to know, but also other methods of trying to research the cognitive aspects of entrepreneurs. In fact, we are seeing this across all disciplines. Increasing university research is not very highly considered nor is it accessible outside universities. This seems to have become a harsh reality on a global level. The monopoly position of universities as institutions where new knowledge is created is increasingly no longer there. This is especially true of academic schools of business administration, not just the STEM subjects.

Role of relevance

We need to take a broader view of topics and approaches if we are to continue to be relevant as business academics. We cannot continue to borrow theories from other disciplines that are years out of date in those home disciplines like psychology, sociology, and economics. For example, we cannot keep doing the same old intentions studies, based on the Theory of Planned Behavior, with a different population and using the same old linear models (even structure equation models are based on linearity). Most of what is submitted to entrepreneurship journals is fine tuning what we already know. In general, very few new questions are being raised and we are not really providing any great answers. If we look at entrepreneurship research, which should be at its core applied work, we find a lot of the research is not really helping entrepreneurs with their problems. As hard as it may sound, take an unbiased look at articles being published in high impact journals in the field of entrepreneurship. Do these studies really create new and potentially useful knowledge? If you challenge the status quo with a new theory or methodology you are not likely to survive the peer review process, at least with reviewers who may have a vested interest in a given theory or approach.

We have argued, mostly unsuccessful to date, that the field of entrepreneurship like psychology, sociology, anthropology, and strategic management are still seeking the illusive unified definition of the field and, consequently, an underlying theory (or more likely multiple theories) to support a given discipline. Often this search has caused us to lose sight of relevance to the subject of our research, the entrepreneur, and their venture. Entrepreneurship lacks not only a unified theory, but also no real consensus on what should be the topics. Frankly, while it is exciting to have a broad range of topics, we still have disagreements on what are the characteristics of an entrepreneur and an entrepreneurial firm. If we are to make advances, we need to start adopting or developing theories that can give it legitimacy within the general study of social phenomena and relevance to those who practice it.

Volume overview

Thus we have asked a number of our colleagues to weigh in on the future direction of the cognitive study of entrepreneurs. They were asked not to review what has been done, but to propose new directions that may be more fruitful and relevant. As a result, we have eleven chapters that cover more traditional areas like intentions and motivations, to new research tools and models, the role culture plays in changing cognitions, and how language impacts the entrepreneur. A brief discussion of the contents of each subsequent chapter to this introductory one follows.

Chapter 2

We begin this edited volume with a chapter that uses a novel way to look at the area of entrepreneurial intentions research that employs a methodology that allows a look at the true complexity of intentions. For over three decades, hundreds of studies have been conducted in a wide range of contexts on entrepreneurial intent and subsequent behavior. As a result, numerous researchers have addressed a wide range of concepts and themes. However, due to the number of articles, chapters, and books, it has become more and more difficult to link all those different concepts. The aim of this chapter, therefore, is to provide a map of the structure topics around entrepreneurial intent and behavior. This allows the reader to develop an appropriate "sightseeing tour" of this entrepreneurial theme that has become increasingly relevant to many researchers and policy makers. You can think of this as a map of the field, the sub-concepts, and the key research players.

Chapter 3

This chapter builds upon the "on again–off again" attempt to find a unique entrepreneurial personality. The authors show how the examination of entrepreneurial personality was largely abandoned when a systematic attempt to study motivation in entrepreneurs, using then "state-of-the-art" theories of achievement motivation, failed to find a "unique model" for entrepreneurs. They also demonstrate that the study of the entrepreneur as *a whole individual* has not usually been the unit of analysis. Too often studies of "personality" at best have been studies of observable behaviors, which some confuse for personality traits. One of the dangers confronting anyone who would borrow theory and method from another discipline is that the borrowing may be incomplete in some critical way. This problem can be exacerbated if the borrowing is done by scholars who, though well-meaning and conscientious, were not originally trained in the parent discipline. The authors then discuss the most recent approach to personality research in psychology, which uses the Big Five (or Six) Factors. One of the objectives of modern personality measurement has been to identify just a few latent dimensions on which people can be characterized. The "Big Five" are Conscientiousness, Agreeableness, Neuroticism, Openness to experience, and Extraversion arranged in one mnemonic order: CANOE.

Chapter 4

In this chapter, our colleagues acknowledge that entrepreneurial intention models are well established in the entrepreneurship literature. However, they note the persistent problem of the low rate of transformation of intentions into action. They note that we still know little about the factors that contribute to this transformation. This chapter focuses on the role of culture in the entrepreneurial process. By identifying two components of culture (values and practices) the authors argue that the mode of influence for each is different. That is, cultural values shape personal motivations, attitudes and intentions, while cultural practices affect the actual start-up behaviors. More importantly they note that the interaction with the economic conditions must also be considered. They conclude by providing an integrative model for the culture's mode of influence on the entrepreneurial process.

Chapter 5

This chapter challenges the vast majority of existing work on intentions by arguing we need to improve our understanding of the role of intentions in start-up teams of entrepreneurs and family firm succession by moving beyond the traditional view of individual intentions in entrepreneurial settings and toward understanding collective intentions. For example, in a start-up there is often a small group whose individual intentions for entering the firm and setting its strategic direction must blend to some form of consensus such as marketing and growth strategy. In addition, in a family firm the intentions toward succession are as much collective as individual. If we seek we-intent to increase the possibility of successful succession, then a focus on "we" intentions allows for a better understanding of the potentially conflicting intentions of key individuals. This chapter argues that the conceptualization of collective intent, such as "we-intentions", offers a better understanding of group processes from a social cognition perspective, especially those of succession. However, collective intentions (and their measurement) are still less understood.

Chapter 6

As in the previous chapter, this one looks at the wide application of the Theory of Planned Behavior (TPB) in entrepreneurship research to predict intention to start a new venture, entrepreneurial intention. It shows that very limited research has examined the relationship between entrepreneurial intentions and the subsequent enactment of those intentions. Even though TPB is considered sufficient and enjoys impressive meta-analytical support, research on the association between intentions and behavior is wanting. What this chapter proposes is the role of Implementation Intentions. This conceptualization holds potential to shed light upon the intention-behavior relationship, conceptually and empirically. Thus, the chapter draws attention to implementation intentions for future research to enhance explanation and prediction of when, where, and how some, but not others, enact their entrepreneurial intentions by launching new ventures.

Chapter 7

The focus of this chapter returns to the role of motivation. As the authors note, research in entrepreneurial motivation often suffers from narrow theoretical articulation and a lack of integration of the psychological, cognitive, and affective aspects. Over the past decade there has been renewed interest in affective components of entrepreneurial motivation, including passion, compassion, and founder's self- and social identities and the role they play in opportunity recognition and venture formation. This chapter provides a new understanding of entrepreneurial motivation based on an integrative review of cognitive and affective motivational constructs and opportunity recognition. The authors conclude with a process model and provide directions for future research.

Chapter 8

In this chapter the focus moves to shifting methodologies for studying entrepreneurial cognitions. The authors acknowledge that understanding entrepreneurial intention has been – and still is – a highly relevant research problem. Traditional approaches in this domain utilize theories rooted in the Theory of Reasoned Action and Theory of Planned Behavior, and rely on tools offered by regression analysis-based approaches. In contrast to this widely used combination, the authors demonstrate why new theoretically justified constructs and a more causal explanation-oriented data analysis approach can complement and improve existing literature. Where previous research tests the individual impact of independent variables on one or two dependent variables, this chapter introduces a method that analyzes the combined effects of variables on an outcome through Fuzzy-set Qualitative Comparative Analysis (FsQCA). FsQCA can be used as a basis of performing classification tasks to identify individuals with entrepreneurial intention potential. With this approach we see that there is more than one solution to a specific outcome. This, in turn, may partially explain why many previous entrepreneurial intention studies have provided mixed results across different samples. The introduced approach also addresses one of the most important methodological shortcomings of FsQCA, namely parameter selection in deriving important sufficient rules. The authors demonstrate this contribution using a dataset collected from eight countries.

Chapter 9

This chapter looks at the contextual variable of organizational culture as a resource that impacts organizational growth and/or success by guiding both structure and function of a venture serving as a source of competitive advantage. The authors note that culture is sometimes directly studied in the entrepreneurship research, but is most likely considered as the creation of an "entrepreneurial culture" in a venture or an entrepreneurial climate for a geographic region. What needs an answer is the question of how the organizational culture of a new venture is created. Given that organizational culture is based on a system of shared values and beliefs, the authors propose an articulated pathway of the cognitive relationship between the values and beliefs of the founder(s) and the eventual culture of the founded organization. In reviewing the literature, they show how the perceptions, expectations, and values of the founder(s) influence the kind of business and its growth patterns over time. However, what is still needed is research that examines how aspects of the entrepreneur's identity are manifested inside the new organization, the processes by which this occurs, and the structure and organizational practices it may lead to for all members. The authors go beyond our current understanding of the pathway between individual identity, entrepreneurial identity, and organizational identity in order to explore organizational culture predicated as a key component of that organizational identity. They finally propose a preliminary conceptual framework and propositions regarding the pathway for culture creation in new ventures and conclude with suggestions for future research as well as the impact on entrepreneurship education and practice.

Chapter 10

Following the previous chapter on entrepreneurial education, this chapter examines the extant literature, which recognizes the important role of learning in the entrepreneurial process. Learning has clearly been a cognitive process that has largely been ignored by entrepreneurship researchers. However, few studies have explored how learning takes place in a mutual interaction with new venture ideas (NVIs). This paper aims to build theoretical understanding about the interplays between the developments of NVIs and how entrepreneurs learn. Using an inductive multiple-case study with six entrepreneurs in Norway, the authors find that NVIs trigger the learning of entrepreneurs at several occasions and, by transforming experiences into knowledge, thus entrepreneurs further develop the new venture ideas. The chapter focuses on the mechanisms of this co-development process.

Chapter 11

This chapter builds on entrepreneurship as narratives and discourse reflecting the thoughts and actions of the entrepreneur. Existing work shows the importance of the entrepreneurial language because the words individuals speak are proxies of their thoughts that guide their behaviors. Words are how entrepreneurs communicate their thoughts and desires to others. By studying language, researchers can gain insights into the entrepreneur's world, and by looking at language, one gains an understanding of the cognitive factors that drive entrepreneurial intention and action during the complex process of new venture creation. Recent work in entrepreneurship has begun to lever linguistic lenses to understand how language influences entrepreneurial behavior. Linguistic theories and analysis build upon and extend the discursive and narrative analysis. The authors note that linguistics differs from narratives and discourse analysis, and is the scientific study of language, focusing on the actual structure of language, patterns, word grouping, among other areas, to demonstrate how the language an actor uses can impact many decisions, including economic decisions, and is an important influential intuitional force.

References

Brännback, M. & Carsrud, A. L. (eds) (2017). *Revisiting the Entrepreneurial Mind: Inside the Black Box.* Springer: New York, NY.

Carsrud, A. L. & Brännback, M. (eds) (2009). *Understanding the Entrepreneurial Mind: Opening the Black Box.* Springer: New York, NY.

Carsrud, A. L. & Brännback, M. (eds) (2014). *Handbook of Research Methods and Applications in Entrepreneurship and Small Business.* Edward Edgar: Cheltenham, UK.

2 "Cruel intention" or "entrepreneurial intention": what did you expect? An overview of research on entrepreneurial intention—an interactive perspective

Adnane Maalaoui, Charles Perez, Gaël Bertrand, Myriam Razgallah and Rony Germon

Introduction

In the past 20 years, many studies have been conducted on entrepreneurial intent and behavior in various contexts (Krueger and Carsrud, 1993; Kolvereid, 1996; Liñán, 2008; Liñán and Chen, 2009; Liñán et al., 2011; Douglas and Fitzsimmons, 2013; Kautonen et al., 2013; Kibler, 2013; Walter et al., 2013; Fayolle and Liñán, 2014). As a result, numerous researchers have addressed these issues. However, due to the number of works now available, it is increasingly difficult to connect their findings. This chapter therefore structures topics around entrepreneurial intent and behavior to gain an appropriate overview of this increasingly relevant entrepreneurial sub-theme.

Conceptual framework

There are many studies on entrepreneurial intention. Some are based on the work of Azjen (1991) and focus on the Theory of Planned Behavior (TPB), whilst others, based on the work of Shapéro and Sokol (1982), examine the Theory of Entrepreneurial Advent. In relation to the former, the structure of such a theory and model essentially leans on reflections around cognitive models. In 1969, Azjen and Fishbein began studying the psychology of intention, and in 1972, 1974, and 1977, they (or at least Azjen) explored the influence of behaviors and social beliefs on intention (Ajzen and Fishbein, 1969, 1972, 1977; Fishbein and Ajzen, 1974).

It was only at the beginning of the 1980s that Azjen explained the influence of attitudes on the behavior and actions of individuals. In 1991, Azjen developed the TPB.

He later proposed the influence of attitudes, social norms, and perceived behavior control on intention and behavior (action). This model has been repeatedly used in studies on entrepreneurship. It became a cornerstone in 2011 when entrepreneurial studies recommended a method to build a referential with which it was possible to test and measure the concept of intention, as employed in this chapter and inspired by the works of Kautonen et al. (2013). The applicability of the Azjen's model (1991), or that of Shapéro and Sokol (1982), makes sense in the field of entrepreneurship.

As Liñán and Chen (2009) explain, cognitive variables may explain decision making (Baron, 2004; Shaver and Scott, 1991) and thus there may be unexplored variables that allow for an understanding of entrepreneurial intent. Many studies, as seen in the works of Carsrud and Brännback (2011) and Krueger and Day (2010), have been conducted based on the connection between cognitive and entrepreneurship (see Bandura, 1997; and other researchers, including Khun, 2008; Liñán, 2008; Liñán and Chen, 2009; Liñán et al., 2011; Douglas and Fitzsimmons, 2013; Walter et al., 2013; Fayolle and Liñán, 2014). Moreover, many studies have been conducted on diverse contexts (see Kautonen et al., 2013 or Kibler, 2013). Such work clarifies specific and singular behaviors and entrepreneurial intentions with regard to a national culture.

It should be emphasized that the concept of entrepreneurial intent is seeking to widen its topics of interest. This can be seen in growth intent, as explained by Kolvereid and Bullvag (1996), education on process or contexts (Liñán and Fayolle, 2015), and with specific entrepreneurial populations, such as seniors (Kautonen et al., 2013).

Entrepreneurial intention is increasingly emerging in the field of entrepreneurship. Several studies have addressed entrepreneurial intention in different contexts. After reviewing the literature of entrepreneurial intention, this study proposes that there are three major types. In general, a major aspect of entrepreneurial intention studies develops antecedents of intention (motivation, values, personal characteristics, culture, etc.). Other authors are interested in exploring the path between intention and action. Some scholars attempt to explain how an entrepreneurial intention can be put into action, examining what motivates an entrepreneur to convert an intention into a concrete action. Others have shown interest in further developing Ajzen's TPB and have tried to find support for its three dimensions, or to extend it with additional dimensions.

In contrast to previous research and compared to Ajzen's TPB, little attention has been paid to the Shapéro Entrepreneurial Event (SEE) model. For this reason, the most famous antecedents of entrepreneurial intention are those of Ajzen's TPB, namely personal attitudes toward behavior, subjective norms, and perceived behavioral control, integrated into self-efficacy by several scholars.

In entrepreneurship literature, different definitions of entrepreneurial intention have been proposed. For instance, Ajzen (2011) defines intention as "a person's readiness to perform a given behavior" (Ajzen cited in Kautonen et al., 2015: 2).

Bird (1988) defined entrepreneurial intention as "a state of mind that directs and guides the actions of the individual toward the development and implementation of a new business concept" (Karimi et al., 2016: 188). Kruger et al. (2000: 420) define intention as "the target behaviors of starting a business". Biraglia and Kadile (2017) argue that entrepreneurial intention predicts entrepreneurial behavior and is action-oriented. Krueger et al. (2000) stipulate that entrepreneurship is an intentional process in the way that individuals plan to undertake an entrepreneurial career. Indeed, it is not *only* a response to certain stimulus, it is a planned behavior (Lortie and Castogiovanni, 2015). Bird (1988) also claims that entrepreneurial intention implies attention, experience with business ideas or concepts, and action (Wurthmann, 2014).

Based on these definitions, it is possible to say that intention is the state of mind that drives an individual to begin a business and that it precedes entrepreneurial behavior (Lortie and Castogiovanni, 2015).

Researchers have been giving increased attention to the study of entrepreneurial intention because they aim to understand what drives some individuals to undertake entrepreneurial careers. The following paragraphs discuss recent research and provide a general overview of studies on intention.

Biraglia and Kadile (2017) investigate the path from practicing entrepreneurship as a hobby to developing an actual entrepreneurial intention based on the role of three factors, namely a person's entrepreneurial creativity, passion, and environmental factors. They have found that entrepreneurial passion is positively associated with entrepreneurial intention. These authors also claim that creativity and entrepreneurial intention are significantly associated. Moreover, self-efficacy is suggested to have an impact on the relationship between creativity and entrepreneurial intention. The more self-efficacy an individual displays the more likely he or she will develop an entrepreneurial intention and undertake an entrepreneurial career (Biraglia and Kadile, 2017).

Some recent studies, such as Hockerts (2017), have investigated entrepreneurial intention in the context of social entrepreneurship. Such studies claim that previous experience with social problems predicts social entrepreneurial intention. According to Hockerts (2017), the relationship between previous experience with social problems and entrepreneurial intention is mediated by four variables, originally developed by Mair and Noboa (2006), and in agreement with Ajzen's TPB, namely social entrepreneurial self-efficacy (internally perceived behavioral control), perceived social support (externally perceived behavioral control), empathy (attitude toward the entrepreneurial behavior), and moral obligation (subjective norms). Hockerts (2017) also finds that social entrepreneurial self-efficacy is the strongest predictor of social entrepreneurial intention.

On the other hand, Al-Jubari et al. (2017) investigate the role of autonomy in the formation of entrepreneurial intention. They highlight the importance of autonomy in predicting entrepreneurial intention, also claiming that the relationship between autonomy and entrepreneurial intention is mediated by subjective norms, attitudes, and perceived behavioral control (entrepreneurial intention antecedents of Ajzen's TPB).

Dheer and Lenartowicz (2016) explore the effect of identity integration, and cognitive and metacognitive intelligence on the formation of entrepreneurial intention among bicultural individuals. They suggest that the integration of bicultural individuals has a positive impact on their entrepreneurial intentions.

Fayolle et al. (2014) explore psychological aspects of entrepreneurship, investigating the role of motivations and values on the connection between intention and action. These authors claim that motivations and values affect the relationship between entrepreneurial intention and action, suggesting that the path from entrepreneurial intention to action depends on a person's level of motivation. Similarly, Carsrud and Brännback (2011) argue that motivation plays an important role in translating intention into action.

Wurthmann (2014) explores the relationship between innovation and entrepreneurial intention among students in the US. He found a positive relationship between attitudes towards innovation and entrepreneurial intention. Wurthmann stipulates that attitudes towards innovation are an antecedent of entrepreneurial intention.

The higher an individual's attitude toward innovation, the greater their entrepreneurial intention. Wurthmann (2014) also claims that the connection between attitudes toward innovation and intention is mediated by perceived feasibility and perceived desirability of starting a business.

Several other researchers have also focused on and further developed Ajzen's model. In previous studies, it has been shown that there are different antecedents of Ajzen's model. For instance, Kolvereid (1996) and Zhao et al. (2005) demonstrate that gender is an antecedent of attitude, social norms, and perceived behavioral control (Lortie and Castogiovanni, 2015). Kolvereid and Isaksen (2006) have also proposed various antecedents of attitude, including autonomy, authority, self-realization, and economic opportunity. Obschonka et al. (2010) note that openness, conscientiousness, extraversion, agreeableness, and neuroticism are antecedents of perceived behavioral control. On the other hand, Cassar (2006) proposes other antecedents of entrepreneurial intention, namely opportunity costs and managerial experience.

Furthermore, it is not possible to speak of intention without discussing the two most influential models of entrepreneurial intention: Ajzen's TPB and the SEE model. Several authors have used the TPB (e.g. Kolvereid, 1996; Carr and Sequeira, 2007; Kovalainen, 2006; Souitaris et al., 2007) to explain new venture creation intention (Lortie and Castogiovanni, 2015). Indeed, this theory explains entrepreneurial intention based on attitudes toward the entrepreneurship act, social norms, and perceived behavioral control. According to Ajzen (1991), attitude toward the act refers to how an individual perceives a behavior (favorably or unfavorably) (Lortie and Castogiovanni, 2015). Attitude toward the behavior influences an individual's entrepreneurial intention and behavior. Social norms refer to the social pressure of significant others toward performing or not performing a behavior (Lortie and Castogiovanni, 2015). As such, the entrepreneurial intention of an individual depends on the perception of significant others given that he or she performs the behavior in question. Finally, Lortie and Castogiovanni (2015) suggest that perceived behavioral control refers to how an individual perceives the behavior, such as whether it will be easy or difficult to perform.

In previous studies, some authors (e.g. Kolvereid, 1996; Carr and Sequeira, 2007) found support for the three elements of the TPB. Others (e.g. Kolvalainen, 2006) have found support for only two elements (social norms and perceived behavioral control). In contrast, some researchers (Schwarz et al., 2009) have argued that there are additional environmental factors that affect entrepreneurial intention (Lortie and Castogiovanni, 2015).

Finally, the SEE model explains entrepreneurial intention based on perceived feasibility, perceived desirability, and a propensity to act (Kautonen et al., 2015). Perceived feasibility refers to a person's ability to perform the behavior; perceived desirability pertains to personal attraction toward performing a behavior; and propensity to act reflects the desire of taking action upon one's decision (Krueger et al., 2000). Krueger et al. (2000) state that perceived feasibility and perceived desirability are associated with self-efficacy. They also claim that a common point between the TPB and the SEE model is that entrepreneurial intention depends, in general, on the attitude toward the behavior (Wurthmann, 2014).

This chapter proposes organizing authors that have contributed to conceptualizing entrepreneurial intent based on their institutions, countries of origin, abstracts, number of citations, title, and keywords. This allows for an observation of the evolution of the concept in the past 20 years in the top 10 ranked entrepreneurship reviews. Such a procedure elucidates areas for further research. The research also highlights the connections between authors in relation to the developed topics.

Methodology

This study proposes a three-step method to gain an overview of the research field. The first step is to identify the most relevant sources from publications related to the field. Second, collect and store all papers related to entrepreneurial intention and belonging to these sources. Third, generate a set of graphs to visualize the various relationships (including a co-authorship graph, topic graph, and author–topic graph, amongst others). The study proposes that this quantitative analysis, combined with an expert and qualitative understanding of these results, can provide the reader with valuable insights.

Based on the Web of Science database, this study identified 14,779 articles related to the topic "Entrepreneur" in up to 100 journals from 2005–2015. Table 2A.1 presents the number of articles and percentages of papers that belong in the top 15 sources.

The research also investigated the main topic of this paper, "Entrepreneur Intention", leading to the identification of 285 articles distributed across up to 100 distinct sources. The results of the top 20 sources are presented in Table 2A.2 (ordered by quantity of papers related to entrepreneurial intention).

A good candidate for analysis is a well-positioned journal in terms of percentage of publications related to the topic of this study (i.e. must belong to Table 2A.2). The study also proposes classifying these candidates into terms of priority based on (1) their Association of Business School (ABS) score and (2) their impact factor. For each of these criteria, the study ranks each source from 1 to N (1=the journal with the best rank, 2=the journal with the second best rank, etc.). Table 2A.3 presents the final ranking calculated as the sum of the ranks of the two criteria.

Table 2A.3 presents a list of journals that are the most appropriate for our analysis. Note that these journals are commonly accepted as the most significant in the entrepreneurial research field.

Data collection

For each publication related to entrepreneurial intention and within the journals listed in Table 2A.3, the following data was collected: title of the contribution, name, affiliation and country of authors, abstract, and keywords. For the purpose of data analysis, a MySQL relational database was designed, the model of which is presented in Figure 2A.1.

This model allows for a broad set of analyses, including (1) topic analysis, (2) co-authorship analysis, (3) topic–author analysis, and (4) topic–topic analysis. The topic analysis highlights the evolution of research topics over time in the field of entrepreneurial intention. It aims to emphasize new trends and is based on analysis of paper title, abstracts, and keywords. The co-authorship analysis aims to highlight collaboration between authors and affiliations over time. It provides a view of key players in the field and the general state of collaboration.

Entity disambiguation

When assessing manually processed data, one of the main issues is typographical mistakes or multiples ways of representing the same entity. This problem is referred to as entity disambiguation in literature (Raad et al., 2013). For example, when trying to build a co-authorship graph, common mistakes are to consider different authors whose names are not strictly identical as distinct entities (nodes). For preventing such problems (Zoltan Acs with Zoltan J. Acs or Alan Carsrud with Alan L. Carsrud), one possibility is to measure the distance of the chains of characters describing these entities.

Note that many algorithms exist for matching entities, but a common approach is to measure the distance between names and identify a match whenever a certain threshold is surpassed. The main difficulty is defining a proper threshold, i.e. a threshold that can optimize the number of detected matches without matching incorrect authors.

For identifying such a threshold, a common approach is to use a training set composed of known match and non-match and to optimize the accuracy of the classification to obtain a good score for the dataset. We applied the Levenshtein distance as a reference for measuring the distance between two authors or institutions (Christen, 2006). The Levenshtein distance between two chains is measured as the minimum number of edits required to change the first chain into the second chain. The authorized edits are insertions, deletions, and substitutions.

In the current study, the best results are obtained by defining a threshold for the Levenshtein distance of 3. Any two authors whose Levenshtein distance is less than or equal to 3 are identified as identical. The number of correctly identified matches was 75–80 (true positives), and the number of incorrectly identified matches was 1 (false negative). The unique incorrectly identified match occurred between *Thomas Hinz* and *Thomas Lans*. Note that there is a final manual inspection of matches to ensure that no misclassified match remains. Increasing the threshold to 4 allows for a reduction of the false negative number, but generated a significantly higher number of incorrectly identified matches (false positives). Two examples are *James E. Post* with *James O. Fiet* and *Robert Smith* with *Robert Sweo*.

The problem is the same for the institutions of authors. This study aimed to match institutions based on the information extracted in the database. The approach used for identifying identical institution is based on the same principles as that for author disambiguation.

Co-authorship analysis methodology

The study proposes modeling the collaboration between authors as a graph denoted $G(N, E)$, where N represents the set of authors and $E \in N \times N$ the set of edges. Note that by construction, the set of edges are couples of nodes (here, couples of authors). These graphs are referred to as co-authorship graphs if the edges are built based on the co-authorship of academic papers (Chen et al., 2001; Newman, 2004).

Such types of graphs are largely used in literature to highlight the structure of scientific collaboration and evaluate the particular positions of authors within a research community (Garfield, 1979).

There are different ways to model a relationship based on co-authorship. This study proposes using a *weighted undirected network* as the main model. This choice is motivated by the fact that co-authoring a paper is, by nature, a symmetric relationship—u publishes with v ≡ v publishes with u (undirected)—and the numbers of papers co-authored can be taken into account to weight a relationship (weighted).

Consider the adjacency matrix A whose element located at row i and column j represents the strength of the weight between an Author i and an Author j; such weight is calculated as the number of co-authored articles. In Figure 2A.2, Author 1 has co-published five papers with Author 2, three papers with Author 5, and two with Authors 4 and 3. Note that Authors 2, 3, 4, and 5 have never published together. The adjacency matrix of the graph is represented as follows:

$$A = \begin{pmatrix} 0 & 5 & 2 & 2 & 3 \\ 5 & 0 & 0 & 0 & 0 \\ 2 & 0 & 0 & 0 & 0 \\ 2 & 0 & 0 & 0 & 0 \\ 3 & 0 & 0 & 0 & 0 \end{pmatrix} \qquad (2.1)$$

Note that such a model has the benefit of allowing the representation of overall relationships between authors in a particular field. Graph theory, network science, and social network analysis are disciplines that focus entirely on algorithms and applications that can be obtained from such a model (Alhajj and Rokne, 2014). This research proposes applying a set of algorithms to this model to gain a concrete view of actors in the field to investigate different aspects of the community.

With the co-authorship graph it is possible to evaluate a set of centrality measures to evaluate how central a given author is for the research field. From Figure 2A.2, one may wonder what are the advantages of Author 1 when compared to the other authors (Freeman, 1977, 1978). Freeman proposes three observations that make Author 1 more central: (1) he is more connected (degree); (2) he is closer to the others (closeness centrality); and (3) he is an intermediate between the others (betweenness centrality). Applying these measures highlights the specific roles that a researcher can achieve in the entrepreneurship research field.

Node degree

The first measure, denoted k_i, corresponds to the degree of a node i. It is measured from the adjacency matrix A as follows:

$$k_i = \sum_{j=1}^{|M|} A_{i,j} \qquad (2.2)$$

This is the sum of the number of co-authored papers by Author i with each author. In this example, this is $k_1 = 12$; $k_2 = 5$; $k_3 = 2$; $k_4 = 2$; $k_5 = 3$. The study highlights the line or row that should be summed to obtain the degree of node 3 in the adjacency matrix. This allows for identifying the author who collaborates the most with other researchers. Paul Erdős is an example of a researcher who has based his entire scientific career collaborating. He has co-authored papers with more than 500 authors, inspiring the Erdős Number.

Betweenness centrality

The betweenness centrality, denoted g_i, is a measure of how "between" others a given author is. This metric relies on the concept of shortest path. A path is defined as a route along the edges of the graph. The associated length of the path is measured as the number of edges contained in the path. The shortest path is considered a path with the fewest edges. The betweenness centrality is measured to highlight authors that regularly appear in the shortest path between any pair of authors. These authors are considered intermediaries and play a unique role in the flow of information passing through the co-authorship graph.

The betweenness centrality is measured as follows:

$$g_i = \sum_{j \neq i \neq k} \frac{\sigma_{jk}(i)}{\sigma_{jk}} \qquad (2.3)$$

where σ_{jk} is the number of shortest paths between nodes j and k, and $\sigma_{jk}(i)$ is the number of shortest paths between nodes j and k that passes through i.

Closeness centrality

Finally, the closeness centrality, denoted h_i, is measured. The variable allows for the identification of authors that appear to have a short distance to others. In other words, they can easily reach any author within a few intermediates. This is the opposite of "farness", which refers to the length of distances between nodes.

The closeness centrality is measured as follows:

$$h_i = \sum_{i \neq j} \frac{1}{d(i,j)} \qquad (2.4)$$

where $d(i, j)$ is the distance between nodes i and j.

Detecting clusters

Beyond the centrality of individuals, this study proposes applying a clustering algorithm to the graph to uncover the communities that exist in the research field. For this purpose, a weighted modularity based algorithm is applied. The weighted modularity is defined as:

$$Q = \frac{1}{2m} \sum_{ij} \left[A_{ij} - \frac{k_i * k_j}{2m} \right] \delta(c_i, c_j) \qquad (2.5)$$

where, Q is the Kronecker delta, k_i is the degree of node I, L is the number of edges in the graph, and $A_{i,j}$ is the element located at row i and column j of the adjacency matrix A.

The resulting value can be used as a reference for clustering (Clauset et al., 2004) by merging communities that allow the best gain in modularity. The following list demonstrates an example clustering algorithm:

1. Each node is a unique community.
2. Identify each community pair, calculate the modularity score Q obtained if they were merged.
3. Merge communities that allow the highest variation in modularity (ΔQ).
4. Repeat steps 2 and 3 until only one community remains.
5. Return partitions that allow for obtaining the highest modularity score.

Many clustering techniques exist, such as the Girvan–Newman algorithm and CFinder. When trying to identify communities, it is necessary to consider the advantages and disadvantages of each technique. Examples of comparison criteria include the computational costs, whether the capacity of the algorithm can scale up for a large dataset, the capacity of the approach to identify the best number of communities, and the possibility of identifying overlapping communities.

Results and discussion

The study identified a set of 955 authors contributing to a total of 600 journal articles. To see the complete list of journals, refer to Table 2A.3. It applied a set of analyses, beginning with a co-authors graph, and then examined keywords and trends over time. The study then examined the relationships between authors and topics. This allowed for a thorough investigation of the research field. It then analyzed the relationships between the main topic "intention" and institutions.

All graphs displayed in this research are available online (see http://goo.gl/6aeKyE). The online version enables searching and interactions, imparting a more comprehensive understanding of the included graphs.

Co-authorship graph

The co-authorship graph, computed from the selected sources, contains 955 authors connected by 1070 edges (Figure 2A.3).

The density of the graph, interpreted as the probability that two researchers in the community have published together, is equal to 0.002. This means that there is only a 0.02 percent chance that two given researchers in the field have published together. This score, although low, illustrates how much novel collaboration is possible for the future. The average degree of the graph, corresponding to the average number of co-authors an author has, is equal to 2.241. Table 2A.5 presents the top 10 authors with respect to their number of co-authors (see also Tables 2A.6 and 2A.7).

The study further investigates the graph, which is composed of a set of authors who are all connected to each other by a certain, but definite, number of intermediates (Figure 2A.4). Note that this co-authorship analysis is extended to build a network of institution collaborations. For this purpose, the study considers authors from the same institution as a single node. The strength of a relationship between two institutions is calculated as the sum over all authors of these institutions of co-authored papers (Table 2A.7).

Term analysis over time

The study proposes identifying variations in trends of research related to authorship intention. For this purpose, the abstract and titles with related years of relevance are extracted from the database. Each word belonging to the title or abstract is a candidate as a term. The importance of a term for a given year is computed using the Z-score (aka the normal score). The first step is to compute the occurrence of each term over each year. A term belonging to a given year is obtained through the keywords as indicated by the authors, but also the words in the abstract and title. A term is defined as a word that is not a linking word. Terms are identified as single words separated by spaces. We obtained terms by deleting all linking words and all punctuation signs and making all letters lowercase.

The abstracts and titles of linking words are removed and the occurrences of each remaining term are computed. These sets of terms are used in combination with the keywords to identify trends over time.

The occurrences of a term at a given year are normalized by the sum of occurrences of the term for this year. This allows the study to obtain the ratio of use of a keyword for a given year (denoted $\rho(term)$). The average and standard deviations of each ratio are finally computed over all years (denoted $\mu(term)$) and $\sigma(term)$), respectively). The Z-score is obtained from the following metrics:

$$Z-score(term_{year}) = \frac{\rho(term_{year}) - \mu(term)}{\sigma(term)} \qquad (2.6)$$

Figure 2A.5 represents terms that occur the most within the dataset.

The final list of relevant terms, examined each year, must satisfy one of the following criteria: it must (1) belong to terms that occur the most (count); (2) belong to the overall most frequent term over the years (average); or (3) belong to the most unequally used terms over the year (standard deviation; see Table 2A.8).

Figure 2A.6 displays the evolution of the use of the following topics: Capital, Culture, Data, and Intention. These topics show the highest increase in use (Z-score) in the past years. Note that these four topics are relatively new to the field of research and have a Z-score of below zero from 1995 to 2006. Figure 2A.6 highlights the importance of intention in entrepreneurial research.

Topic–author and topic–topic analysis

This study proposes enriching the term analysis by taking into account authors that refer to such terms. To this end, a link is created between an author and a term whenever the author mentions this term in a title or abstract. The weight of the link is proportional to the number of times the author mentions the term. This analysis allows for the capture of the research interests of authors (Figure 2A.7).

The connections of Alan L. Carsrud allow for an elucidation of some aspects of his related research interests. It is possible to identify a primary focus on entrepreneurship and entrepreneurial intentions. This research implies analysis of influences and understanding of behavior and is closely related to business and ventures (Figure 2A.8).

The connections of Norris Krueger highlight aspects of his related research interests. The connections reveal a main focus on entrepreneurship and entrepreneurial intentions. His work involves understanding behavior and process in relation to the influences of entrepreneurs. Opportunity is highlighted as one possible factor (Figure 2A.9).

Figures 2A.10, 2A.11, and 2A.12 show the main authors related to intention. These are authors for whom the keyword "intention" is often referenced in publications. The important authors for this topic include Francisco Liñán, Alan L. Carsrud, Dean Shepherd, Michael Reilly, Norris Krueger, and Kelly Shaver.

It is important to emphasize that Carsrud and Krueger continue to work together on applied and related issues to the Theory of the Entrepreneurial Event model from Shapéro and Sokol (1982). Their developments around the concept of entrepreneurial intent via Azjen's model fully support their presence within the field of research on entrepreneurial intention, as shown in Figure 2A.13.

Another author who cannot be missed in the results (as seen in Figure 2A.11) is Francisco Liñán. Indeed, through his numerous works on the TPB, his name appears to be essential in the field of research on entrepreneurial intent and fully justifies his significant presence in Figure 2A.11.

Moreover, Teemu Kautonen appears to be a potential contributor to the concept and can be seen as gradually emerging in Figure 2A.11.

The author–topic graph allows this study to generate a novel version of the author graph, which remains on the common research interests (topics). Two authors are connected by an edge that has a high weight when an author often refers to the same terms. This is obtained through a projection of the author–topic graph (multiplication matrix method).

The proximities of authors related by common research topics are displayed in Figure 2A.7. This graph is built from topics extracted from abstracts, titles, and keywords. It allows for the identification of different used terms and potential research fields for different groups of authors. The groups of authors are highlighted in Figure 2A.11, which shows six majors communities of researchers. These communities are the result of cooperation between research topics and authors. The six communities of research concerning entrepreneurial intent are driven by many international researchers, such as Thurik, Gartner, Davidsson, Gupta, Carsrud, and Krueger, all of whom substantially contribute to this field. This graph also provides information on a group of researchers, which is not highlighted in Figure 2A.14 but is essential to gain an overview of research on entrepreneurship. Some authors are, in fact, essential links between authors of different communities and may explain the constitution of communities around the issue of entrepreneurial intent.

Authors such as Kautonen or Liñán are essential for completing the picture of research on entrepreneurial intent in the last 20 years and demonstrate connections between many major communities and lead authors. This finding may help to explain how the concept of the entrepreneurial intent has grown in the past 20 years (see Figure 2A.11).

Similar to the authors' graph, a topic similarity graph is included. These graphs connect topics that are often used by the same authors. Two topics are closely tied when many authors have conjointly used these topics. This graph allows for the capture of the proximity between research topics, highlighting the multiple dimensions of given research in the field (Figure 2A.12).

The cartography of topics is displayed in the upper portion of the graph whose connections reveal the proximity of the topics. This proximity is measured by the co-occurrence of these topics in papers. Entrepreneurial, entrepreneurship, business, and intention are the most common topics.

Interest by individuals can be observed for effort, ambition, aspiration, and motivation, and also by non-entrepreneurs for ventures, belief, chances, motivations, and funding. A focus on understanding is related to behavior, as well as feasibility, perceptions. These aspects are viewed as critical and aimed to be integrated into a model. Figure 2A.13 highlights topics related to intention.

The topic of intention is related to many different dimensions, such as behavior and opportunity, but also multiple influential factors, including gender, differences between individuals, education, studies, activities, motivations and reasons, and perceptions of success.

Double network dimension between researchers

Past research, as demonstrated in the literature review, has become increasingly richer in recent decades, suggesting that the research community has made substantial efforts to examine particular themes in more depth. Figure 2A.4 exhibits a surprising result related to the top three authors of the discipline: it appears they have not directly collaborated within the period of analysis and over the analyzed articles. The network appears to be structured in a particular way. Figure 2A.4 highlights specific external nodes of collaboration between Roy Thurik, Candida Brush, and Dean Shepherd.

Moreover, analyzing Figure 2A.4 and Tables 2A.4, 2A.5, and 2A.6 together shows some connections between the top three authors. Connections are captured as nodes that are identified on the shortest paths between these authors. The top three authors have many co-authors, but only two have specific connections between each other. Researchers who are nodes of collaboration between the top three authors appear to be Paul Reynolds, Erkko Autio, Ronald Mitchell, William B. Gartner, and Johan Wiklund. Although not directly identified as top authors, these researchers play an important role in the overall cohesiveness of the network and a key role in the development of the entrepreneurship research community. These authors logically have a relatively high betweenness centrality score. For further information, the geographical dimension between these authors is sampled and a specific "belt" is drawn by means of the shortest paths between the top authors.

A clear axis emerges between northern Europe with Roy Thurik and the US with Candida Brush and Dean Shepherd. This organization appears to promote the diffusion of new results and theories within the research community. One can only wonder what would emerge with more direct collaborations between those authors. Furthermore, the axis designed by this sub-network appears to be restrained to the US and Europe (see Figure 2A.14). It is logical to consider geographically broadening the network to enrich understandings of entrepreneurial intention and entrepreneurship. This result is in agreement with a call by Shepherd (2015) in *Journal of Business Venturing* "for a more interactive" research in entrepreneurship. In some ways, the results of this study also appear as a possible solution to limitations highlighted by Liñán and Fayolle (2015).

Another surprising result related to networks dimensions emerges when jointly analyzing Figures 2A.3, 2A.4, 2A.10, and 2A.11. Figures 2A.10 and 2A.11 reveal that the top three authors extracted from Tables 2A.4–2A.6 are not closer to the intention topic like Liñán, Carsrud, Krueger or Shaver. Moreover, Thurik does not appear in this topic graph. These results may imply a double organization inside the author network—one that structures co-authorship in a geographical way (with linkers) and the other that structures topics inside the entrepreneurial intention thematic field. Consequently, this method for analyzing connections and networks on the basis of topic and co-authorship may help the community gain a better understanding of the structure of the community and may, in the close future, help young researchers better position themselves in the community to gain visibility with their research.

Finally, an interesting observation can be made by studying Figures 2A.3 and 2A.4 in relation to the organization of networks in the community. Figure 2A.3 shows that the majority of the community does not belong to the *first core* main component of the network (63.55 percent). The core component is composed of a small sample of the full community of researchers (about 25 percent). This result can also be seen by analyzing the average number of connections between researchers, consequently leading to the observation that the first level of the network implies more than 1.57 connections per author, unlike the second level of the network with 0.96 connections per author.

This result leads to the conclusion that there may be some entry barriers into the first level of the network, which may be related to the capacity of a researcher to communicate, discuss, and connect themselves with other members of the community to publish their research. Consequently, the recommendation can be made to young researchers, who aim to contribute to the field of entrepreneurial intention, to have networking activities that enlarge their publication capacities and contribute to the overall cohesiveness of the research field.

Emerging topics and future research

A surprising result emerges from analyzing the most commonly used keywords (Figure 2A.5). Observing last year's publications (especially for *Entrepreneurship Theory & Practice* reviews) shows the importance of family business, although this development may be too recent to be definitive.

Moreover, Figure 2A.5 is in line with Shepherd (2015), who requested entrepreneurship research to be further oriented to interactivity (as shown in the network analysis earlier), cognition, compassion, and social entrepreneurship. However, these topics do not clearly appear in Figure 2A.5, and only some keywords related to social entrepreneurship can be extracted from this graph. This result can be logically explained by our database, which only considers papers published before 2016. Nonetheless, cognitive, social topics have perspectives for future studies according to Shepherd (2015) and these appear clearly in Figure 2A.12. Furthermore, particularly for cognitive topics, it can be seen that entrepreneurial–intention–perception(s)–behavior–influence and many other related aspects are closer in the entrepreneurship research field, which would also confirm Shepherd's call to action.

Figure 2A.6—in conjunction with topics that exhibit a growing interest in the past few years—shows that data and culture are being studied more often, especially between 2011 and 2015. This result is unsurprising given the large emergence of big data in this period. Furthermore, culture and intention are recurring topics in entrepreneurship literature. From 2013 to 2015, intention, motivations, values, and other cognitive approaches appear to emerge, echoing the request by Shepherd (2015) for an increasingly cognitive-based approach to entrepreneurship.

Figure 2A.13 reveals three major thematic blocks. The first (red) is linked to the entrepreneurial and entrepreneurship topic, implying a broader viewpoint of entrepreneurial intention, starting from the general entrepreneurship field level. This first level encompasses many dimensions related to entrepreneurship, on the one hand, and entrepreneurial intention, on the other hand. Indeed, some can be assimilated to cognitive approach, like perceptions, attitudes, behavior, values, influence, motivations, cognition, and self-efficacy. Other related topics concern a specific student population (student, school, and education). Surprisingly, this second subtheme is not included in the second thematic block, related to an individual level of analysis. This may suggest that entrepreneurial intention education contains a broad viewpoint and not analysis from an individual perspective.

The second thematic block (green) is related to the entrepreneur and business topics, representing a more individual level of topic research. This level of analysis likely allows for a deeper insight into the entrepreneurship intention topic. Finally, the third major thematic block (purple) is at the interface of the first two thematic blocs, analyzing topics which are positioned between the first two dimensions, such as the social, careers, and differences.

The entrepreneurial intention topic appears through our results as structured around three thematic blocks. This structure can be designed as shown in Figure 2A.15. Taking into account such a structure may allow for a broader analysis of research on entrepreneurial intention. Researchers should consider this structure when further developing this specific field of research.

Conclusion and implications

Research on entrepreneurial intent has become increasingly important for understanding entrepreneurship. Interest in the cognitive aspects of business creation in research on entrepreneurship produces results that help both researchers and practitioners gain a more complete understanding of the process. This bibliometric work attempts to shed light on the concept and, moreover, proposes a better understanding of the phenomenon by considering a large volume of papers on this topic from the past 20 years.

At this time, several researchers avoid the study of this concept. Others have arrived at new methods of understanding, including factors of time, the entrepreneurial ecosystem, and entrepreneurial orientation, amongst others.

This research attempts to shed light on work conducted on the concept of entrepreneurial intention in the past 20 years and in the top 10 entrepreneurship journals. The descriptive work is based on an innovative methodology, namely network science, and the study builds a bibliometric database of more than 650 papers with direct and indirect links to the concept of entrepreneurial intent. The work highlights communities of researchers, collaboration between researchers, and connections between the entrepreneurial intent and other topics in entrepreneurship. The study also demonstrates the most influential researchers who have provided substantial contributions to the concept.

In addition, it reveals existing gaps in literature and identifies potential research for future work. This is enhanced by various concepts developed by Elfving et al. (2009) or by Liñán and Fayolle (2015), leading to a better understanding of entrepreneurial intention.

The study emphasizes various concepts that are directly and indirectly related to entrepreneurial intention, including education, alertness and opportunities, entrepreneurial orientation, motivation, self-efficacy, entrepreneurial behavior, entrepreneurial process, implementation, SME growth, and internationalization. These concepts show that the concept of entrepreneurial intention is a vibrant source for comprehensively analyzing the entrepreneurial ecosystem.

The main limits of this research are its descriptive aspects. This work would be stronger if it highlighted the methodologies used in each mobilized paper, model, or theory. It would allow for a more detailed and accurate analysis and would be complementary to the work of Liñán and Fayolle (2015).

So what?

This chapter proposes exploring the evolution of the understanding of entrepreneurial intention over the past 20 years. Research has given substantial focus to entrepreneurship, and in 2015, entrepreneurship emerged as a multidimensional concept that requires organization and structure for a comprehensive overview of the concept.

This analysis presents a global vision of research on entrepreneurial intention. Instead of exclusively providing analysis through bibliometrics, the study proposes a different investigation by analyzing interactions between its data. The attempt is to understand different dimensions analyzed around this concept, as well as collaboration between researchers, their institutions, and communities developed around entrepreneurship.

Although this chapter contains descriptive research, its methodology is nonetheless original and based on data-mining and cloud analysis.

Finally, this work opens new possibilities for future research by further examining the concept of entrepreneurial intention. Indeed, it allows for stronger analysis via an identical methodology and the inclusion of models, theories, and research methodologies (conceptual, qualitative, quantitative, and qualitative/quantitative) found in previous literature.

This would be useful for a deeper perspective on entrepreneurial intent.

References

Ajzen, I. (1991). The Theory of Planned Behavior. *Organizational Behavior and Human Decision Processes*, 50(2), 179–211.

Ajzen, I. (2011). The Theory of Planned Behaviour: Reactions and reflections. *Psychology & Health*, 26, 1113–27.

Ajzen, I. and Fishbein, M. (1969). The prediction of behavioral intentions in a choice situation. *Journal of Experimental Social Psychology*, 5(4), 400–16.

Ajzen, I. and Fishbein, M. (1972). Attitudes and normative beliefs as factors influencing behavioral intentions. *Journal of Personality and Social Psychology*, 21(1), 1.

Ajzen, I. and Fishbein, M. (1977). Attitude-behavior relations: A theoretical analysis and review of empirical research. *Psychological bulletin*, 84(5), 888.

Al-Jubari, I., Hassan, A. and Hashim, J. (2017). The role of autonomy as a predictor of entrepreneurial intention among university students in Yemen. *International Journal of Entrepreneurship and Small Business*, 30(3), 325–40.

Alhajj, R. and Rokne, J. (2014). *Encyclopedia of Social Network Analysis and Mining*. Springer-Verlag: New York, NY.

Bandura, A. (1997). *Self-Efficacy: The Exercise of Control*. Macmillan: Basingstoke, UK.

Baron, R.A. (2004). The cognitive perspective: A valuable tool for answering entrepreneurship's basic "why" questions. *Journal of Business Venturing*, 19(2), 221–39.

Biraglia, A. and Kadile, V. (2017). The role of entrepreneurial passion and creativity in developing entre-preneurial intentions: Insights from American homebrewers. *Journal of Small Business Management*, 55(1), 170–88.

Bird, B. (1988). Implementing entrepreneurial ideas: The case for intention. *Academy of Management Review*, 13(3), 442–53.

Carr, J.C. and Sequeira, J.M. (2007). Prior family business exposure as intergenerational influence and entrepreneurial intent: A theory of planned behavior approach. *Journal of Business Research*, 60, 1090–98.

Carsrud, A. and Brännback, M. (2011). Entrepreneurial motivations: What do we still need to know? *Journal of Small Business Management*, 49(1), 9–26.

Cassar, G. (2006). Entrepreneur opportunity costs and intended venture growth. *Journal of Business Venturing*, 21(5), 610–32.

Chen, C., Paul, R.J., & O'Keefe, B. (2001). Fitting the jigsaw of citation: Information visualization in domain analysis. *Journal of the Association for Information Science and Technology*, 52(4), 315–30.

Christen, P. (2006). A comparison of personal name matching: Techniques and practical issues. In Workshop on Mining Complex Data (MCD), at IEEE ICDM 2006, Hong Kong, pp. 290–4.

Clauset, A., Newman, M.E.J. and Moore, C. (2004). Finding community structure in very large networks. *Physical Review-E*, 70(6), 066111.

Dheer, R.J.S. and Lenartowicz, T. (2016). Multiculturalism and entrepreneurial intentions: Understanding the mediating role of cognitions. *Entrepreneurship Theory & Practice*, 41.

Douglas, E.J. and Fitzsimmons, J.R. (2013). Intrapreneurial intentions versus entrepreneurial intentions: Distinct constructs with different antecedents. *Small Business Economics*, 41(1), 115–32.

Elfving, J., Brännback, M. and Carsrud, A.L. (2009). Toward a contextual model of entrepreneurial intentions. In A.L. Carsrud and M. Brännback (Eds), *Understanding the Entrepreneurial Mind.* Springer: New York, NY, pp. 23–33.

Fayolle, A. and Liñán, F. (2014). The future of research on entrepreneurial intentions. *Journal of Business Research*, 67(5), 663–66.

Fayolle, A., Liñán, F. and Moriano, J.A. (2014). Beyond entrepreneurial intentions: Values and motivations in entrepreneurship. *International Entrepreneurship and Management Journal*, 10(4), 679–89.

Fishbein, M. and Ajzen, I. (1974). Attitudes towards objects as predictors of single and multiple behavioral criteria. *Psychological Review*, 81(1), 59.

Freeman, L.C. (1977). A set of measures of centrality based on betweenness. *Sociometry*, 40(1), 35–41.

Freeman, L.C. (1978). Centrality in social networks conceptual clarification. *Social Networks*, 1(3), 215–39.

Garfield, E. (1979). Is citation analysis a legitimate evaluation tool? *Scientometrics*, 1(4), 359–75.

Hockerts, K. (2017). Determinants of social entrepreneurial intentions. *Entrepreneurship Theory & Practice*, 41(1), 105–30.

Karimi, S., Biemans, H.J.A., Lans, T., Chizari, M. and Mulder, M. (2016). The impact of entrepreneurship education: A study of Iranian students' entrepreneurial intentions and opportunity identification. *Journal of Small Business Management*, 54(1), 187–209.

Kautonen, T., Van Gelderen, M. and Fink, M. (2015). Robustness of the theory of planned behavior in predicting entrepreneurial intentions and actions. *Entrepreneurship Theory & Practice*, 39(3), 655–74.

Kautonen, T., Van Gelderen, M. and Tornikoski, E.T. (2013). Predicting entrepreneurial behaviour: A test of the theory of planned behaviour. *Applied Economics*, 45(6), 697–707.

Kibler, E. (2013). Formation of entrepreneurial intentions in a regional context. *Entrepreneurship & Regional Development*, 25(3–4), 293–323.

Kolvereid, L. (1996). Prediction of employment status choice intentions. *Entrepreneurship Theory & Practice*, 21(1), 47–57.

Kolvereid, L. and Bullvag, E. (1996). Growth intentions and actual growth: The impact of entrepreneurial choice. *Journal of Enterprising Culture*, 4(1), 1–17.

Kolvereid, L. and Isaksen, E. (2006). New business start-up and subsequent entry into self-employment. *Journal of Business Venturing*, 21, 866–85.

Kovalainen, A. (2006). Influencing attitudes and skills for entrepreneurship and SME growth. *Promoting Entrepreneurship in South East Europe: Policies and Tools*, 89–103.

Krueger, N.F. and Carsrud, A.L. (1993). Entrepreneurial intentions: Applying the theory of planned behaviour. *Entrepreneurship and Regional Development*, 5, 315–30.

Krueger, N.F. and Day, M. (2010). Looking forward, looking backward: From entrepreneurial cognition to neuroentrepreneurship. In Z. Acs and D.B. Audretsch (Eds), *Handbook of Entrepreneurship Research*. Springer: New York, NY, pp. 321–57.

Krueger, N.F., Reilly, M.D. and Carsrud, A.L. (2000). Competing models of entrepreneurial intentions. *Journal of Business Venturing*, 15(5–6), 411–32.

Liñán, F. (2008). Skill and value perceptions: How do they affect entrepreneurial intentions? *International Entrepreneurship and Management Journal*, 4(3), 257–72.

Liñán, F. and Chen, Y.W. (2009). Development and cross-cultural application of a specific instrument to measure entrepreneurial intentions. *Entrepreneurship Theory & Practice*, 33(3), 593–617.

Liñán, F. and Fayolle, A. (2015). A systematic literature review on entrepreneurial intentions: Citation, thematic analyses, and research agenda. *International Entrepreneurship and Management Journal*, 11(4), 907–33.

Liñán, F., Urbano, D. and Guerrero, M. (2011). Regional variations in entrepreneurial cognitions: Start-up intentions of university students in Spain. *Entrepreneurship and Regional Development*, 23(3–4), 187–215.

Lortie, J. and Castogiovanni, G. (2015). The theory of planned behavior in entrepreneurship research:

What we know and future directions. *International Entrepreneurship and Management Journal*, 11(4), 935–57.

Maalaoui, A., Perez, C., Bertrand, G., Razgallah, M. and Germon, R. (2016). "Cruel Intention" or "Entrepreneurship Intention": What did you expect? An overview of the Entrepreneurship Intention research field—an interaction perspective. Conference Proceedings, United States Association for Small Business and Entrepreneurship, pp. ED1.

Mair, J. and Noboa, E. (2006). Social entrepreneurship: How intentions to create a social venture are formed. In J. Mair, J. Robinson and K. Hockerts (Eds), *Social Entrepreneurship*. Palgrave Macmillan, Basingstoke, UK, pp. 121–35.

Newman, M.E. (2004). Fast algorithm for detecting community structure in networks. *Physical Review E*, 69(6), 066133.

Obschonka, M., Silbereisen, R.K. and Schmitt-Rodermund, E. (2010). Entrepreneurial intention as developmental outcome. *Journal of Vocational Behavior*, 77, 63–72.

Raad, E., Chbeir, R. and Dipanda, A. (2013). Discovering relationship types between users using profiles and shared photos in a social network. *Multimedia Tools Applications*, 64(1), 141–70.

Schwarz, E.J., Wdowiak, M.A., Almer-Jarz, D.A. and Breitenecker, R.J. (2009). The effects of attitudes and perceived environment conditions on students' entrepreneurial intent: An Austrian perspective. *Education + Training*, 51(4), 272–91.

Shapéro, A. and Sokol, L. (1982). The social dimensions of entrepreneurship. In C.A. Kent, D.L. Sexton, and K.H. Vesper (Eds), *Encyclopedia of Entrepreneurship*. Prentice-Hall: Englewood Cliffs, NJ, pp. 72–90.

Shaver, K.G. and Scott, L.R. (1991). Person, process, and choice: The psychology of new venture creation. *Entrepreneurship Theory & Practice*, Winter, 23–42.

Shepherd, D. (2015). Party on! A call for entrepreneurship research that is more interactive, activity based, cognitively hot, compassionate, and prosocial. *Journal of Business Venturing*, 30, 489–507.

Souitaris, V., Zerbinati, S. and Al-Laham, A. (2007). Do entrepreneurship programmes raise entrepreneurial intention of science and engineering students? The effect of learning, inspiration and resources. *Journal of Business Venturing*, 22(4), 566–91.

Walter, S.G., Parboteeah, K.P. and Walter, A. (2013). University departments and self-employment intentions of business students: A cross-level analysis. *Entrepreneurship Theory & Practice*, 37(2), 175–200.

Wurthmann, K. (2014). Business students toward innovation and intentions to start their own businesses. *International Entrepreneurship and Management Journal*, 10, 691–711.

Zhao, H., Seibert, S.E. and Hills, G.E. (2005). The mediating role of self-efficacy in the development of entrepreneurial intentions. *Journal of Applied Psychology*, 90(6), 1265.

Appendix*

Table 2A.1   Top 15 sources regarding number of published papers from 2005 to 2015 related to the "Entrepreneur" topic

Journal	Number of articles	Percentage	5Y impact factor	ABS[1] rank
Journal of Business Venturing	357	2.42	4.571	4
Small Business Economics	259	1.75	1.641	3
Entrepreneurship Theory and Practice	169	1.14	2.598	4
Entrepreneurship and Regional Development	134	0.91	1.000	3
Forbes	116	0.78	0.07	NA
International Small Business Journal	114	0.77	1.397	3
Journal of Small Business Management	112	0.76	1.361	3
Harvard Business Review	101	0.68	1.831	4
Procedia Social and Behavioral Sciences	93	0.63	0.000	NA
Technovation	76	0.51	3.251	3
Journal of Business Ethics	72	0.49	1.552	3
Strategic Entrepreneurship Journal	62	0.42	2.80	3
International Entrepreneurship and Management Journal	61	0.41	5.053	1
Research Policy	59	0.40	3.989	4
International Journal of Technology Management	36	0.24	0.64	2
Total	1821	12.32		

Note: [1]Journal rankings based on the tiered lists from several schools that are members of the UK Association of Business Schools.

Source: Retrieved from Web of Science, 21 February 2015

---

*   Interactive versions of Figure 2A.7 and Figure 2A.12 are available at: http://goo.gl/6aeKyE

Table 2A.2   Top 20 sources regarding number of published papers from 2005 to 2015 related to the "Entrepreneur Intention" topic

Journal	Percentage	5Y impact factor	ABS rank[1]
Entrepreneurship Theory and Practice	5.26	2.598	4
Journal of Business Venturing	4.91	4.571	4
Procedia Social and Behavioral Sciences	4.21	NA	NA
Small Business Economics	3.51	1.641	3
Journal of the Korean Entrepreneurship Society	3.51	0.425	NA
International Entrepreneurship and Management Journal	3.16	5.053	1
Entrepreneurship and Regional Development	3.16	1.00	3
Journal of Korea Academia Industrial Cooperation Society	2.46	0.262	NA
International Small Business Journal	2.11	1.397	3
Journal of Foodservice Management	1.40	NA	NA
Journal of Small Business Management	1.40	1.361	3
Technovation	1.40	3.449	3
Journal of Vocational Behavior	1.40	3.079	4
Asia Pacific Journal of Business Venturing and Entrepreneurship	1.40	NA	NA
Transformations in Business Economics	1.40	0.26	NA
Proceedings of the 4th European Conference on Entrepreneurship and Innovation	1.40	NA	NA
Journal of Korea Academia Industrial Cooperation Society	1.40	0.262	NA
International Journal of Technology Management	1.40	0.49	2
Strategic Entrepreneurship Journal	1.40	1.744	3
Journal of International Entrepreneurship	1.40	5.053	1
Total	33.68		

Note: [1]Journal rankings based on the tiered lists from several schools that are members of the UK Association of Business Schools.

Source: Maalaoui et al. (2016).

Table 2A.3   Top 10 sources

Journal	5Y impact factor	ABS rank[1]	Total	Ranking
Journal of Business Venturing	3	1	4	1
Entrepreneurship Theory and Practice	5	1	6	2
Technovation	4	3	7	3
Strategic Entrepreneurship Journal	6	3	9	4
Small Business Economics	7	3	10	5
International Entrepreneurship and Management Journal	1	10	11	6
International Small Business Journal	8	3	11	7
Journal of International Entrepreneurship	1	10	11	8
Journal of Small Business Management	9	3	12	9
Entrepreneurship and Regional Development	10	3	13	10

Note: [1]Journal rankings based on the tiered lists from several schools that are members of the UK Association of Business Schools.

Source: Maalaoui et al. (2016).

Table 2A.4   Top 10 authors that have the highest number of co-authors

Id	Degree[1]
Roy Thurik	16
Candida Brush	15
Dean Shepherd	14
Melissa Cardon	13
Ronald Mitchell	11
Johan Wiklund	11
Holger Patzelt	10
Nancy Carter	10
Vishal Gupta	10
Kelly Shaver	9

Note: [1]Number of co-authors.

Source: Maalaoui et al. (2016).

Table 2A.5   Top 10 authors that have the highest betweenness centrality score

Id	Betweenness centrality
Johan Wiklund	16634
Erkko Autio	15636.81587
Jonathan Levie	14520
Niels Bosma	9896.529225
Dean Shepherd	9788.333333
Paul Reynolds	9361.933987
Roy Thurik	5492.333333
Melissa Cardon	5386.5
Candida Brush	4245.63582
Holger Patzelt	4235.833333

Source: Maalaoui et al. (2016).

Table 2A.6   Top 10 authors that have the highest weighted degree score

Id	Weighted degree[1]
Roy Thurik	52
Candida Brush	38
Dean Shepherd	34
Kelly Shaver	30
Ronald Mitchell	28
Johan Wiklund	26
Melissa Cardon	26
William Gartner	26
Holger Patzelt	24
Nancy Carter	24

Note: [1]This score corresponds to the total number of articles of each given author.

Source: Maalaoui et al. (2016).

Table 2A.7   Institutions and collaborations

Institutions	Number of collaborators
Indiana University	26
Syracuse University	15
Babson College	13
Texas Tech University	10
Jönköping International Business School (JIBS)	10
University of Strathclyde	9
Concordia University	9
Brigham Young University	8
University of Seville	7
University of Colorado at Boulder	7

Id	Betweenness centrality
Indiana University	18372.17244
Syracuse University	7645.174328
Texas Tech University	6809.01453
Jönköping International Business School (JIBS)	6432.726435
Brock University	5264.633181
University of Oklahoma	5238.422222
University of Alberta	5084.617582
Concordia University	5012.961508
University of Strathclyde	4723
Babson College	4524.782937

Id	Closeness centrality
Florida International University/Stockholm School of Economics	9.288321168
National University of Singapore and Leuphana University of Lueneburg	9.197080292
University of Minnesota Duluth	9.010948905
University of North Carolina at Greensboro	8.886861314
University College London	8.857664234
Aston University	8.843065693
University of Colorado	8.452554745
Lally School of Management and Technology	8.452554745
University of Wisconsin Oshkosh	8.332116788
Teesside University	8.313868613

Source: Maalaoui et al. (2016).

Table 2A.8 Top keywords with respect to the occurrence and average and standard deviation usage over the years

Top terms for different metrics		
Number of occurrences	Average over the years	Standard deviation over the years
Entrepreneurial (1248)	Entrepreneurial (46.22222)	Entrepreneurial (58.933685)
Entrepreneurship (872)	Entrepreneurship (34.88)	Entrepreneurship (42.28211)
Entrepreneurs (503)	Entrepreneurs (19.346153)	Business (16.84682)
Business (498)	Business (19.153847)	Entrepreneurs (14.666812)
Research (353)	Research (14.12)	Intentions (11.752972)
Venture (197)	Intentions (11.411765)	Family (10.744766)
Intentions (194)	Capital (10.307693)	Intention (10.293317)
Education (183)	Institutional (10)	Institutional (9.60324)
Development (158)	Learning (9.7)	Learning (8.756585)
International (144)	International (9.6)	Students (8.75051)
Women (139)	Family (9.375)	Factors (7.809557)
Capital (134)	Education (9.15)	Influence (7.727826)
Influence (134)	Venture (8.954545)	Orientation (7.6753016)
Intention (125)	Role (8.35)	Perceived (7.3128667)
Small (124)	Intention (8.333333)	International (6.9570107)
Entrepreneur (123)	Factors (8.318182)	Relationship (6.9470787)
Relationship (122)	Women (8.176471)	Culture (6.7844796)
Process (121)	Orientation (7.923077)	Knowledge (6.7712626)
Individuals (106)	Opportunity (7.769231)	Data (6.7334375)

Source: Maalaoui et al. (2016).

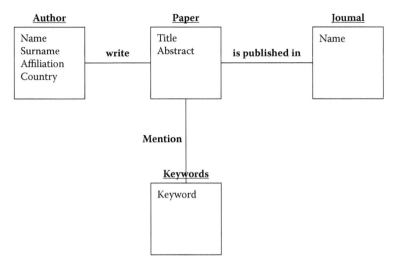

Figure 2A.1   Model of the data collected

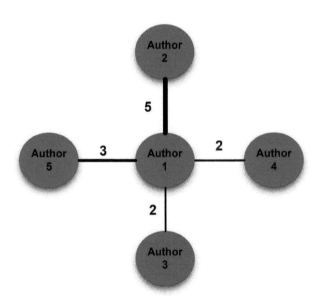

Figure 2A.2   Example of co-authorship composed of three authors

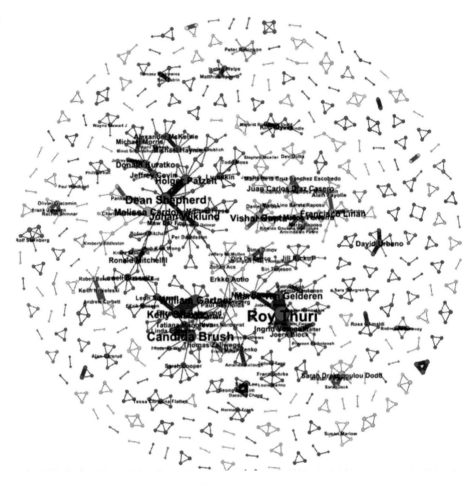

Figure 2A.3   The co-authorship graph (it contains 955 authors connected through 1070 connections)

Figure 2A.4   The giant component of the co-authorship graph composed of 247 authors linked through 390 connections

Figure 2A.5 Cloud representing the most common terms (used as keywords, in titles or in abstracts) and related to the "entrepreneurship intention" research field

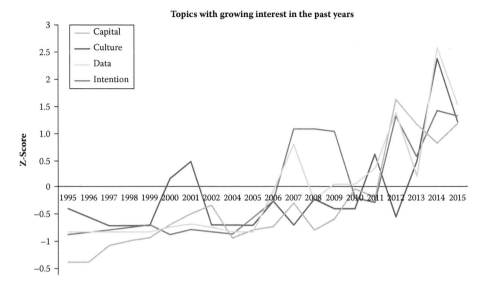

Figure 2A.6   This picture represents the Z-score of topics that have observed a growing interest in the research community over the past few years (the Z-score of the topic is displayed for each year)

Note: Authors are represented in blue and topics are represented in red.

Figure 2A.7 Representation of relationships between topics and authors

An interactive version of this figure is available at: http://goo.gl/6aeKyE

38

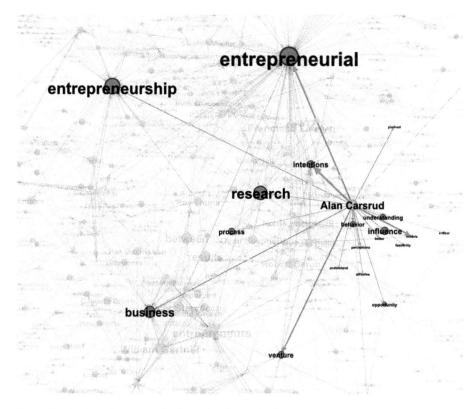

Figure 2A.8   Intention research, Carsrud and main topics

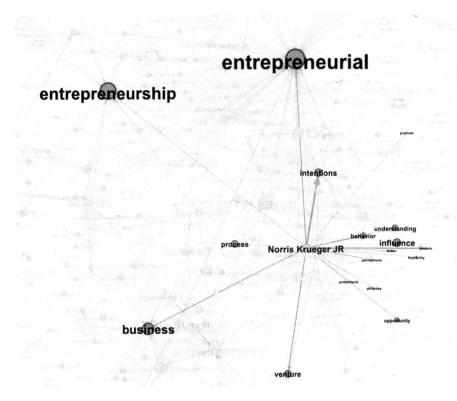

Figure 2A.9   Intention, Krueger and main topics

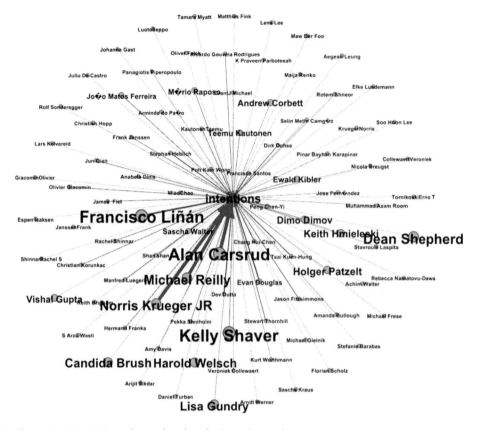

Figure 2A.10   Main authors related to the intention topic

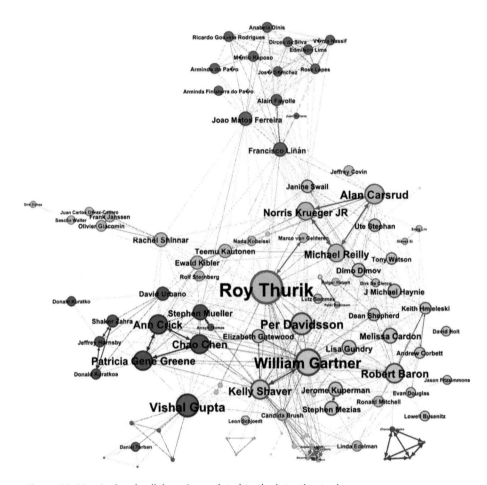

Figure 2A.11   Authors' collaborations related to the intention topic

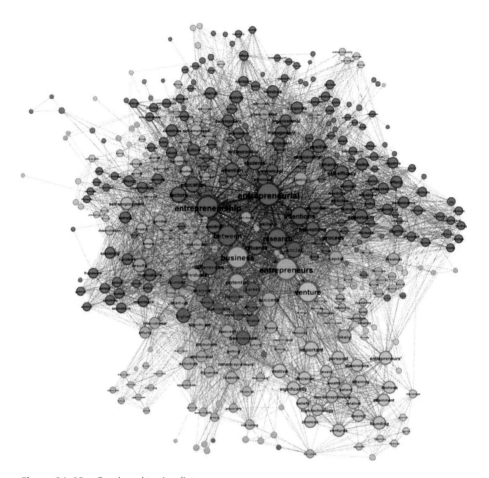

Figure 2A.12   Graph and topics distance

An interactive version of this figure is available at: http://goo.gl/6aeKyE

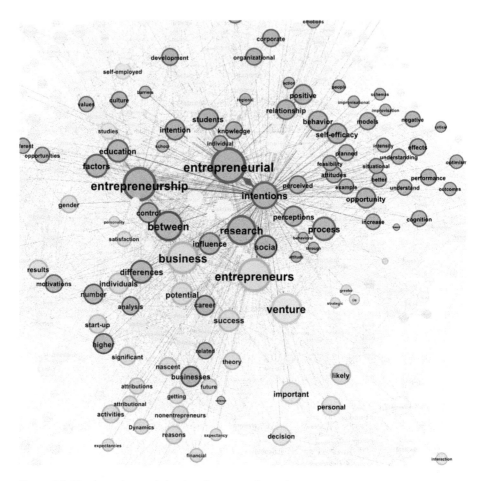

Figure 2A.13 Intention topic is related to some dimensions

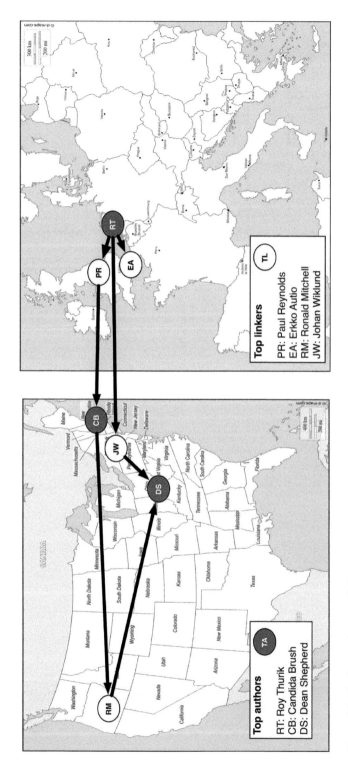

Figure 2A.14 Top authors and linkers

45

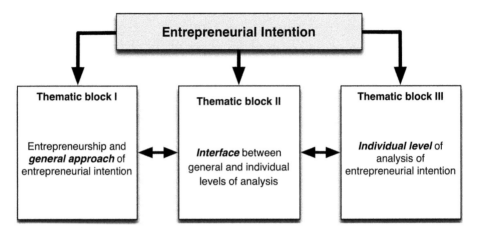

Figure 2A.15   General topic structure for the entrepreneurial intention theme

3   Who is the entrepreneur? The right question has been asked, in the wrong way

Kelly G. Shaver and Alan L. Carsrud

Introduction

Economic conditions do not create new firms, market opportunities do not create new firms, and disruptive technologies do not create new firms. Rather, it is *people*, more specifically *individuals*, who create new firms. A thorough understanding of the process of entrepreneurship requires at least some – if not central – attention to the personal characteristics of the individuals who perform the activities necessary to launch a new venture. Clearly, Birch's (1987) seminal research has driven the growth of research in small business and entrepreneurship and, in particular, the focus on understanding the entrepreneur. Among some of the first empirical and theoretical work on the psychology of entrepreneurs are two edited volumes that predate Birch's work. These are *The Art and Science of Entrepreneurship* (Sexton & Smilor, 1986) and *Managing Take-off in Fast Growth Firms* (Smilor & Kuhn, 1986). The papers in these volumes focused on Achievement Motivation as a personality trait of the entrepreneur.

Achievement motivation in the entrepreneur

The earliest known work on achievement motivation (NAch) conducted by McClelland and his colleagues (McClelland, 1961; McClelland et al., 1953) was an early examination of one personality characteristic and its relationship to entrepreneurial behaviors that would go on to influence some important findings through a number of systematic studies. Among these papers were studies in the 1970s and 1980s that showed how the quality and quantity of academic and vocational success, including entrepreneurial performance, can be significantly predicted by varying combinations of multi-dimensional factors of NAch (Carsrud et al., 1982; Carsrud & Olm, 1986; Carsrud et al., 1989; Helmreich, 1982; Helmreich et al., 1978; Helmreich et al., 1986; Helmreich et al., 1980; Helmreich & Spence, 1978; Spence & Helmreich, 1978).

These studies indicate that the best performance is typically exhibited by those individuals scoring *high* in mastery needs and work orientation, but *low* in interpersonal competitiveness. The latter is counter to the myth of the competitive entrepreneur many people hold. That is, interpersonal competitiveness, popularly considered a trait of entrepreneurs, is not related to actual entrepreneurial success in US samples of entrepreneurs (Carsrud et al., 2009; Carsrud & Olm, 1986; Carsrud et al., 1989). More recent work indicates that these patterns may have cultural difference (Carsrud & Brännback, 2011). Elfving (2008) has also demonstrated that context has a significant impact on entrepreneurs' motivations, an area that still needs to be adequately researched.

Thus, for a period in time from the 1950s to the 1980s NAch in entrepreneurs was rather systematically studied by individuals trained in psychology. While NAch is seen as an important element in driving entrepreneurial behavior, research results showed considerable variations (Brockhaus, 1980, 1982; Carland et al., 1984; Carsrud & Olm, 1986; Carsrud et al., 1989; Gasse, 1982; McClelland, 1961, 1965; McClelland et al., 1953). Some of this difference can be attributed to looking at NAch as unidimensional versus multi-dimensional. In addition, some of the differences could be attributed to different measurement approaches.

Carland et al. (1984) argued that small business owners perceived their businesses as an extension of their personalities, whereas entrepreneurs were characterized by innovative business behavior. Frankly, this latter assumption seems to take the individual out of the entrepreneur. It also assumes that entrepreneurs are not managers, which is likewise absurd. This view is especially interesting considering that McClelland and Winter (1969) much earlier found that NAch was the differentiating factor between small business entrepreneurs and other business leaders. As noted earlier, Carsrud and Olm (1986) studied multi-dimensional NAch in samples of male and female entrepreneurs finding patterns similar to other successful professionals such as academic researchers and airline pilots. Over the years the role of NAch in entrepreneurial behavior has continued to attract interest among entrepreneurship scholars (Carsrud et al., 2009; Collins et al., 2004; Hart et al., 2007; Langen-Fox & Roth, 1995; Lumpkin & Erdogan, 2004; Stewart & Roth, 2007; Tuuanaen, 1997). Carsrud and Brännback (2011) note in their review of the literature on entrepreneurial motivations there is still more research that needs to be done.

The move to individual cognitions and specific behaviors

As promising as these early endeavors on NAch as a personality trait driving entrepreneurial performance were, there were also dissenting voices. These notably included Aldrich & Wiedenmayer's (1993) view that what was really important in entrepreneurship were "rates, not traits," and Gartner's (1988) argument that "'Who is an entrepreneur?' is the wrong question." Alternatively, while accepting the idea that there was no single "entrepreneurial personality," Shaver and Scott (1991) nevertheless asserted the importance of the "person, in whose mind all of the possibilities come together, who believes that innovation is possible, and who has the motivation to persist until the job is done" (p. 39). Indeed, acting on this belief that psychology had much to say about entrepreneurial behavior, Shaver created the first course known to have carried the title "Psychology of Entrepreneurship" at the College of William & Mary in 1993.

When the search for an "entrepreneurial personality" went out of fashion, some researchers interested in person-related variables turned to much smaller pieces of the puzzle in the form of cognitions and behaviors such as intentions, attitudes, or specific firm-creating behaviors. As Carsrud and Brännback (2011) have shown when work on the personality of the entrepreneur fell out of favor, the study of cognitive factors took up some of the slack. This can be seen by the study of the intentions of individuals to become entrepreneurs, beginning with Krueger and Carsrud (1993) and later Krueger et al. (2000). However, it took over five years before research on entrepreneurial intentions really took off seriously.

As Carsrud and Brännback (2011) demonstrated the study of the entrepreneur as *a whole individual* has usually not been the unit of analysis. Firms have often been the unit of analysis, but firms don't make decisions, individuals in the firm do. Too often studies of "personality" at best have really been studies of observable behaviors which some confuse for personality traits. For example, the entrepreneur is seen as an *innovator, creator* (Schumpeter, 1934), *locator* and *implementer* of ideas through *exerciser* of leadership (Baumol, 1968). Kirzner (1973, 1979) saw the entrepreneur as an actor who exhibited deliberate behaviors. These are very typical views of those trained as economists looking at the individual but naïve in the theories of personality and social psychology. Others see the entrepreneur as the *possessor* of idiosyncratic knowledge which impacts opportunity recognition (Eckhardt & Shane, 2003; Gaglio & Katz, 2001; Shane, 2003; Shane & Venkatarman, 2000). Yet none of these characterizations is really looking at the whole entrepreneurial personality.

Why return to the personality of the entrepreneur?

It is the whole person – with all of his or her cognitions, beliefs, attitudes, motivations, emotions, skills, and capabilities – that is the subject matter for both classical social psychology and personality theories. We contend that all of these dimensions, taken in concert, need to form the foundation for the future study of the psychology of the entrepreneur as proposed by Carsrud and Brännback (2009) in their book *Understanding the Entrepreneurial Mind* and in Brännback and Carsrud, (2017) *Revisiting the Entrepreneurial Mind*. We believe that it is time to return to the study of the *Entrepreneurial Personality*.

As Carsrud and Brännback (2011), Carsrud et al. (2009) and McMullan and Kenworthy (2015) note, entrepreneurship studies have taken extensively and unquestioningly from the existing theories in the behavioral and social science disciplines in an attempt to answer the question of what it is that uniquely makes one an entrepreneur. A major reason for abandoning this line of inquiry was that significant portions of research on the psychology of the entrepreneur were unsystematic and opportunistic, with the rare exception of the work on NAch. True personality traits were rarely studied. One also must remember that economists and management researchers conceive of personality in rather naïve ways or assume the individual is not that critical to the new venture process.

However, even worse was the flawed assumption that there was some factor that was unique to just entrepreneurs. Researchers assumed it was possible to identify personality traits that would *uniquely define an entrepreneur,* and when this was not easily demonstrated this line of research was quickly abandoned because that assumption or "myth" failed to be supported. What entrepreneurship researchers, not trained in psychology, did not understand was that personality traits, including motivations, could still be a way to understand entrepreneurial behavior and performance outcomes. As Carsrud and Brännback (2011) have shown, what drives success in other professions also drives success in entrepreneurs. This reflects once again an uncritical adaption of theories from other disciplines without an adequate understanding of the underlying work in that area.

The result of failing to appreciate the appropriate general nature of personality traits and motivation was predictable. Productive lines of research were readily abandoned, including motivations. Even work on cognitive factors like intentions was largely ignored for decades (Carsrud & Brännback, 2011; Carsrud et al., 2009). Most researchers, like lemmings, turned their attention instead to the firm as the unit of analysis as if the individual entrepreneur was merely a fungible asset and interchangeable part. That is, one entrepreneur is as good as any other. It was the firm or innovation that was critical. This was especially the case if studying particular entrepreneurial processes and activities at the firm level (Gartner, 1988). Frankly, this should not be seen as surprising because as most entrepreneurship researchers in business schools come from strategy or organizational behavior as their academic backgrounds, the number of entrepreneurship researchers academically trained in psychology still remains low.

History has a way of repeating itself—today the entrepreneur, as an individual, has once again become a focal point of research not only in terms of cognitive terms like intentions, passions, attitudes, beliefs and behaviors (Carsrud & Brännback, 2009), but also in terms of how those affect others via entrepreneurial leadership (Renko et al., 2015). Clearly the focus on the firm alone did not address the issue of what makes someone an entrepreneur. One cannot see the entrepreneur as the emotionally uninvolved agent as many economists would like to portray. Not all the lemmings went off the cliff chasing the firm as the unit of analysis. The 1980s did provide a lesson on the dangers of uncritical borrowing of theories, a lesson that still has largely gone unlearned (Kenworthy & McMullen, 2014; McMullen & Kenworthy, 2015).

The danger of borrowing

One of the dangers confronting anyone who would borrow theory and method from another discipline is that the borrowing may be incomplete in some critical ways. This problem can be exacerbated if the borrowing is done by scholars who, though well-meaning and conscientious, were not originally trained in the parent discipline. That is not the case for the present authors, one of whom was trained as an experimental social psychologist, and the other was trained in personality and social psychology and was a licensed clinical psychologist with additional post-doctoral training in industrial and applied social psychology. Together, both have contributed significantly to the parent discipline, including service on editorial boards (the *Journal of Personality and Social Psychology* and the *Journal of Applied Social Psychology*). They have published in these journals, as well as in the *Journal of Applied Psychology, Journal of Consulting and Clinical Psychology,* and the *American Psychologist.* One has also published textbooks in the parent discipline (Shaver, 1987; Shaver & Tarpy, 1993).

The problem of indiscriminate borrowing has been illustrated by Shaver (2014), who examined articles that had been published in the *Entrepreneurship: Theory & Practice* (ET&P) and the *Journal of Business Venturing* (JBV) in the four-year period between 2007 and 2010 (inclusive). During this time frame ET&P published more than 225 articles and JBV published more than 150. Of this total, 61 (15 percent) were psychologically relevant and contained dependent variables at the level of the individual (as opposed to a team, a network, or a firm). These 61 articles could be classified into those dealing specifically with cognitive processes (19), those involving decision making (12), those dealing with self-efficacy or identity (16), and those involving motives or emotions (14). Well over half of these articles deal almost exclusively with cognitive processes that were not reflected in the performance of any identifiable entrepreneurial *behavior.* As a discipline, social psychology has certainly been criticized for being the study of the behavior of college sophomores, but it is still the study of their behavior, not merely their thought processes, which seems to be the issue for entrepreneurship work in this area, i.e. what drives intentions. How intentions and cognitions impact entrepreneurial behavior has been largely ignored (Bird & Schjoedt, 2009).

In addition to an over-reliance on cognitive—not behavioral—dependent variables, psychologically informed work in entrepreneurship has also suffered from what Shaver (2014) calls the "liability of oldness." Specifically, when psychological principles are adopted for use in entrepreneurship research, too frequently they are not the most current statements of those principles. First consider the time lag between the original contribution in psychology and its entry into the entrepreneurship literature. Consider two examples: entrepreneurial intentions and self-efficacy. Each of these is a very popular topic in current work on entrepreneurial behavior. The use of Ajzen's (1985) Theory of Planned Behavior (TPB) as an account for the development of entrepreneurial intentions was most prominently introduced by Krueger and his colleagues (e.g. Krueger & Brazeal, 1994; Krueger & Carsrud,

1993). That time frame is roughly 10 years from the publication of Ajzen's book, but his work was really based on a much earlier book by Fishbein and Ajzen (1975). Thus, the initial use of behavioral intentions in entrepreneurship follows their use in social psychology by nearly 20 years; today that is now 40 years from the basic research. Only a few entrepreneurship researchers have adopted the much newer and more nuanced psychological thinking proposed in Theory of Trying (Bagozzi et al., 2003), which still builds on Ajzen's work but moves beyond it significantly.

Much the same is true for the field's use of self-efficacy. This concept entered entrepreneurship research in the 1990s. For example, the concept was used in the work of Boyd and Vozikis (1994) and an "entrepreneurial self-efficacy" scale developed by Chen et al. (1998). But Bandura's work on social learning that provided the conceptual background had begun in the 1960s, and his outline of self-efficacy was published in the *Psychological Review* in 1977, at least 15 years earlier. In other words, entrepreneurship researchers are rather delayed in adopting from psychology. But this is also true of research adopted from sociology, organizational behavior, or even strategy. They often do not keep up with the latest thinking in the field of psychology and then subsequently cite only other entrepreneurship research, not changes in the conceptualization that is going on within psychology. Thus entrepreneurship research, not surprisingly, has no impact on the "mother" discipline and is not consistent with the newest conceptualizations within the base discipline.

The liability of oldness

The real problem created by the *liability of oldness* is, as Shaver (2014) points out, that scholars in the derivative field (entrepreneurship) run the distinct risk of not using the most recent versions of the theoretical tools provided by the originating discipline. For example, there are recent meta-analyses of topics dear to the hearts of entrepreneurship scholars, such as locus of control (Twenge et al., 2004) or choice effects on intrinsic motivation (Patall et al., 2008), that are largely missing from current work on "the psychology of entrepreneurship." As Shaver (2014) noted, there are other examples (motivation as noted by Carsrud & Brännback, 2011), but these are sufficient to make the point that those of us who would borrow from a parent discipline need to do a better job of borrowing the most recent thinking from that parent discipline. True scholarship requires reading broadly and in depth.

Personal and situational influences on behavior

Building on the title of this paper, in what ways was "Who is an entrepreneur?" the wrong question? The answer to that question is primarily only one way. At the time of Gartner's commentary, the expectation was that there was a single, coherent "entrepreneurial personality," a specific collection of traits that would be found among entrepreneurs but not among other people. That was clearly naïve. Even at the time, this expectation should have been contradicted by other things we knew about entrepreneurial careers. For example, although it is true that having entrepreneurial parents increases the likelihood that the adult child of such parents will become an entrepreneur, the connection is far from perfect. Is it the example that entrepreneurial parents provide? Is it the social networks and social capital they provide? Is it the financial capital they provide? Or, as has been suggested recently, is there truly a genetic component (Shane & Nicolaou, 2013)? Whatever the contribution of entrepreneurial parents might be, two key facts remain: (a) not all children of entrepreneurial parents become entrepreneurs, and (b) over a working lifetime, a person may go from corporate employment to entrepreneurship, and perhaps even back to corporate employment.

The evidence against a single, coherent, entrepreneurial personality is even stronger today thanks to the research accomplished by teams associated with the Global Entrepreneurship Monitor (2013; Amorós & Bosma, 2014). If there were truly a specific entrepreneurial personality, then it stands to reason that such people would be randomly distributed across all societies and cultures and there would be very little in the way of cross-country differences in the levels of entrepreneurial behavior. But the GEM research – which now covers 70 countries accounting for 90 percent of the world's GDP – shows vast differences in total early-stage entrepreneurial activity, ranging from a low of less than 4 percent (in Italy and Japan) to a high of nearly 40 percent (in Zambia and Nigeria). It is simply implausible to argue, for example, that Zambia and Nigeria are where all of the entrepreneurial personalities live. Rather, the world's economies can be split into three large groups. "Factor-driven" economies depend on their natural resources and unskilled labor; "efficiency-driven" economies depend on more effective production and more skilled labor capable of employing existing technologies; and "innovation-driven" economies can sustain their higher wages only if their businesses are able to compete with new and unique products (Schwab & Sala-i-Martín, 2014). Higher levels of entrepreneurial activity occur in the factor-driven economies than in the innovation-driven economies.

The old view that there might be a single "entrepreneurial personality" obviously overlooked any role that might have been played by the cultural context or the country's resources. It also overlooked the much more "local" influences provided by the situations in which people find themselves. In addition, the roles of family, local, and societal norms as contextual variables have not adequately been researched (Elfving et al., 2009; Brännback & Carsrud, 2016). It is clear that *context* is critical in understanding entrepreneurial cognitions and behaviors (Welter & Gartner, 2016).

The influence of situations on behavior has a long history in psychology, beginning with the strict behaviorism of Watson (1913) and continued in the operant conditioning approach of Skinner (1938). Indeed, the situational approach held such sway for so long that in a controversial book on personality assessment, Mischel (1968) minimized the importance of intra-psychic factors in favor of the power of situations. Not surprisingly, other writers soon countered the purely situationist view (e.g. Bowers, 1973). Over the intervening years, psychologists interested in personality dynamics have attempted to specify more carefully the conditions favorable to intra-psychic influences on human action. This work includes the research by Cattell (1980) on the "data box" (Individuals? Traits? Occasions?) and a more extended formulation by Ozer (1986) that involves a four-dimensional matrix: Individuals, Response Classes, Situations, and Time. From our perspective, the true personality of an entrepreneur would effectively be what remains after variations in situation and time have been removed and multiple potential responses have been considered. In other words, when contextual factors have been taken into account what remains is the impact of personality traits.

Traits and types

Psychological research in personality has always been concerned with how the intra-psychic targets (e.g. traits) have been measured. Where do the measurement scales we use come from? An early paper by Goldberg (1972) established three basic methods for constructing personality assessment scales. As described by Johnson (2014), these are the external strategy, the internal strategy, and the intuitive strategy. The external approach examines the consistency of correlations among items, especially in the context of other information about the respondents. Applied to entrepreneurs, this strategy would have us ask questions of experienced and successful entrepreneurs and compare those answers to ones provided by individuals who have never even considered entrepreneurial activity. Items that were answered differently by the two sorts of respondent groups would then be taken as a measure of entrepreneurial tendencies.

The internal strategy examines the consistency of items answered by a large group of research participants (not selected for any particular behavior). A large pool of items is administered to a sample and factor analytic techniques are then employed to create separate scales. The relative independence of these scales from one another can indicate whether the concept involved is a narrow one or a broad one.

Finally, the intuitive method relies on the investigator's professional judgment. In the entrepreneurship domain one might expect that a scale should include some assessment of risk propensity, of locus of control, or of achievement motivation. The difficulty, of course, is that the professional's judgment could be more or less highly influenced by a stereotype of what an entrepreneur *should* be. This "*should*" is clearly subject to cultural expectations. Readers will recognize this approach as having been employed – often with mixed results – by some of the early research in entrepreneurship that led to Gartner's question.

In practice, however, it is common to find a mixture of strategies involved in the construction of an inventory, and then to have the subject be the result to refinement through methods derived from Item Response Theory (IRT; Morizot et al., 2007). An example might be found in work that combines items from the Panel Studies of Entrepreneurial Dynamics (PSED; Gartner et al., 2004, p. 325; Reynolds & Curtin, 2009) expected to apply to everyone, with items expected to differ between entrepreneurs and non-entrepreneurs.

The "Big Five" (or six) factors

One of the objectives of modern personality measurement has been to identify just a few latent dimensions on which people can be characterized. Given that the public domain International Personality Item Pool (IPIP) now contains 2,413 separate items (http://ipip.ori.org/newIPIPitemsTOC.htm, accessed September 24, 2014), the challenge to find "a few" latent dimensions would seem to be a daunting one. Nevertheless, as Lewis and Bates (2014) note, "it is now uncontroversial to assert that a small number of latent factors – often five (Costa & McCrae, 1992) or, less frequently, three (Eysenck & Eysenck, 1975), or six (Lee & Ashton, 2004) – account for the bulk of reliable variance in a wide spectrum of traits and behaviors" (p. 9).

The "Big Five" are Conscientiousness, Agreeableness, Neuroticism, Openness to experience, and Extraversion (Costa & McCrae, 1992) arranged here in one mnemonic order: CANOE. Each of these is a dimension that consists of separate elements. Conscientiousness represents the poles of efficient/organized versus easy-going/careless. Conscientious people are dependable, organized, prefer planned to spontaneous behavior, and are interested in achievement. Agreeableness represents the difference between friendliness/compassion and a detached, analytical nature. Neuroticism is the dimension that runs from sensitive/nervous to secure/confident. Openness to experience distinguishes people who are naturally curious and inventive from those who are cautious and consistent. Finally, extraversion differentiates people who are gregarious and outgoing from those who are solitary and reserved. At least one study has tested for differences in entrepreneurial performance based on the Big Five (Ciavarella et al., 2004). Not surprisingly, these investigators found that conscientiousness was positively related to venture survival. There was, however, an unanticipated negative relationship between openness to experience and long-term venture survival. Extraversion, emotional stability (the positive end of neuroticism), and agreeableness were unrelated to venture success. Before concluding that an extraverted, emotionally stable, and agreeable person would make a terrible entrepreneur, it is worth noting that one study is rarely sufficient as a basis for such general conclusions. We have a tradition in entrepreneurship (and management research in general) of failing to publish replication studies, which leads us into the earlier noted problem of being unsystematic and opportunistic in how research is conducted.

Linguistic issues

The five-factor model has typically been found when the personality descriptors used in the English language are a version of the internal strategy described earlier. Specifically, the factors emerge from analyses of the descriptive words, not from examination of the behaviors of individuals selected for being at the extreme on some dimension. Recently, however, analyses of the lexical structure of personality descriptors used in languages other than English have suggested that there should be a sixth latent personality trait in addition to the Big Five (Ashton & Lee, 2007). This sixth is Honesty/Humility: the degree to which a person is sincere, honest, loyal, and modest versus sly, deceitful, greedy, and pretentious. When the sixth dimension is added, the group of traits is identified by the acronym HEXACO. This stands for Honesty/Humility, Emotionality, eXtraversion, Agreeableness, Conscientiousness, and Openness to experience. Extraversion, Conscientiousness, and Openness to experience are essentially the same in the two trait systems. By contrast, the three HEXACO dimensions of Humility, Agreeableness, and Emotionality together correspond to the elements of the Big Five's Agreeableness and Neuroticism.

Given that so much of contemporary research in entrepreneurship takes place in countries where the native language is not English, it might serve us well to use the HEXACO factors, rather than the Big Five factors, as dimensions on which to characterize entrepreneurs. For an extended discussion on cultural and language issues in the study of the entrepreneur one is referred to Brännback et al. (2014).

Personality structure and entrepreneurship research

By now it should be clear that we believe that answering the question of "Who is an entrepreneur?" requires study of more than a single – or even a few – isolated cognitive processes. Rather, it requires using several personality and motivational *dimensions* in concert to "locate" the entrepreneur in a theoretical space that also contains – in different locations – all the rest of those people who have no interest in starting their own businesses. A good start would be to ask how many studies in our leading entrepreneurship journals involve either the Big Five or the HEXACO personality factors. Unfortunately, the list is exceedingly short. In *Entrepreneurship Theory & Practice* an EBSCO search using Business Source Complete reveals no articles using either the Big Five or the HEXACO model. In the *Journal of Business Venturing*, the only Big Five article is the Ciavarella et al. (2004) study cited earlier; HEXACO does not appear. In the *Journal of Small Business Management*, there are two studies by Morrison (1996, 1997) on the job satisfaction of franchisees that involve some dimensions in the Big Five; there is nothing involving the HEXACO dimensions. In *Entrepreneurship and Regional Development* there are no articles involving either the Big Five or HEXACO. In *Small Business Economics* there is one study by Chlosta et al. (2012) that involves Openness to experience. The list could go on, but this is probably sufficient to make the point: to date there has been almost no research that the psychological community would think provided answers to the question, "Who is an entrepreneur?" In the psychological literature, personality is studied for its own sake, but also because it is presumed to provide much of the internal *motivation* for behavior. With a definite sense of déjà vu, we now turn to the only broad motivational pattern that has received significant, if sporadic, attention in the entrepreneurship literature: achievement motivation.

Conclusions

In this chapter we have argued that "Who is an entrepreneur?" is really one of the *right* questions to ask, but that to date, it has not been asked in the right way. We agree that there are identifiable differences in both cognitive and metacognitive processes between entrepreneurs and non-entrepreneurs (Gaglio & Katz, 2001; Haynie et al., 2012; Mitchell et al., 2009; Stewart & Roth, 2007). We agree that entrepreneurs may have a level of passion not found among their corporate-employed counterparts (Cardon et al., 2013). We believe that some of the reasons entrepreneurs give for doing what they do are different from the work-based reasons provided by people who are not starting businesses (Carter et al., 2003) and even that those reasons may change over time (Davis & Shaver, 2012). We have shown the importance of a particular motive, NAch, derived directly from classical personality theory. But the full concept of a person encompasses more than his or her cognitions, passion, or reasons for acting: it also includes that essence that persists across time, context, and circumstances. It includes the individual's personality. And in everyday language, *that* is the most complete answer to "Who is an entrepreneur?" Other chapters in this book will delve into the role of language as it impacts entrepreneurial cognitions and behaviors.

If the psychological study of entrepreneurship is to progress to the next level, we argue that it must begin to consider – much more fully than in the past – the personality characteristics of the entrepreneur. We argue that future research on entrepreneurs begin to consider the five or six latent personality factors that to date have received virtually no attention from entrepreneurship researchers. And when these future studies begin to consider personality dimensions, we hope that they will do so mindful of the most recent advances in the home discipline. The future psychology of the entrepreneur needs to be a contemporary version, not an historical one.

References

Ajzen, I. (1985). From intentions to actions: A theory of planned behavior. In J. Kuhl & J. Beckmann (Eds), *Action Control: From Cognition to Behavior* (pp. 11–39). Berlin: Springer-Verlag.
Aldrich, H. & Wiedenmayer, G. (1993). From traits to rates: An ecological perspective on organization foundings. In J. A. Katz & R. H. Brockhaus Sr. (Eds), *Advances in Entrepreneurship, Firm Emergence, and Growth* (pp. 145–195). Greenwich, CT: JAI Press.

Amorós, J. E. & Bosma, N. (2014). *Global Entrepreneurship Monitor 2013 Global Report: Fifteen Years of Assessing Entrepreneurship across the Globe*. Concepción, Chile: Universidad del Desarrollo and Global Entrepreneurship Research Association.

Ashton, M. C. & Lee, K. (2007). Empirical, theoretical, and practical advantages of the HEXACO model of personality structure. *Personality and Social Psychology Review, 11*, 150–66.

Bagozzi, R. P., Dholakia, U. & Basuroy, S. (2003). How effortful decisions get enacted: The motivating role of decision processes, desires & anticipated emotions. *Journal of Behavioral Decision Making, 16* (4), 273–95.

Bandura, A. (1977). Self-efficacy: Toward a unifying theory of behavioral change. *Psychological Review, 84*, 191–215.

Baumol, W. J. (1968). Entrepreneurship in economic theory. *The American Economic Review, 58*, 64–71.

Birch, D. (1987). *Job Creation in America: How Our Smallest Companies Put the Most People to Work*. New York, NY: Free Press.

Bird, B. & Schjoedt, L. (2009). Entrepreneurial behavior: Its nature, scope, recent research, and agenda for future research. In A. L. Carsrud & M. Brännback (Eds), *Understanding the Entrepreneurial Mind: Opening the Black Box* (pp. 327–58). New York, NY: Springer.

Bowers, K. S. (1973). Situationism in psychology: An analysis and critique. *Psychological Review, 80*, 307–36.

Boyd, N. G. & Vozikis, G. S. (1994). The influence of self-efficacy on the development of entrepreneurial intentions and actions. *Entrepreneurship Theory & Practice, 18* (4), 63–77.

Brännback, M. & Carsrud, A. L. (2016). Understanding entrepreneurial cognitions through the lenses of context. In F. Welter & W. B. Gartner (Eds), *A Research Agenda for Entrepreneurship and Context* (pp. 16–27). Cheltenham, UK: Edward Elgar.

Brännback, M. & Carsrud, A. L. (Eds) (2017). *Revisiting the Entrepreneurial Mind: Inside the Black Box*. New York, NY: Springer-Verlag.

Brännback, M., Lång, S., Carsrud, A. L. & Terjesen, S. (2014). Cross-cultural studies in entrepreneurship: A note on culture and language. In A. L. Carsrud & M. Brännback (Eds), *Handbook of Research Methods and Applications in Entrepreneurship and Small Business* (pp. 156–76). Cheltenham, UK: Edward Elgar.

Brockhaus, R. H. (1980). Risk taking propensity of entrepreneurs. *Academy of Management Journal, 23*, 509–20.

Brockhaus, R. H. (1982). The psychology of the entrepreneur. In C. A. Kent, D. A. Sexton & K. H. Vesper, (Eds), *Encyclopedia of Entrepreneurship* (pp. 39–55). Englewood Cliffs, NJ: Prentice-Hall.

Cardona, M. S., Grégoire, D. A., Stevens, C. E. & Patel, P. C. (2013). Measuring entrepreneurial passion: Conceptual foundations and scale validation. *Journal of Business Venturing, 28* (3), 373–96.

Carland, J. W., Hoy, F., Boulton, W. R. & Carland, J. A. C. (1984). Differentiating entrepreneurs from small business owners: A conceptualization. *Academy of Management Review, 9*, 351–59.

Carsrud, A. L. & Brännback, M. (2009). *Understanding the Entrepreneurial Mind: Opening the Black Box*. New York, NY: Springer.

Carsrud, A. L. & Brännback, M. (2011). Entrepreneurial motivations: What do we still need to know? *Journal of Small Business Management, 49*, 9–26.

Carsrud, A. L. & Olm, K. W. (1986). The success of male and female entrepreneurs: A comparative analysis of the effects of multi-dimensional achievement motivation and personality traits. In R. Smilor & R. L. Kuhn (Eds), *Managing Take-Off in Fast Growth Firms* (pp. 147–62). New York, NY: Praeger.

Carsrud, A. L., Brännback, M., Elfving, J. & Brandt, K. (2009). Motivations: The entrepreneurial mind and behavior. In A. L. Carsrud & M. Brännback (Eds), *Understanding the Entrepreneurial Mind: Opening the Black Box* (pp. 141–65). New York, NY: Springer.

Carsrud, A. L., Dodd, B. G., Helmreich, R. L. & Spence J. T. (1982, August). *Predicting Performance: Effects of Scholastic Aptitude, Achievement Motivation, Past Performance, and Attributions*. Presented at the American Psychological Association, Washington, DC.

Carsrud, A. L., Olm, K. & Thomas, J. (1989). Predicting entrepreneurial success: Effects of multi-dimensional achievement motivation, levels of ownership, and cooperative relationships. *Entrepreneurship and Regional Development, 1* (3), 237–44.

Carter, N. M., Gartner, W. B., Shaver, K. G. & Gatewood, E. J. (2003). The career reasons of nascent entrepreneurs. *Journal of Business Venturing, 18,* 13–39.

Cattell, R. B. (1980). The separation and evaluation of personal and environmental contributions to behavior by the person-centered model (PCER). *Multivariate Behavioral Research, 15,* 371–402.

Chen, C. C., Greene, P. G. & Crick, A. (1998). Does entrepreneurial self-efficacy distinguish entrepreneurs from managers? *Journal of Business Venturing, 13,* 295–316.

Chlosta, S., Patzelt, H., Klein, S. & Dormann, C. (2012). Parental roles and the decision to become self-employed: The moderating effect of personality. *Small Business Economics, 38,* 121–38.

Ciavarella, M. A., Buchholtz, A. K., Riordan, C. M., Gatewood, R. D. & Stokes, G. S. (2004). The Big Five and venture survival: Is there a linkage? *Journal of Business Venturing, 19,* 465–83.

Collins, C., Hanges, P. & Locke, E. A. (2004). The relationship of achievement motivation to entrepreneurial behavior: A meta-analysis. *Human Performance, 17,* 95–117.

Costa, P. T. & McCrae, R. R. (1992). *NEO Personality Inventory-Revised (NEO-PI-R) and NEO Five-Factor Inventory (NEO-FFI) Professional Manual.* Odessa, FL: Psychological Assessment Resources.

Davis, A. E. & Shaver, K. G. (2012). Understanding gendered variations in business growth intentions across the life course. *Entrepreneurship Theory & Practice, 36,* 495–512.

Eckhardt, J. T. & Shane, S. (2003). Opportunities and entrepreneurship. *Journal of Management, 29* (3), 333–49.

Elfving, J. (2008). *Contextualizing Entrepreneurial Intentions: A Multiple Case Study on Entrepreneurial Cognitions and Perceptions.* Turku, Finland: Åbo Akademi förlag.

Elfving, J., Brännback, M. & Carsrud, A. L. (2009). Towards a contextual model of entrepreneurial intentions. In A. L. Carsrud & M. Brännback (Eds), *Understanding the Entrepreneurial Mind: Opening the Black Box* (pp. 23–34). New York, NY: Springer.

Eysenck, H. J. & Eysenck, S. B. G. (1975). *Manual of the Eysenck Personality Questionnaire.* San Diego, CA: Educational and Industrial Testing Service.

Fishbein, M. & Ajzen, I. (1975). *Belief, Attitude, Intention, and Behavior.* Reading, MA: Addison-Wesley.

Gaglio, C. M. & Katz, J. A. (2001). The psychological basis of opportunity identification: Entrepreneurial alertness. *Small Business Economics, 16* (2), 95–111.

Gartner, W. B. (1988). "Who is an entrepreneur?" is the wrong question. *American Journal of Small Business, 12* (4), 11–32.

Gartner, W. B., Shaver, K. G., Carter, N. M. & Reynolds, P. D. (Eds), (2004). *The Handbook of Entrepreneurial Dynamics: The Process of Business Creation* (p. 325). Thousand Oaks, CA: Sage Publications.

Gasse, Y. (1982). Elaborations on the psychology of the entrepreneur. In C. A. Kent, D. A. Sexton & K. H. Vesper (Eds), *Encyclopedia of Entrepreneurship* (pp. 57–66). Englewood Cliffs, NJ: Prentice-Hall.

Global Entrepreneurship Monitor (2013). *GEM 2013 Global Report,* accessed March 10, 2017 at www.gemconsortium.org/report.

Goldberg, L. R. (1972). Parameters of personality inventory construction and utilization: A comparison of prediction strategies and tactics. *Multivariate Behavioral Research Monographs, 72* (2), 59.

Hart, J. W., Stasson, M. F. & Mahoney, J. M. (2007). The Big Five and achievement motivation: Exploring the relationship between personality and a two-factor model of motivation. *Individual Differences Research, 5* (2), 267–74.

Haynie, J. M., Shepherd, D. A. & Holger, P. (2012). Cognitive adaptability and an entrepreneurial task: The role of metacognitive ability and feedback. *Entrepreneurship Theory & Practice, 36* (2), 237–65.

Helmreich, R. L. (1982, August). *Pilot Selection and Training.* Presented at the American Psychological Association, Washington, DC.

Helmreich, R. L. & Spence, J. T. (1978). The Work and Family Orientation Questionnaire: An objective instrument to assess components of achievement motivation and attitudes towards family and career. *JSAS Catalog of Selected Documents in Psychology, 8*, 35, (Ms. No. 1677).

Helmreich, R. L., Beane, W. E., Lucker, G. W. & Spence, J. T. (1978). Achievement motivation and scientific attainment. *Personality and Social Psychology Bulletin, 4*, 222–6.

Helmreich, R. L., Sawin, L. L. & Carsrud, A. L. (1986). The honeymoon effect in job performance: Temporal increases in the predictive power of achievement motivation. *Journal of Applied Psychology, 71* (2), 185–8.

Helmreich, R. L., Spence, J. T., Beane, W. E., Lucker, G. W. & Matthews, K. A. (1980). Making it in academic psychology: Demographic and personality correlates of attainment. *Journal of Personality and Social Psychology, 39*, 896–908.

International Personality Item Pool, accessed March 10, 2017 at http://ipip.ori.org/.

Johnson, J. A. (2014). Measuring thirty facets of the Five Factor Model with a 120-item public domain inventory: Development of the IPIP-NEO-120. *Journal of Research in Personality, 51*, 78–89.

Kenworthy, T. P. & McMullen, W. E. (2014). From philosophy of science to theory testing: Generating practical knowledge in entrepreneurship. In A. L. Carsrud & M. Brännback (Eds), *Handbook of Research Methods and Applications in Entrepreneurship and Small Business* (pp. 20–55). Cheltenham, UK: Edward Elgar.

Kirzner, I. (1973). *Competition and Entrepreneurship.* Chicago, IL: University of Chicago Press.

Kirzner, I. (1979). *Perception, Opportunity and Profit.* Chicago, IL: University of Chicago Press.

Krueger, N. F. & Brazeal, D. (1994). Entrepreneurial potential and potential entrepreneurs. *Entrepreneurship Theory & Practice, 18* (1), 5–21.

Krueger, N. F. & Carsrud, A. L. (1993). Entrepreneurial intentions: Applying the theory of planned behaviour. *Entrepreneurship and Regional Development, 5*, 315–30.

Krueger, N. F., Reilly, M. & Carsrud, A. L. (2000). Competing models of entrepreneurial intentions. *Journal of Business Venturing, 15* (5/6), 411–532.

Langen-Fox, J. L. & Roth, S. (1995). Achievement motivation and female entrepreneurs. *Journal of Occupational and Organizational Psychology, 68*, 209–18.

Lee, K. & Ashton, M. C. (2004). Psychometric properties of the HEXACO personality inventory. *Multivariate Behavioral Research, 39*, 329–58.

Lewis, G. J. & Bates, T. C. (2014). How genes influence personality: Evidence from multi-facet twin analyses of the HEXACO dimensions. *Journal of Research in Personality, 51*, 9–17.

Lumpkin, G. T. & Erdogan, B. (2004). If not entrepreneurship, can psychological characteristics predict entrepreneurial orientation? – A Pilot Study. *ICFAI Journal of Entrepreneurship Development, 1*, 21–33.

McClelland, D. C. (1961). *The Achieving Society.* Princeton, NJ: D. Van Nostrand.

McClelland, D. C. (1965). Achievement motivation can be developed. *Harvard Business Review, 43* (6), 6–17.

McClelland, D. C. & Winter, D. G. (1969). *Motivating Economic Achievement.* New York, NY: Free Press.

McClelland, D. C., Atkinson, J. W., Clark, R. A. & Lowell, E. I. (1953). *The Achievement Motive.* New York, NY: Appleton-Century-Crofts.

McMullan, W. E. & Kenworthy, T. P. (2015). *Creativity and Entrepreneurial Performance: A General Scientific Theory.* New York, NY: Springer-Verlag.

Mischel, W. (1968). *Personality and Assessment.* New York, NY: Wiley.

Mitchell, R. K., Mitchell, B. T. & Mitchell, J. R. (2009). Entrepreneurial scripts and entrepreneurial expertise: The information processing perspective. In A. L. Carsrud & M. Brännback (Eds), *Understanding the Entrepreneurial Mind: Opening the Black Box* (pp. 97–140). New York, NY: Springer.

Morizot, J., Ainsworth, A. T. & Reise, S. P. (2007). Toward modern psychometrics: Application of item response theory models in personality research. In R. W. Robins, R. C. Fraley & R. F. Krueger (Eds), *Handbook of Research Methods in Personality Psychology* (pp. 407–23). New York, NY: Guilford Press.

Morrison, K. A. (1996). An empirical test of a model of franchisee job satisfaction. *Journal of Small Business Management, 34*, 27–41.

Morrison, K. A. (1997). How franchise job satisfaction and personality affects performance, organizational commitment, franchisor relations, and intention to remain. *Journal of Small Business Management, 35*, 39–67.

Ozer, D. J. (1986). *Consistency in Personality: A Methodological Framework.* Heidelberg: Springer-Verlag.

Panel Studies of Entrepreneurial Dynamics, accessed March 10, 2017 at www.psed.isr.umich.edu/psed/home.

Patall, E. A., Cooper, H. & Robinson, J. C. (2008). The effects of choice on intrinsic motivation and related outcomes: A meta-analysis of research findings. *Psychological Bulletin, 134*, 270–300.

Renko, M., El-Tarabishy, A., Carsrud, A. L. & Brännback, M. (2015). Understanding and measuring entrepreneurial leadership. *Journal of Small Business Management, 53* (1), 54–74.

Reynolds, P. D. & Curtin, R. T. (Eds) (2009). *New Firm Creation in the United States: Initial Explorations with the PSED II Data Set.* New York, NY: Springer.

Schumpeter, J. A. (1934). *The Theory of Economic Development.* Oxford, UK: Oxford University Press.

Schwab, K. & Sala-i-Martín, X. (2014). *The Global Competitiveness Report 2014–2015.* Geneva: World Economic Forum.

Sexton, D. & Smilor, R. (Eds) (1986). *The Art and Science of Entrepreneurship.* Cambridge, MA: Ballinger.

Shane, S. (2003). *A General Theory of Entrepreneurship.* Cheltenham, UK: Edward Elgar.

Shane, S. & Nicolaou, N. (2013). The genetics of entrepreneurial performance. *International Small Business Journal, 31*, 473–95.

Shane, S. & Venkataraman, S. (2000). The promise of entrepreneurship as a field of research. *Academy of Management Review, 25*, 217–26.

Shaver, K. G. (1987). *Principles of Social Psychology* (3rd edn.). Hillsdale, NJ: Lawrence Erlbaum Associates.

Shaver, K. G. (2014). Psychology of entrepreneurial behavior. In A. Fayolle (Ed.), *Handbook of Research on Entrepreneurship: What We Know and What We Need to Know* (pp. 262–80). Cheltenham, UK: Edward Elgar.

Shaver, K. G. & Scott, L. R. (1991). Person, process, choice: The psychology of new venture creation. *Entrepreneurship Theory & Practice, 16* (2), 23–45.

Shaver, K. G. & Tarpy, R. M. (1993). *Psychology.* New York, NY: Macmillan.

Skinner, B. F. (1938). *The Behavior of Organisms.* New York, NY: Appleton-Century-Crofts.

Smilor, R. & Kuhn, R. L. (Eds) (1986). *Managing Take-Off in Fast Growth Firms.* New York, NY: Praeger.

Spence, J. T. & Helmreich, R. L. (1978). *Masculinity and Femininity: Their Psychological Dimensions, Correlates, and Antecedents.* Austin, TX: The University of Texas Press.

Stewart, W. J., Jr. & Roth P. L. (2007). A meta-analysis of achievement motivation differences between entrepreneurs and managers. *Journal of Small Business Management, 45* (4), 401–21.

Tuuanaen, M. (1997). Finnish and US entrepreneurs' need for achievement: A cross-cultural analysis. In A. J. Carland & J. W. Carland (Eds), *The Proceedings of the Academy of Entrepreneurship* (pp. 8–20). Cullowhee, NC: Academy of Entrepreneurship.

Twenge, J. M., Zhang, L. & Im, C. (2004). It's beyond my control: A cross-temporal meta-analysis of increasing externality in locus of control, 1960–2002. *Personality and Social Psychology Review, 8*, 308–19.

Watson, J. B. (1913). Psychology as the behaviorist views it. *Psychological Review, 20*, 158–77.

Welter, F. & Gartner, W. B. (Eds) (2016). *A Research Agenda for Entrepreneurship and Context.* Cheltenham, UK: Edward Elgar.

4   A proposed model for the culture's mode of influence on the entrepreneurial process

Francisco Liñán and Inmaculada Jaén

Introduction

Entrepreneurial intentions are considered a very relevant predictor of start-up behaviour (Kautonen et al., 2015). This has so far served as a justification to focus solely on the study of entrepreneurial intentions. In contrast, the research specifically focusing on the transformation from intention to action is still scarce. Few longitudinal analyses have been performed to test the predictive capacity of intention. A recent literature review (Liñán & Fayolle, 2015) found only 24 longitudinal studies out of 409 articles on entrepreneurial intentions, and only 20 of them focused on new venture creation (with the remaining addressing firm growth). These limited results, nevertheless, overwhelmingly confirm that intention is a significant predictor of entrepreneurial action.

At the same time, the extant research also finds that the rate of transformation from intention to action is considerably low. Van Gelderen et al. (2015) find that nearly 70 per cent of intentional entrepreneurs have not taken real action to start their ventures after one year. Thus, in order to actually understand how to transform entrepreneurial intention into action, there is a need to develop more complex models, taking into account other relevant variables. Many such variables have been proposed in the literature. Some authors have considered demographic/background elements, such as age, gender, experience and education (Langowitz & Minniti, 2007; Levesque & Minniti, 2006). Others have analysed the role of psychological variables (Van Gelderen et al., 2015). The analysis of economic conditions is relatively frequent (Carree et al., 2007), and the role of culture and social conditions is also attracting considerable attention (Kibler et al., 2014; Liñán & Fernandez-Serrano, 2014).

Regarding this latter element, culture is proposed in this chapter as an encompassing contextual element playing a very relevant role in explaining the process from intention to action. While a number of contributions have studied the role of culture in the configuration of entrepreneurial intentions (Liñán et al., 2016), others have analysed culture's effect on start-up rates (Pinillos & Reyes, 2011). Elements such as the social legitimacy of entrepreneurship have been found to affect actual venture creation (Kibler et al., 2014).

Still, the question remains as to how culture affects the transformation of entrepreneurial intention into action. In this chapter, we focus on understanding how and to what extent national culture influences entrepreneurship, including entrepreneurial beliefs, motives, intentions and behaviours (Hayton & Cacciotti, 2013). We argue that culture is made up of at least two elements: social cognition and societal legitimation. Each of these elements would have a different effect on either the entrepreneurial intention or its transformation into action. The relative influence exerted by each of these two components will determine the aggregate effect of culture on the entrepreneurial process.

This proposed model of cultural influence on entrepreneurship can also help explain some of the apparent paradoxes that have been found in the literature. In particular, there is considerable evidence that individualist values favour entrepreneurship (Liñán et al., 2016; Moriano et al., 2007; Yang et al., 2015). At the same time, however, countries with a less individualistic culture exhibit higher levels of entrepreneurial intentions and start-up rates (Xavier et al., 2013). Despite several attempts to explain this contradiction (Pinillos & Reyes, 2011), the issue is still far from settled.

Measuring culture

Culture may be defined as the set of basic common values which contributes to shaping people's behaviour in a society (Inglehart, 1997). It also includes patterns of thinking, feeling and acting, which are learned and shared by people living within the same social environment (Hofstede & Hofstede, 2005). Hence, at least two components of culture are identified: values and behaviours. Regarding its effect on entrepreneurship, few consolidated 'truths' may still be claimed. In fact, the interdisciplinarity inherent to this field of research can lead to substantial challenges in theory development because scholars may emphasise different theoretical lenses, languages, research questions and methods (Hayton & Cacciotti, 2013).

The first and most common classification of cultures distinguishes between individualist and collectivist ones (Hofstede, 1980; Schwartz, 1999; Triandis, 1995). Yet, alternative characterisations have also been made. From an empirical point of view, Hofstede's cultural dimensions of individualism, uncertainty avoidance, power distance and masculinity (Hofstede, 1980, 2003; Hofstede & Hofstede, 2005) have been frequently used as a reference in research about the influence of culture on entrepreneurship (Hayton et al., 2002; Liñán & Chen, 2009; Mueller et al., 2002). Results have confirmed their influence on national start-up rates, innovation or entrepreneurial intentions. Notwithstanding, conflicting results have recently emerged (Hayton & Cacciotti, 2013). Hofstede's measures have been criticised as having methodological weaknesses, being very old and lacking a theory-driven development base (Cullen et al., 2014; Jabri, 2005; Tang & Koveos, 2008).

More recently, scholars have also applied Schwartz's (1990) cultural value structure to the study of entrepreneurship (De Clercq et al., 2014; Hirschi & Fischer, 2013;

Holland & Shepherd, 2013; Liñán & Fernandez-Serrano, 2014; Liñán et al., 2013; Yang et al., 2015). Its seven cultural value orientations are classified into three bipolar dimensions addressing three basic social problems: (a) individuality vs. group membership (opposing autonomy and embeddedness orientations), (b) getting societal tasks done (opposing egalitarianism and hierarchy) and (c) mode of interaction with others and with nature (opposing harmony and mastery) (Schwartz, 2006, 2008). Recent work has shown that they interact with wealth in influencing different types of entrepreneurial activity (Liñán et al., 2013). At the same time, they are also useful in explaining international investment decisions (Siegel et al., 2013), and seem to moderate the impact of regulatory barriers on entrepreneurship (Fernández-Serrano & Romero, 2014).

Steenkamp (2001) proposes an empirical integration of both theories, for which there seems to be some theoretical basis (Schwartz, 2009). So, for the purposes of this chapter, we will follow most of Steenkamp's (2001) recommendations by considering four aspects or dimensions of culture. Accordingly, we will first consider 'individualism–collectivism' as related to the corresponding Hofstede's dimension, and to Schwartz's autonomy–embeddedness dimension. Second, we will refer to 'power and social stratification' as encompassing power distance[1] (Hofstede) and egalitarianism–hierarchy (Schwartz). Third, Hofstede's masculinity and Schwartz's harmony–mastery dimensions will be considered under the label of 'competitiveness and attitude to others'. Finally, 'attitude to risk and uncertainty' will also be considered as a cultural dimension potentially affecting entrepreneurship. We are conscious that this integration is not without problems, but it will serve to illustrate the different mechanisms through which culture may operate affecting the entrepreneurial process, without diverting attention from the debate between alternative cultural theories.

Understanding the influence of culture

In a recent review, Hayton and Cacciotti (2013) identify two main research streams regarding the impact of national culture. First, it may influence aggregate entrepreneurial activity by either promoting innovation (Williams & McGuire, 2010) or by facilitating the actual starting of new ventures (Pinillos & Reyes, 2011). Second, it may affect the individual characteristics of entrepreneurs – either modifying their values and motives (Pruett et al., 2009) or the mechanism conforming each person's entrepreneurial intention and the level of this variable (Jaén & Liñán, 2015). In this sense, culture may be seen as 'both values and actual ways in which members of a culture go about dealing with their collective challenges' (Javidan et al., 2006, p. 899). Consequently, as mentioned earlier, culture should be considered as comprised of two main elements: values and practices (Autio et al., 2013; Krueger et al., 2013; Stephan et al., 2015).

The first such element relies on the definition of culture as shared values. According to this, the majority of individuals in that society will share some personal values that are similar to the predominant cultural values (Schwartz, 2008). Therefore, if some cultural values are identified as leading to an entrepreneurially supportive culture, we can expect a larger fraction of that culture's members to stress those values and, for this reason, be themselves classified as more pro-entrepreneurial individuals.

This influence corresponds to what Davidsson (1995) calls the 'psychological traits approach', and has more recently been termed as social cognition (Fiske & Taylor, 2013). It refers to the transmission of values, beliefs and motivations among the different members of society (Autio et al., 2013). Family and peer group shape the socialisation process of persons and transmit their values and beliefs to new members (Boehnke, 2001; Phalet & Schonpflug, 2001). Of course, there is a wide intra-social variation in personal preferences (Fischer, 2006; Fischer & Schwartz, 2011), but there is a cultural element in the intergenerational transmission of values and beliefs. From this perspective, a more pro-entrepreneurial culture should reflect itself in more prevalent pro-entrepreneurial motivations of society members (Jaén & Liñán, 2013). Thus, more individuals will exhibit the kind of values and attitudes that are associated with entrepreneurial activity (McGrath et al., 1992; Mueller & Thomas, 2001; Stephan et al., 2015). As a result, they will be more likely to develop individual cognitive processes leading to the formation of strong entrepreneurial intentions (Bird, 1988; Busenitz & Lau, 1996).

The second transmission mechanism from culture to entrepreneurship is societal legitimation. This implies the predominance of certain cultural values leading to the social acceptance and support of entrepreneurship (Autio et al., 2013). Even if individuals do exhibit a high entrepreneurial intention, acting on this personal intention implies several forms of social interaction, and the decision will be affected by the expected reactions of others (Leung & Morris, 2015). A supportive culture makes an entrepreneurial career more valued and socially recognised, hence creating a favourable institutional environment (Thornton et al., 2011; Urbano & Alvarez, 2014). This mechanism works through social institutions and their actions (via legislation, government directives or the education system), selecting and prioritising some behaviours over the others. Accordingly, the formal (and informal) institutional framework will be conformed in such a way so as to facilitate the implementation of entrepreneurial behaviours on the part of any citizen (Liñán et al., 2013). In this regard, institutions are shaped to make entrepreneurship a socially appropriate behaviour (Bourdieu, 1991; Markus & Kitayama, 1991; Schwartz, 1994).

Societal legitimation establishes what is socially accepted and what is not (Javidan et al., 2006). It works through societal compliance mechanisms, represented by formal and informal institutions (Autio et al., 2013). That is, we are referring to objective norms and rules – either formal, such as the start-up procedures, or the legal regulation of business activity; or informal, such as the existence of trust, the functioning of social networks, or the so-called 'trade practices' (Thornton et al., 2011; Urbano & Alvarez, 2014). As Leung & Morris (2015, p. 1034) explain, 'cultural differences in judgement patterns are carried more by perceived descriptive norms than by personal beliefs or values'. That is, perceived cultural practices are more important in determining what the individual feels as accepted by society.

Recent research has confirmed that the social legitimacy of entrepreneurship is a relevant variable in predicting entrepreneurial behaviour (Kibler & Kautonen, 2014; Kibler et al., 2014). If the creation of new firms becomes easier (socially legitimate), more ventures will be launched (Etzioni, 1987). Positive societal legitimation of entrepreneurship facilitates access to social capital and other external resources (Liao & Welsch, 2005), and it results in speedier and simpler procedures to start a venture (Fernández-Serrano & Romero, 2014). Thus, this will contribute to individuals perceiving their environment to be more favourable (munificent) for entrepreneurial activity (Kibler et al., 2014). In turn, opposing cultural practices will make the individual face greater difficulties and 'social sanctions' in starting up, consequently reducing actual start-up rates (Stephan et al., 2015).

On the other hand, cultural values (social cognition) would be a stronger element shaping personal behaviour in situations where there are no established social rules of conduct. In this case, personal preference (values and beliefs) would become the relevant variable. 'An implication of this argument is that values would shape behaviour more in situations lacking strong signals of social adaptation' (Leung & Morris, 2015, p. 1038). That is, where there is no social interdependence and no perceived pressure to behave in any given direction, personal values are the important element.[2]

In this study, we argue that both social cognition and societal legitimation mechanisms play a crucial role in the entrepreneurial process, as shown in Figure 4.1.

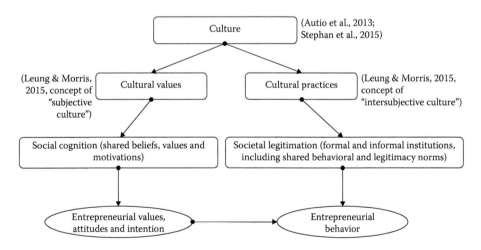

Source: Self-elaboration based on Autio et al. (2013), Leung & Morris (2015) and Stephan et al. (2015).

Figure 4.1 Culture's influence on the entrepreneurial process

Social cognition will be reflected in the personal values, attitudes and intentions of individuals, making them more or less inclined towards entrepreneurship (Autio et al., 2013; Leung & Morris, 2015). In contrast, societal legitimation will have a direct effect on the evaluation of the social rewards and sanctions involved in actually acting on this intention (Stephan et al., 2015). Thus, the influence of culture on entrepreneurship would be the result of both social cognition and societal legitimation mechanisms functioning together. In the next section, we argue that this influence of culture will also depend on the specific economic conditions of each country. Accordingly, we expect to find relevant interaction effects between the income level and culture in explaining entrepreneurship.

Economic development and entrepreneurship

Entrepreneurship plays a very important role in the process of economic development. It increases employment opportunities, enhances the level of technical innovations, and promotes economic growth (Audretsch & Fritsch, 1999; Fritsch & Mueller, 2004; Reynolds et al., 2002; Van Stel & Storey, 2004). From a dynamic perspective, entrepreneurs are agents of change because entrepreneurship implies starting new businesses, experimenting with new techniques and a new organisation of production, introducing new products or even creating new markets (Wennekers et al., 2002).

However, development is generally accompanied by an increased demand for labour – especially qualified labour – and, therefore, higher real wages. Hence, the opportunity costs of self-employment would rise. Consequently, higher Gross Domestic Product per capita (GDPpc) could reduce the entrepreneurial activity (Bjornskov & Foss, 2006; Noorderhaven et al., 2004). In particular, the more complex characteristics of the economic system may require successful ventures to be started by highly qualified individuals (Cullen et al., 2014), who, in turn, are those with better prospects in the labour market. This negative effect of income on entrepreneurship could thus be even more relevant for opportunity-based entrepreneurial activity.

At the same time, Minniti et al. (2006) and Lee and Peterson (2000) argue that there may be a positive effect of the income level on entrepreneurial activity, at least for industrialised economies. In these economies, it is argued, a higher GDPpc favours entrepreneurship (Fishman & Sarria-Allende, 2004; Parker & Robson, 2004). Economic development induces new firm formation because the opportunities and expected rewards of starting a business are higher (Carree et al., 2002; Reynolds et al., 1994). Furthermore, the level of income and wealth determines the variety of consumer demand. A high differentiation in demand benefits the suppliers of new and specialised products and diminishes the scale advantages of large incumbent firms (Jovanovic, 1993; Wennekers et al., 2002).

Nevertheless, the relative importance of these positive effects of higher income on entrepreneurship are expected to be relatively small when compared to the increase in the opportunity costs of entrepreneurship as labour markets and organisations are developed. In particular, for developing countries, the increased demand for labour should outweigh any positive effects of income growth on the supply of entrepreneurs (Naudé, 2010; Poschke, 2013). Consequently, we expect a generally negative relationship between the GDPpc and entrepreneurship. Nonetheless, it could be less so for higher levels of income (Carree et al., 2002; Liñán et al., 2013; Sternberg & Wennekers, 2005; Wennekers et al., 2005). In this sense, some authors (Van Stel et al., 2003; Verheul et al., 2002) suggest a U-shaped influence of income on entrepreneurship; yet recent data fail to confirm this relationship (Kelley et al., 2016). Additionally, we argue that culture and its possible interactions with the income level may be relevant in this respect, as will be discussed later. For this reason, the following proposition is formulated:

P1: The income level is negatively related to entrepreneurship, but the effect may be weaker for higher levels of income.

The interaction of culture and economic conditions in entrepreneurship

A considerable interdependence between culture and economic development is found in practice (Liñán & Fernandez-Serrano, 2014; Mueller et al., 2002; Ros, 2002). Less developed countries are typically characterised by a predominance of collectivism and high power and social stratification, while individualism and low stratification tend to prevail in developed countries (Schwartz, 2008; Tang & Koveos, 2008). In turn, when competiveness and attitude to others and attitude to uncertainty and risk are considered, no evidence of a clear relationship with economic development is found (Schwartz, 2008; Tang & Koveos, 2008).

In low-income countries, where economic activity is relatively simpler and formal economic institutions are less developed, there is a greater need for economic actors to resort to social (non-economic) interactions to be able to carry out economic activity (Bianchi, 2010; Naudé, 2010). In this sense, societal norms and practices are probably more important in determining personal actions. According to Baker et al. (2005), the perceived societal legitimation (cultural practices) will shape the expected (and actual) results of the social interactions needed to start a firm. Cultural practices shape formal and informal institutions, making new venture creation easier (or more difficult). This, in turn, is more strongly related to actual economic activity and the income level. Since entrepreneurship is an inevitably social activity, societal legitimation will probably play a predominant role, in interaction with the income level, when determining entrepreneurship. For this reason, societal legitimation (cultural practices) will be more relevant in determining individual entrepreneurial behaviour, especially in developing countries.

As the economy advances towards higher stages of development, former practices and regulations become obsolete and inadequate (North, 1995; Williamson, 2000).

Cultural practices are adapted to new forms of activity, leading to a transformation of formal and informal institutions. The specific forms that this institutional transformation take will differ depending on the predominant culture in that society (Tabellini, 2010). While it is often relatively easier to modify formal economic institutions by policy action, informal institutions are likely to resist change and take time to evolve towards new social norms (Stephan et al., 2015; Thornton et al., 2011). Informal institutions act as the background conditions against which the more proximate formal institutions operate (De Clercq et al., 2014). Therefore, different combinations of the cultural dimension and income level will result in different practices. This, in turn, will have an effect on entrepreneurship, depending on whether the practices have changed in a direction that is more or less favourable to entrepreneurship.

In contrast, the effect of social cognition (cultural values) could be expected to remain stable across different economic conditions. Both in developing and developed countries, pro-entrepreneurial values –when transmitted to individuals in the society – will result in the development of more favourable entrepreneurial beliefs, attitudes and intentions by these individuals (Iakovleva et al., 2011). That is, for any given combination of income and cultural practices, a more favourable social cognition will result in a larger share of society members exhibiting a high entrepreneurial intention and (all else being equal) higher start-up rates (Kautonen et al., 2013; Kibler & Kautonen, 2014; Krueger et al., 2000).

In the case of high-income countries, institutions are highly developed and economic activity is carried out through market interactions (Bianchi, 2010; Naudé, 2010). Greater economic development will imply better functioning institutions, which will be better aligned with the needs of modern economic activity. In this context, there is relatively less social exposure when taking economic decisions and a personal preference (partly determined by the predominant cultural values) becomes more prominent (Leung & Morris, 2015). Accordingly, the contribution of social cognition (cultural values and beliefs) to determining individual entrepreneurial behaviour is relatively more important than societal legitimation, as compared to the case for developing countries.

P2: The relative influence of social cognition (cultural values) and societal legitimation (cultural practices) on entrepreneurship changes with the economic development level. In developing countries, societal legitimation prevails. In developed countries, the relative importance of social cognition is higher.

Individualism, income level and entrepreneurship

There is considerable evidence regarding the relationship between the cultural dimension of individualism–collectivism and entrepreneurial activity (Liñán et al., 2013; Shane, 1993; Tiessen, 1997). In collectivistic countries, cultural values will stress prioritising group interest over personal aims (Earley & Gibson, 1998). This could be initially conducive to lower entrepreneurial intention, through the social cognition effect. In this respect, personal-level individualism is found to promote entrepreneurial intention and action (Hirschi & Fischer, 2013; Holland & Shepherd, 2013; Liñán et al., 2016; Yang et al., 2015), while the opposite is true for personal-level collectivistic values. At the same time, however, cultural practices stress the importance of group membership, solidarity and cooperation. This implies that economic activities will be carried out to pursue group interests and any group member will feel an obligation to contribute to its success (Earley & Gibson, 1998).

The level of economic development will, in this respect, play a significant role. In developing countries, where formal markets and institutions are often lacking, strong embeddedness could strengthen and promote entrepreneurial behaviour. The sense of community would provide support for in-group nascent entrepreneurs, facilitating the access to basic resources within the group (Cullen et al., 2014; De Clercq et al., 2014). In a context where markets for most resources do not exist, are inefficient, or subject to corruption, the resources controlled by in-group members (not only funding, but also labour, land, or even machinery which is not easily accessible through the market) are essential for the venture to be able to survive (Bianchi, 2010; Naudé, 2010). Without them, the viability of the new venture is impossible. Thus, entrepreneurship becomes necessarily a collective endeavour. Group members consider entrepreneurial activity as the socially legitimate practice in this environment.

In this context, the inexistence of a well-developed labour market in which offering themselves as employees will make them take entrepreneurship as the socially expected route, irrespective of their personal values and inclinations. The opportunity cost of entering into entrepreneurship is very low or inexistent, due to the undeveloped (or insufficiently developed) labour market (Poschke, 2013).

Additionally, the sense of obligation to the group makes its members more willing to start up if this is what other group members expect from them, and guarantees support from the remaining members of the family or group (Earley & Gibson, 1998). Hence, to the extent that entrepreneurial activity involves participation by group members in providing resources, funding and support, collectivism facilitates entrepreneurship. Nascent entrepreneurs have access to resources (funding, labour, etc.) through in-group relationships (Cullen et al., 2014; De Clercq et al., 2014). In particular, these kinds of ventures created out of a sense of obligation to the family or inner group are facilitated by the economic characteristics of these countries (Bianchi, 2010; Naudé, 2010).

In contrast, a culture stressing individualism in developing countries does not help entrepreneurship. It may lead to individuals with positive entrepreneurial attitudes and intention (through cultural values). All the same, the economic conditions make entrepreneurship more difficult due to the lack of institutions and markets (Bianchi, 2010; Naudé, 2010). In this sense, societal practices will discourage entrepreneurship, since attempting a new venture faces high obstacles. The predominance of individualistic values would lead to less support and solidarity within the family or in-group (Earley & Gibson, 1998). The nascent entrepreneur will receive less help from other group members (in the form of providing resources needed by the venture), who will not feel any obligation to contribute to the project. In this context, given the difficulties in accessing the necessary resources through alternative routes (market, public provision, etc.) (Bianchi, 2010), the entrepreneur will feel the individualistic cultural practices to be negative and detrimental and will be less likely to decide to act (Noseleit, 2010; Wdowiak et al., 2007).

As the economy advances, the institutional environment improves and formal and informal institutions work better, facilitating a normalised access to resources through well-developed markets (De Clercq et al., 2014). In this alternative environment, collectivism imposes cultural practices that are detrimental to entrepreneurial action. The need to abide by collective decisions is seen here more as an impediment than a facilitating factor. In this situation, people perceiving that the society attaches too much importance to groups may feel constrained to pursue their inner goals. Pressure to conform to group interests, to hire in-group workers or suppliers, to trade within the group or to use only group-resources will limit the options to develop their projects' potential fully (Cullen et al., 2014; De Clercq et al., 2014). In a highly developed but collectivistic society, the expected difficulty in the access to quality and less costly resources, due to perceived pressure to conform to group-member suppliers, workers, etc., will reduce the expected profitability and chances of survival (Bianchi, 2010; Naudé, 2010). In addition, resource acquisition by entrepreneurs is likely to be more difficult in collectivist societies (Henrekson, 2005), as key stakeholders may withhold important resources necessary for the start-up process. This, in turn, reduces the likelihood of entrepreneurial intentions being transformed into entrepreneurial behaviour (Cullen et al., 2014; De Clercq et al., 2014).

Entrepreneurs will see a conflict between either pursuing their projects at the expense of opposing what they feel are the prevailing social norms (thus risking social sanctions), or pursuing a project that is weakened by group pressure limitations, or will simply abandon the project. Overall, then, acting on their intentions may increase the perceived potential loss and as a result cause anxiety to these individuals in relation to implementing gestation activities (Van Gelderen et al., 2015). Consequently, higher perceived in-group collectivism is likely to affect start-up behaviours negatively. The entrepreneur perceives that this kind of entrepreneurial behaviour will not be appreciated and accepted by society, which leads to higher legitimacy costs of entrepreneurship (Kibler et al., 2014).

In the case of social cognition, its role will be more relevant in developed countries. In them, an individualistic culture is associated with the values of stimulation and self-direction (Schwartz, 1999). Individuals sharing these values appreciate independent thought and action and enjoy the excitement and challenge of life (Schwartz, 1992). They explore new ways of doing things (Holland & Shepherd, 2013), using their intellectual capacity to develop new products and services (Shane et al., 1991). Berings and Adriaenssens (2012) find that the values of innovation and creativity have a positive influence on the enterprising interest of students. So, when individualism prevails, more people will exhibit entrepreneurial values, attitudes and intention, leading to higher start-up rates (all else being equal) (Yang et al., 2015). In contrast, collectivistic cultural values are related to stability, preservation of traditions, and moderation in action (Schwartz, 1992). Individuals sharing these values will be inclined to preserve the status quo, sticking with traditional roles (Lyons et al., 2007). A strongly collectivistic culture is less likely to be identified with individuals stressing favourable attitudes towards entrepreneurship, leading to a lower entrepreneurial intention and for this reason negatively affecting start-up behaviour.

P3a: Individualism (as opposed to collectivism) increases entrepreneurial motivation and intention irrespective of the level of economic development, through the social cognition mechanism (cultural values).

P3b: Individualism (as opposed to collectivism) affects entrepreneurial action differently depending on the level of economic development through the societal legitimation mechanism (cultural practices). In developing countries, a collectivistic culture favours entrepreneurial action, while in developed countries individualism favours entrepreneurial action.

Power and social stratification, income level and entrepreneurship

In hierarchy-prevalent societies, powerful incumbents feel entitled to protect their position and privileges, limiting access to the resources and information for entrepreneurial activity, and to the knowledge structures needed to exploit them (De Clercq et al., 2014). Thus, individuals considering the starting of a new venture will perceive cultural practices as making it difficult to secure the resources needed. Highly stratified societies tend to stress the need to accept the position one has in society (Schwartz, 2006). The position and privileges of powerful incumbents are taken for granted and not challenged. In this context, entrepreneurship represents a threat to this position. It will accordingly be seen as socially deviant behaviour with high legitimacy costs (Autio et al., 2013). Meanwhile, in low power and stratification societies, societal practices will tolerate entrepreneurship as an acceptable path to vertical mobility. For these reasons, societies that are more egalitarian should tolerate entrepreneurship by means of societal legitimation (cultural practices).

Regarding social cognition, the values transmitted to society members by high power distant cultures would stress power and wealth (Schwartz, 2006), rather than the opposite values of universalism and commitment. They will stress the preservation of the status quo and the assumption of traditional roles. In contrast, in less stratified or less power distant societies, individuals' attempts to improve their social and economic status would be seen as legitimate goals (Schwartz, 2006). Social status is not 'given' from birth (as is the case in hierarchy-dominated cultures), but rather it is considered to be the result of personal effort and contribution to society. Hence, cultural values stress contribution and responsibility, which would lead to higher entrepreneurial motivations and intentions through social cognition mechanisms. It may be argued that universalism and commitment would be related to social entrepreneurship as a way to contribute to society's wellbeing (Hoogendoorn, 2016). In this sense, Yang et al. (2015) found universalism to positively relate to entrepreneurial intentions, while power values were negatively related. Overall, then, we could expect egalitarianism cultures to transmit values contributing to individuals exhibiting higher entrepreneurial intentions.

Therefore, since both societal legitimation and social cognition mechanisms concur, a generally positive relationship between low power and social stratification (egalitarianism or low power distance) and entrepreneurship should be expected. However, we argue that this relation will be stronger in developed countries. The predominance of fewer social stratification cultural practices (egalitarianism) will lead to a functioning of formal and informal institutions in a way that facilitates responsible action, and a contribution to society and honesty (Schwartz, 1999). This environment is especially beneficial in a complex economic system, where the role of education and human capital is more important in explaining economic activity (Gennaioli et al., 2013). In this context, a fairer access to education and equal rights allows the best-prepared individuals to be able to take advantage of spotted entrepreneurial opportunities (Shane & Venkataraman, 2000).

In contrast, a predominance of hierarchy practices is more detrimental to entrepreneurship in highly developed countries because an unequal distribution of roles and power will prevent those more qualified from launching their ventures (De Clercq et al., 2014). In turn, less skilled individuals from the smaller elite groups will be granted a 'natural' right to start up. This is probably inefficient in any situation, but it may be more so in developed countries, where more complex opportunities are available and the skills needed are more specialised (Shane & Venkataraman, 2000). In developing countries, in turn, simpler ventures are created and there would be less difference in the endowment of the basic skills needed. In high-income countries, therefore, privileged access to entrepreneurship by less skilled individuals is more of a problem.

P4a: Low power and social stratification (as opposed to hierarchy and power distance) increase entrepreneurial motivation and intention irrespective of the level of economic development, through the social cognition mechanism (cultural values).

P4b: Low power and social stratification (as opposed to hierarchy and power distance) facilitate entrepreneurial action through the societal legitimation mechanism (cultural practices). This effect is stronger for highly developed countries due to the economic system and entrepreneurial opportunities being more complex and demanding higher skills and specialised resources.

Competitiveness and attitude to others, income level and entrepreneurship

In this dimension, a predominance of competitive (masculinity or mastery) social values will lead to institutions (both formal and informal) legitimising the active pursuit of individual betterment, even at the expense of others (Schwartz, 2006). 'Exploitation of resources and people for the sake of progress and change takes precedence' (Schwartz, 2009, p.142). Individuals are seen as having to compete and it is legitimate to use others, and nature, as a means to reach one's own aims. Starting a venture will be seen as a viable practice to try to improve the individuals' personal situation (Liñán & Fernandez-Serrano, 2014). This is compatible with a weaker network of social protection (Schwartz, 2009), and difficulties in the labour market will thus result in a higher start-up rate (necessity entrepreneurship). As a result one would expect cultural practices and institutions that facilitate the creation of new ventures. This should promote entrepreneurship in both developing and developed countries.

Regarding the role of social cognition, the predominance of mastery values should be associated with a higher need for achievement at the individual level (Schwartz, 2006). This personal value has been related to entrepreneurship (Yang et al., 2015). People stressing achievement values are often prepared to invest time and effort to demonstrate competence and success in their endeavours (Bardi & Schwartz, 2003). They believe that building a successful venture can result in a positive public image and influential positions in social circles (McGrath et al., 1992).

For this reason, both through social cognition and societal legitimation, a positive relationship between a competitiveness-dominated culture and entrepreneurship should be expected. Since entrepreneurship represents the attempt to change economic and competition conditions in the market, it would be favourably valued in societies stressing masculinity or mastery values. In contrast, harmony-prevalent cultures would be associated with a lower entrepreneurial activity. No significant interaction effect with the income level is expected in explaining entrepreneurial activity.

P5a: A high competitiveness attitude towards others (as opposed to harmony and low masculinity values) increases entrepreneurial motivation and intention irrespective of the level of economic development, through the social cognition mechanism (cultural values).

P5b: A high competitiveness attitude to others (as opposed to harmony and low masculinity values) facilitates entrepreneurial action through the societal legitimation mechanism (cultural practices).

Attitude to uncertainty and risk, income level and entrepreneurship

This cultural dimension refers to the extent to which the members of a culture feel threatened by uncertain or unknown situations (Hofstede & Hofstede, 2005). In cultures with a highly negative attitude to uncertainty and risk, people are more easily threatened by ambiguous situations. These societies tend to develop institutional mechanisms to reduce the perceived ambiguity. In them, there is a tendency to rely on more extensive forms of planning (Shane, 1993) and explicit plans and predictions are of greater normative importance (Hofstede & Hofstede, 2005).

From a social cognition perspective, one should expect that a negative attitude to uncertainty would lead people to exhibit lower entrepreneurial intentions. In particular, the attitude to entrepreneurship would be negative, implying some risk of failure and uncertain prospects of success (Douglas & Shepherd, 2000, 2002). In this sense, the attitude to risk has been found to be negatively related to the entrepreneurial intention and its motivational antecedents (Douglas & Shepherd, 2002; Van Gelderen et al., 2008).

Similarly, in the case of societal legitimation, uncertainty acceptant societies will have less detailed social norms regulating social interactions. Consequently, there will be more opportunities in which no strong social rules exist and the importance of cultural values would be more prevalent in determining action (Leung & Morris, 2015). In turn, a negative attitude to uncertainty will lead to more regulated social interactions, with a prescribed course of action for almost every situation. So, societal legitimation will be the most important element in determining action, and the influence of personal values will be the lowest (Leung & Morris, 2015).

P6a: A tolerant attitude to uncertainty and risk increases entrepreneurial motivation and intention irrespective of the level of economic development, through the social cognition mechanism (cultural values).

P6b: A tolerant attitude to uncertainty and risk diminishes the presence and importance of the societal legitimation mechanism (cultural practices) in entrepreneurship.

Discussion

Probably the first question to be addressed is related to the cultural theory adopted. In this chapter, we have embraced a hybrid model based on Steenkamp (2001), which integrates Hofstede's (1980) and Schwartz's (1999) approaches. Yet our purpose is not to claim its superiority over each of the original theories. On the contrary, we have aimed to skip the debate about competing cultural theories, and focus exclusively on its influence on the entrepreneurial process. We leave it for future research to adapt this model to each one of these original theories, or to a third one.

A second element to be addressed relates to the specific effect of social cognition on the different motivational antecedents of intention. It may be relatively straightforward to argue that individualist values will contribute to developing a favourable personal attitude towards entrepreneurship (Yang et al., 2015). The effect on perceived behavioural control, or self-efficacy, may not be so obvious. Still, it may be argued that achievement-related values (such as those stressed by the competitive – masculine or mastery – cultural dimension) could be positively related to perceived behavioural control (McClelland, 1961; Rauch & Frese, 2007).

In contrast, the effect of cultural values on subjective norms via social cognition is expected to be substantially more complex. In this chapter, we have assumed that the effect of the social cognition mechanism on entrepreneurial intention is unidirectional and consistent across cultures (pro-entrepreneurial values increase intention). However, it may be argued that collectivism and high social stratification contribute to increasing the perceived subjective norm because it represents the expected approval of the entrepreneurial decision by important referent people (Ajzen, 1991; Krueger et al., 2000). Hence, collectivistic and socially stratified societies would be contributing to increasing the entrepreneurial intention of its citizens through the effect of cultural values on subjective norms. This will be particularly relevant to the extent that subjective norms are more important predictors of the entrepreneurial intention in collectivistic societies (Liñán & Chen, 2009). Nonetheless, this latter result has not been confirmed in a more recent multi-country study (Moriano et al., 2012). Much research is still needed to gain a deeper understanding of the role of subjective norms in the culture–intention relationship.

The implications that may be derived from this approach are numerous. First, the relationship from economic development to entrepreneurship can no longer be considered on its own. Attention has to be paid to culture, especially in multi-country studies or international comparisons. The conflicting results found in the literature (Kelley et al., 2016; Pinillos & Reyes, 2011; Van Stel et al., 2003; Verheul et al., 2002) might be explained through the inclusion of culture. If this latter variable is not adequately reflected, the analysis would suffer from a potentially substantial omitted-variable bias.

Second, the role of culture has to be investigated much further. We have enunciated some propositions about the modes of influence of each cultural dimension on the entrepreneurial process. Notwithstanding, these propositions are still general and need to be operationalised to empirically test their applicability. Nevertheless, the data on cultural values and practices is difficult to gather. The GLOBE project includes differentiated data on values and practices (House et al., 2002); but culture is not measured by strictly following either Hofstede's (1980) or Schwartz's (1999) theories. The compatibility of the GLOBE's measures with the cultural dimensions considered in this chapter needs to be investigated accordingly.

Additionally, a third mechanism of influence from culture to entrepreneurship has also been proposed, and is not considered in this chapter. This relates to the idea that entrepreneurs are 'different' to other people. It has been argued that the level of value-congruence between individuals and their culture is important in explaining entrepreneurial behaviour (Noorderhaven et al., 2004). In particular, 'outlier individuals' –not sharing predominant cultural values – may be more prone to becoming entrepreneurs. In this sense, Rauch et al. (2013) find that both personal and cultural values affect the innovation–growth relationship in firms, with the strongest effect occurring when the difference between some of the personal and cultural values is highest. All the same, little is yet known about the 'social deviance' between personal and cultural values, and the interaction process (Fayolle et al., 2014; Liñán et al., 2016). The extent to which this phenomenon is relevant in entrepreneurship research remains to be investigated.

Finally, even though most of the existing research has tended to identify culture with nation, some studies have challenged this traditional identification (García-Cabrera & García-Soto, 2008). The existence of intra-national cultural differences should be acknowledged (Sackmann & Phillips, 2004). Thus, regional variations in cultural values may contribute to explaining differences in entrepreneurship levels within a country (Davidsson, 1995; Davidsson & Wiklund, 1997; Jaén & Liñán, 2013). Therefore, sub-national cultures (regions, ethnic groups) have to be considered, as well as the interplay between different levels of culture (Fayolle et al., 2010).

Conclusion

This chapter proposes a detailed explanation of the mechanisms through which culture may affect the entrepreneurial process. In this endeavour, we have built on several previous contributions, and particularly on the work of Autio et al. (2013), Leung and Morris (2015) and Stephan et al. (2015). As far as we know, this is the first attempt to develop a complete model to explain the different effects of alternative cultural elements (in interaction with the economic conditions) in the process from entrepreneurial intention to start-up behaviour. Nevertheless, a large number of questions remain open and need to be addressed. In particular, the propositions posed need to be developed as testable hypotheses and checked against data. Additionally, the implications of this model need to be derived. We call for researchers to work on, develop or refute these propositions and the model upon which they are based.

NOTES

1   Steenkamp (2001) found power distance to correlate with the individualism–collectivism dimension. Nevertheless, Hofstede also had difficulties in empirically differentiating both dimensions and still proposed power distance as an independent dimension (Earley & Gibson, 1998). Our decision is based on conceptual proximity between power distance and the egalitarianism–hierarchy dimension.

2   Autio et al. (2013) identify a middle mechanism labelled as 'collective action'. This refers to collective expectations and shared norms. It includes an element of social cognition (helping establish the personal values and beliefs about optimal social situations and interactions), and an element of societal legitimation (establishing tacit norms about expected behaviours in society). In what follows, for reasons of clarity, we will only consider the two main mechanisms described – social cognition and societal legitimation.

References

Ajzen, I. (1991). The Theory of Planned Behavior. *Organizational Behavior and Human Decision Processes, 50*(2), 179–211.

Audretsch, D. B. & Fritsch, M. (1999). The industry component of regional new firm formation processes. *Review of Industrial Organization, 15*(3), 239–52.

Autio, E., Pathak, S. & Wennberg, K. (2013). Consequences of cultural practices for entrepreneurial behaviors. *Journal of International Business Studies, 44*(4), 334–62.

Baker, T., Gedajlovic, E. & Lubatkin, M. (2005). A framework for comparing entrepreneurship processes across nations. *Journal of International Business Studies, 36*(5), 492–504.

Bardi, A. & Schwartz, S. H. (2003). Values and behavior: strength and structure of relations. *Personality and Social Psychology Bulletin, 29*(10), 1207–20.

Berings, D. & Adriaenssens, S. (2012). The role of business ethics, personality, work values and gender in vocational interests from adolescents. *Journal of Business Ethics, 106*(3), 325–35.

Bianchi, M. (2010). Credit constraints, entrepreneurial talent, and economic development. *Small Business Economics, 34*(1), 93–104. doi:10.1007/s11187-009-9197-3

Bird, B. (1988). Implementing entrepreneurial ideas: the case for intention. *Academy of Management Review, 13*(3), 442–53.

Bjornskov, C. & Foss, N. J. (2006). Economic freedom and entrepreneurial activity: some cross-country evidence. *DRUID Working Paper, 06–18.*

Boehnke, K. (2001). Parent–offspring value transmission in a societal context: suggestions for a utopian research design – with empirical underpinnings. *Journal of Cross-Cultural Psychology, 32*(2), 241–55.

Bourdieu, P. (1991). *Language and Symbolic Power.* Cambridge: Polity Press.

Busenitz, L. W. & Lau, C. M. (1996). A cross-cultural cognitive model of new venture creation. *Entrepreneurship Theory & Practice, 20*(4), 25–39.

Carree, M. A., Van Stel, A., Thurik, A. R. & Wennekers, A. R. M. (2002). Economic development and business ownership: an analysis using data of 23 OECD countries in the period 1976–1996. *Small Business Economics, 19*(3), 271–90.

Carree, M. A., Van Stel, A., Thurik, A. R. & Wennekers, A. R. M. (2007). The relationship between economic development and business ownership revisited. *Entrepreneurship and Regional Development, 19*(3), 281–91.

Cullen, J. B., Johnson, J. L. & Parboteeah, K. P. (2014). National rates of opportunity entrepreneurship activity: insights from Institutional Anomie Theory. *Entrepreneurship Theory & Practice, 38*(4), 775–806. doi:10.1111/etap.12018

Davidsson, P. (1995). Culture, structure and regional levels of entrepreneurship. *Entrepreneurship and Regional Development, 7*(1), 41–62.

Davidsson, P. & Wiklund, J. (1997). Values, beliefs and regional variations in new firm formation rates. *Journal of Economic Psychology, 18*(2–3), 179–99.

De Clercq, D., Lim, D. S. K. & Oh, C. H. (2014). Hierarchy and conservatism in the contributions of resources to entrepreneurial activity. *Small Business Economics, 42*(3), 507–22. doi:10.1007/s11187-013-9515-7

Douglas, E. J. & Shepherd, D. A. (2000). Entrepreneurship as a utility maximizing response. *Journal of Business Venturing, 15*(3), 231–51.

Douglas, E. J. & Shepherd, D. A. (2002). Self-employment as a career choice: attitudes, entrepreneurial intentions, and utility maximization. *Entrepreneurship Theory & Practice, 26*(3), 81–90.

Earley, P. C. & Gibson, C. B. (1998). Taking stock in our progress on individualism-collectivism: 100 years of solidarity and community. *Journal of Management, 24*(3), 265–304.

Etzioni, A. (1987). Entrepreneurship, adaptation and legitimation: a macro-behavioral perspective. *Journal of Economic Behavior & Organization, 8*(2), 175–89.

Fayolle, A., Basso, O. & Bouchard, V. (2010). Three levels of culture and firms' entrepreneurial orientation: a research agenda. *Entrepreneurship and Regional Development, 22*(7–8), 707–30.

Fayolle, A., Liñán, F. & Moriano, J. A. (2014). Beyond entrepreneurial intentions: values and motivations in entrepreneurship. *International Entrepreneurship and Management Journal, 10*(4), 679–89. doi:10.1007/s11365-014-0306-7

Fernández-Serrano, J. & Romero, I. (2014). About the interactive influence of culture and regulatory barriers on entrepreneurial activity. *International Entrepreneurship and Management Journal, 10*(4), 781–802. doi:10.1007/s11365-014-0296-5

Fischer, R. (2006). Congruence and functions of personal and cultural values: do my values reflect my culture's values? *Personal and Social Psychology Bulletin, 32*(11), 1419–31.

Fischer, R. & Schwartz, S. H. (2011). Whence differences in value priorities? Individual, cultural, or artifactual sources. *Journal of Cross-Cultural Psychology, 42*(7), 1127–44. doi:10.1177/0022022110381429

Fishman, R. & Sarria-Allende, V. (2004). *Regulation of entry and the distortion of industrial organization. Working Paper No. 10929.* Cambridge, MA: National Bureau of Economic Research.

Fiske, S. T. & Taylor, S. E. (2013). *Social Cognition: From Brains to Culture* (2nd edn.). Thousand Oaks, CA: Sage Publications.

Fritsch, M. & Mueller, P. (2004). Effects of new business formation on regional development over time. *Regional Studies, 38*(8), 961–75.

García-Cabrera, A. M. & García-Soto, M. G. (2008). Cultural differences and entrepreneurial behaviour: an intra-country cross-cultural analysis in Cape Verde. *Entrepreneurship and Regional Development, 20*(5), 451.

Gennaioli, N., La Porta, R., Lopez-de-Silanes, F. & Shleifer, A. (2013). Human capital and regional development. *Quarterly Journal of Economics, 128*(1), 105–64. doi:10.1093/qje/qjs050

Hayton, J. C. & Cacciotti, G. (2013). Is there an entrepreneurial culture? A review of empirical research. *Entrepreneurship & Regional Development, 25*(9–10), 708–31. doi:10.1080/08985626.2013.862962

Hayton, J. C., George, G. & Zahra, S. A. (2002). National culture and entrepreneurship: a review of behavioral research. *Entrepreneurship Theory & Practice, 26*(4), 33–52.

Henrekson, M. (2005). Entrepreneurship: a weak link in the welfare state? *Industrial and Corporate Change, 14*(3), 437–67.

Hirschi, A. & Fischer, S. (2013). Work values as predictors of entrepreneurial career intentions: a longitudinal analysis of gender effects. *Career Development International, 18*(3), 216–231.

Hofstede, G. (1980). *Culture's Consequences: International Differences in Work-Related Values.* Beverly Hills, CA: Sage Publications.

Hofstede, G. (2003). *Culture's Consequences: Comparing Values, Behaviors, Institutions and Organizations Across Nations* (2nd edn.). Thousand Oaks, CA: Sage Publications.

Hofstede, G. & Hofstede, G. J. (2005). *Cultures and Organizations, Software of the Mind.* New York, NY: McGraw-Hill.

Holland, D. V. & Shepherd, D. A. (2013). Deciding to persist: adversity, values, and entrepreneurs' decision policies. *Entrepreneurship Theory & Practice, 37*(2), 331–58. doi:10.1111/j.1540-6520.2011.00468.x

Hoogendoorn, B. (2016). The prevalence and determinants of social entrepreneurship at the macro level. *Journal of Small Business Management, 54*(S1), 278–96.

House, R., Javidan, M., Hanges, P. & Dorfman, P. (2002). Understanding cultures and implicit leadership theories across the globe: an introduction to project GLOBE. *Journal of World Business, 37*(1), 3–10.

Iakovleva, T., Kolvereid, L. & Stephan, U. (2011). Entrepreneurial intentions in developing and developed countries. *Education + Training, 53*(5), 353–70. doi:10.1108/00400911111147686

Inglehart, R. (1997). *Modernization and Postmodernization.* Princeton, NJ: Princeton University Press.

Jabri, M. M. (2005). Commentaries and critical articles: text-context relationships and their implications for cross cultural management. *International Journal of Cross Cultural Management, 5*(3), 349–60.

Jaén, I. & Liñán, F. (2013). Work values in a changing economic environment: the role of entrepreneurial capital. *International Journal of Manpower, 34*(8), 939–60. doi:10.1108/IJM-07-2013-0166

Jaén, I. & Liñán, F. (2015). Cultural values in the study of a society's entrepreneurial potential. In

A. Fayolle, P. Kyro, & F. Liñán (Eds), *Developing, Shaping and Growing Entrepreneurship* (pp. 154–77). Cheltenham, UK: Edward Elgar. doi:10.4337/9781784713584.00015

Javidan, M., House, R. J., Dorfman, P. W., Hanges, P. J. & De Luquet, M. S. (2006). Conceptualizing and measuring cultures and their consequences: a comparative review of GLOBE's and Hofstede's approaches. *Journal of International Business Studies*, 37(6), 897–914.

Jovanovic, T. B. (1993). The diversification of production. *Brookings Papers on Economic Activity, Microeconomics*, 1993(1), 197–235.

Kautonen, T., Van Gelderen, M. & Fink, M. (2015). Robustness of the theory of planned behavior in predicting entrepreneurial intentions and actions. *Entrepreneurship Theory & Practice*, 39(3), 655–74. doi:10.1111/etap.12056

Kautonen, T., Van Gelderen, M. & Tornikoski, E. T. (2013). Predicting entrepreneurial behaviour: a test of the theory of planned behaviour. *Applied Economics*, 45(6), 697–707. doi:10.1080/00036846.2011 .610750

Kelley, D., Singer, S. & Herrington, M. (2016). *Global Entrepreneuship Monitor 2015/16 Global Report*. London.

Kibler, E. & Kautonen, T. (2014). The moral legitimacy of entrepreneurs: an analysis of early-stage entrepreneurship across 26 countries. *International Small Business Journal*, 34(1), 34–50. doi:10.1177/0266242614541844

Kibler, E., Kautonen, T. & Fink, M. (2014). Regional social legitimacy of entrepreneurship: implications for entrepreneurial intention and start-up behaviour. *Regional Studies*, 48(6), 995–1015. doi:10.1080 /00343404.2013.851373

Krueger, N. F., Liñán, F. & Nabi, G. (2013). Cultural values and entrepreneurship. *Entrepreneurship and Regional Development*, 25(9–10), 703–707. doi:10.1080/08985626.2013.862961

Krueger, N. F., Reilly, M. D. & Carsrud, A. L. (2000). Competing models of entrepreneurial intentions. *Journal of Business Venturing*, 15(5–6), 411–32.

Langowitz, N. & Minniti, M. (2007). The entrepreneurial propensity of women. *Entrepreneurship Theory & Practice*, 31(3), 341–64.

Lee, S. M. & Peterson, S. J. (2000). Culture, entrepreneurial orientation, and global competitiveness. *Journal of World Business*, 35(4), 401–16.

Leung, K. & Morris, M. W. (2015). Values, schemas, and norms in the culture–behavior nexus: a situated dynamics framework. *Journal of International Business Studies*, 46(9), 1028–50.

Levesque, M. & Minniti, M. (2006). The effect of aging on entrepreneurial behavior. *Journal of Business Venturing*, 21(2), 177–94.

Liao, J. W. & Welsch, H. (2005). Roles of social capital in venture creation: key dimensions and research implications. *Journal of Small Business Management*, 43(4), 345–62.

Liñán, F. & Chen, Y. W. (2009). Development and cross-cultural application of a specific instrument to measure entrepreneurial intentions. *Entrepreneurship: Theory and Practice*, 33(3), 593–617. doi:10.1111/j.1540-6520.2009.00318.x

Liñán, F. & Fayolle, A. (2015). A systematic literature review on entrepreneurial intentions: citation, thematic analyses, and research agenda. *International Entrepreneurship and Management Journal*, 11(4), 907–33. doi:10.1007/s11365-015-0356-5

Liñán, F. & Fernandez-Serrano, J. (2014). National culture, entrepreneurship and economic development: different patterns across the European Union. *Small Business Economics*, 42(4), 685–701. doi:10.1007/s11187-013-9520-x

Liñán, F., Fernández-Serrano, J. & Romero, I. (2013). Necessity and opportunity entrepreneurship: the mediating effect of culture. *Revista de Economía Mundial*, 33, 21–47.

Liñán, F., Moriano, J. A. & Jaén, I. (2016). Individualism and entrepreneurship: does the pattern depend on the social context? *International Small Business Journal*, 34(6), 760–76.

Lyons, S. T., Duxbury, L. & Higgins, C. (2007). An empirical assessment of generational differences in basic human values. *Psychological Reports*, 101(2), 339–52. doi:10.2466/pro.101.2.339-352

Markus, H. R. & Kitayama, S. (1991). Culture and the self: implications for cognition, emotion and motivation. *Psychological Review*, *98*, 224–253.

McClelland, D. C. (1961). *The Achieving Society*. Princeton, NJ: London: Van Nostrand.

McGrath, R. G., MacMillan, I. C., Yang, E. A. & Tsai, W. (1992). Does culture endure, or is it malleable? Issues for entrepreneurial economic development. *Journal of Business Venturing*, *7*(6), 441–58.

Minniti, M., Bygrave, W. D. & Autio, E. (2006). *GEM, Global Entrepreneurship Monitor, 2005 Executive Report*. London, UK & Babson Park, MA: London Business School & Babson College.

Moriano, J. A., Gorgievski, M., Laguna, M., Stephan, U. & Zarafshani, K. (2012). A cross-cultural approach to understanding entrepreneurial intention. *Journal of Career Development*, *39*(2), 162–85. doi:10.1177/0894845310384481

Moriano, J. A., Palací, F. J. & Morales, J. F. (2007). The psychosocial profile of the university entrepreneur. *Psychology in Spain*, *11*, 72–84.

Mueller, S. L. & Thomas, A. S. (2001). Culture and entrepreneurial potential: a nine country study of locus of control and innovativeness. *Journal of Business Venturing*, *16*(1), 51–75.

Mueller, S. L., Thomas, A. S. & Jaeger, A. M. (2002). National entrepreneurial potential: the role of culture, economic development and political history. In M. A. Hitt & J. L. C. Cheng (Eds), *Managing Transnational Firms: Resources, Market Entry and Strategic Alliances* (Vol. 14, pp. 221–57). Amsterdam: JAI Press.

Naudé, W. (2010). Entrepreneurship, developing countries, and development economics: new approaches and insights. *Small Business Economics*, *34*(1), 1–12. doi:10.1007/s11187-009-9198-2

Noorderhaven, N., Thurik, R., Wennekers, A. R. M. & Van Stel, A. (2004). The role of dissatisfaction and per capita income in explaining self-employment across 15 European countries. *Entrepreneurship: Theory and Practice*, *28*(5), 447–66.

North, D. C. (1995). The new institutional economics and Third World development. In J. Harris, J. Hunter, & C. M. Lewis (Eds), *The New Institutional Economics and Third World Development* (pp. 17–26). London: Routledge. doi:10.1080/713701070

Noseleit, F. (2010). The entrepreneurial culture: guiding principles of the self-employed. In A. Freytag & A. R. Thurik (Eds), *Entrepreneurship and Culture* (pp. 41–54). New York, NY: Springer.

Parker, S. C. & Robson, M. (2004). Explaining international variations in self-employment: evidence from a panel of OECD countries. *Southern Economic Journal*, *71*(2), 287–301.

Phalet, K. & Schonpflug, U. (2001). Intergenerational transmission of collectivism and achievement values in two acculturation contexts: the case of Turkish families in Germany and Turkish and Moroccan families in the Netherlands. *Journal of Cross-Cultural Psychology*, *32*(2), 186–201.

Pinillos, M.-J. J. & Reyes, L. (2011). Relationship between individualist–collectivist culture and entrepreneurial activity: evidence from Global Entrepreneurship Monitor data. *Small Business Economics*, *37*(1), 23–37. doi:10.1007/s11187-009-9230-6

Poschke, M. (2013). Who becomes an entrepreneur? Labor market prospects and occupational choice. *Journal of Economic Dynamics and Control*, *37*(3), 693–710.

Pruett, M., Shinnar, R., Toney, B., Llopis, F., Fox, J. (2009). Explaining entrepreneurial intentions of university students: a cross-cultural study. *International Journal of Entrepreneurial Behaviour & Research*, *15*(6), 571–94.

Rauch, A. & Frese, M. (2007). Let's put the person back into entrepreneurship research: a meta-analysis on the relationship between business owners' personality traits, business creation, and success. *European Journal of Work and Organizational Psychology*, *16*(4), 353–385.

Rauch, A., Frese, M., Wang, Z.-M., Unger, J., Lozada, M., Kupcha, V. & Spirina, T. (2013). National culture and cultural orientations of owners affecting the innovation–growth relationship in five countries. *Entrepreneurship & Regional Development*, *25*(9–10), 732–55.

Reynolds, P. D., Bygrave, W., Autio, E. & Hay, M. (2002). *Global Entrepreneurship Monitor. 2002 summary report*. Kansas City, KS: Ewin Marion Kauffman Foundation.

Reynolds, P. D., Storey, D. J. & Westhead, P. (1994). Cross-national comparison of the variation in new firm rates. *Regional Studies, 28*(4), 443–56.

Ros, M. (2002). Los valores culturales y el desarrollo socioeconómico: una comparación entre teorías culturales. *Revista Española de Investigaciones Sociológicas, 99*, 9–33.

Sackmann, S. A. & Phillips, M. E. (2004). Contextual influences on culture research: shifting assumptions for new workplace realities. *International Journal of Cross Cultural Management, 4*(3), 370–90. doi:10.1177/1470595804047820

Schwartz, S. H. (1990). Individualism–collectivism. Critique and proposed refinements. *Journal of Cross-Cultural Psychology, 21*(2), 139–57.

Schwartz, S. H. (1992). Universals in the content and structure of values: theoretical advances and empirical tests in 20 countries. In M. P. Zanna (Ed.), *Advances in Experimental Social Psychology* (Vol. 25, pp. 1–65). New York, NY: Academic Press.

Schwartz, S. H. (1994). Are there universal aspects in the structure and contents of human values? *Journal of Social Issues, 50*, 19–45.

Schwartz, S. H. (1999). A theory of cultural values and some implications for work. *Applied Psychology: An International Review, 48*(1), 23–47.

Schwartz, S. H. (2006). A theory of cultural value orientations: explication and applications. *Comparative Sociology, 5*(2–3), 137–82.

Schwartz, S. H. (2008). *Cultural Value Orientations: Nature and Implications of National Differences.* Moscow: Publishing House of SU HSE.

Schwartz, S. H. (2009). Culture matters. National value cultures, sources and consequences. In R. S. Wyer, C.-Y. Chiu, & Y.-Y. Hong (Eds), *Understanding Culture: Theory, Research, and Application* (pp. 127–50). New York, NY: Psychology Press.

Shane, S. A. (1993). Cultural influences on national rates of innovation. *Journal of Business Venturing, 8*(1), 59–73.

Shane, S. A. & Venkataraman, S. (2000). The promise of entrepreneurship as a field of research. *Academy of Management Review, 25*(1), 217–26.

Shane, S. A., Kolvereid, L. & Westhead, P. (1991). An exploratory examination of the reasons leading to new firm formation across country and gender. *Journal of Business Venturing, 6*(6), 431–46.

Siegel, J. I., Licht, A. N. & Schwartz, S. H. (2013). Egalitarianism, cultural distance, and foreign direct investment: a new approach. *Organization Science, 24*(4), 1174–94. doi:10.1287/orsc.1120.0776

Steenkamp, J. B. (2001). The role of national culture in international marketing research. *International Marketing Review, 18*(1), 30–44.

Stephan, U., Uhlaner, L. M. & Stride, C. (2015). Institutions and social entrepreneurship: the role of institutional voids, institutional support, and institutional configurations. *Journal of International Business Studies, 46*(3), 308–31.

Sternberg, R. & Wennekers, A. R. M. (2005). Determinants and effects of new business creation using global entrepreneurship monitor data. *Small Business Economics, 24*(3), 193–203.

Tabellini, G. (2010). Culture and institutions: economic development in the regions of Europe. *Journal of the European Economic Association, 8*(4), 677–716.

Tang, L. & Koveos, P. E. (2008). A framework to update Hofstede's cultural value indices: economic dynamics and institutional stability. *Journal of International Business Studies, 39*(6), 1045–63.

Thornton, P. H., Ribeiro-Soriano, D. & Urbano, D. (2011). Socio-cultural factors and entrepreneurial activity. *International Small Business Journal, 29*(2), 105–18. doi:10.1177/0266242610391930

Tiessen, J. H. (1997). Individualism, collectivism and entrepreneurship: a framework for international comparative research. *Journal of Business Venturing, 12*(5), 367–84.

Triandis, H. C. (1995). *Individualism & Collectivism. New Directions in Social Psychology.* Boulder, CO: Westview.

Urbano, D. & Alvarez, C. (2014). Institutional dimensions and entrepreneurial activity: an international study. *Small Business Economics, 42*(4), 703–16.

Van Gelderen, M., Brand, M., Van Praag, M., Bodewes, W., Poutsma, E. & Van Gils, A. (2008). Explaining entrepreneurial intentions by means of the theory of planned behaviour. *Career Development International, 13*(6), 538–59. doi:10.1108/13620430810901688

Van Gelderen, M., Kautonen, T. & Fink, M. (2015). From entrepreneurial intentions to actions: self-control and action-related doubt, fear, and aversion. *Journal of Business Venturing, 30*(5), 655–73.

Van Stel, A. & Storey, D. J. (2004). The link between firm births and job creation: is there a Upas Tree Effect? *Regional Studies, 38*(8), 893–909.

Van Stel, A., Wennekers, A. R. M., Thurik, A. R., Reynolds, P. D., Turik, R. & de Wit, G. (2003). *Explaining nascent entrepreneurship across countries. SCALES-paper* (Vol. SCALES). Zoetermeer, Netherlands: EIM Business and Policy Research.

Verheul, I., Wennekers, A. R. M., Audretsch, D. B. & Thurik, A. R. (2002). An eclectic theory of entrepreneurship. In D. B. Audretsch, A. R. Thurik, I. Verheul, & A. R. M. Wennekers (Eds), *Entrepreneurship: Determinants and Policy in a European–US Comparison.* Boston, MA: Kluwer Academic Publishers.

Wdowiak, M. A., Schwarz, E. J., Breitenecker, R. J. & Wright, R. W. (2007). Linking the cultural capital of the entrepreneur and early performance of new ventures: a cross-country comparison. *Journal for East European Management Studies, 17*(2), 149–83.

Wennekers, A. R. M., Uhlaner, L. M. & Thurik, A. R. (2002). Entrepreneurship and its conditions: a macro perspective. *International Journal of Entrepreneurship Education, 1*(1), 25–64.

Wennekers, A. R. M., Van Stel, A., Thurik, A. R. & Reynolds, P. D. (2005). Nascent entrepreneurship and the level of economic development. *Small Business Economics, 24*(3), 293–309.

Williams, L. K. & McGuire, S. J. (2010). Economic creativity and innovation implementation: the entrepreneurial drivers of growth? Evidence from 63 countries. *Small Business Economics, 34*(4), 391–412.

Williamson, O. E. (2000). The new institutional economics: taking stock, looking ahead. *Journal of Economic Literature, 38*(3), 595–613. doi:10.2307/2565421

Xavier, S. R., Kelley, D., Kew, J., Herrington, M. & Vorderwülbecke, A. (2013). *Global Entrepreneurship Monitor (GEM) 2012 Global Report.* Accessed 30 August, 2017 at www.gemconsortium.org/report/48545

Yang, K. P., Hsiung, H. H. & Chiu, Y. J. (2015). The comfort zone of the value circumplex for entrepreneurship: a structural analysis. *Career Development International, 20*(6), 663–83.

Theory of trying and "we-intentions": from individual to collective intentions in entrepreneurship and family business

Malin Brännback, Alan L. Carsrud and Norris Krueger

Introduction

There exists a wide variety of articles on the role of intentions within family business. A classic example of the traditional intention studies in family business research is that by Stavrou (1999). In that study university students were asked about their intentions to join or not join their family's firm. Results showed their individual intentions were significantly related to their individual needs, goals, skills, and abilities. Intentions have also even been used to define "what is a family firm" (Chua et al., 1999). Other topics in family business with a focus on intentions include the intention to control the family firm (Chrisman et al., 2003); the role of tactical intentions (Stewart, 2003); intentions within the capital decision making of the firm (Romano et al., 2001); transfer of wealth intentions (Schulze et al., 2003), as well as succession intentions (Zellweger et al., 2011). In this chapter the focus is on intentions and succession, but the paper has wider implications for research on start-up teams and their collective intentions regarding the firm.

Why "we" supersedes "I" in family firm research

In most studies, intentions are conceptualized as a singular subject concept, not as a plural subject concept as in "we-intentions." Searle (1990) has argued that collective intentions are either a discernible function of the individuals' intentions or could only be understood as driven by different forces. Further, he argues persuasively that the latter is the case. In short, if intentions toward a shared objective are poorly understood from individual intentions then we must shift our focus if we hope to influence phenomena like succession more skillfully. On the other hand, that means phenomena like family firm succession afford us significant opportunities to advance research in social cognition and intentions in particular.

Nonetheless, the dominant theoretical and empirical model for success intent remains the Theory of Planned Behavior (Ajzen, 1991) even though many of the studies imply collective intentions. For example, when discussing stewardship of firm resources, as in the case of the study by Romano et al. (2001), we-intentions are not directly studied. It is from the area of succession that this paper uses as examples to explore the role of "we-intentions".

This conceptual paper presents another perspective on the role of intentions, as described in the Theory of Trying (Bagozzi, 2000), which we then apply to the management of succession intentions. Most previous succession research has focused on factors that influence succession, or a potential successor's career choices. In their chapter on intentions in family firms, Brännback and Carsrud (2012) discuss the problem of multiple players' intentions and their potential for conflict with regard to succession. They focused their discussion on how this potential for conflict is mediated by the strength of specific social norms held by the business-owning family. That is, being part of a given social group (a business-owning family) has an impact on one's individual intentions, as well as subsequent actions or behaviors (Miller and Le Breton-Miller, 2011; Centola, 2015). This paper goes beyond the idea of multiple layers of intentions to propose the concept of "we-intentions" as a vehicle for conceptualizing collective intentions as drivers of social action (Gilbert, 1992; Tuomela, 1995; Bagozzi, 2000, 2005). Family firm succession is inherently a social action that occurs usually in a group with very tight boundaries of influence, the firm-owning family (Centola, 2015).

What both Brännback and Carsrud (2012) and Miller and Le Breton-Miller (2011) assume is there is some form of collective intention whose foundation is in a commonly held social norm within the family which results in a collective "we-intention". Interestingly, this group-level intention has yet to be adequately studied in either family business or entrepreneurship, even though it is widely studied in consumer behavior (Bagozzi, 2000; 2005). However, work in social cognition has begun to expand our conceptual and empirical tool kit (ProtoSociology, 2003) and entrepreneurial phenomena are particularly useful domains for research (e.g. entrepreneurial teams). If entrepreneurial start-ups are team based, then "we-intentions" have not been studied, with almost all research focused on the intentions of a single person within the team often described as a "founder." What about the collection intentions of the "founding team"? Likewise, the bulk of the succession literature either studies the intention of the current CEO to transfer leadership/ownership or the intentions of the potential successor. Little, if any, empirical work has been done on the interaction of these individual intentions. However, there are numerous case studies, which clearly demonstrate various intentional states in a family firm (Carsrud and Brännback, 2011). This article will refer to several published case studies on succession.

The role of "us", as will be discussed later, is based upon the philosophical work of Gilbert (1992), Tuomela (1995) and Velleman (1997) on collective or shared intentions. Tuomela's work, and much of the study of intentions (Ajzen, 1991), have been influenced by the work of Searle (1983) who examined a variety of intentional states. This paper builds on various intentions theories (e.g. Theory of Reasoned Action, Theory of Planned Behavior, and Theory of Trying) as well as theories of social norms and social identity. The research question addressed in this paper is: *In what way does a plural conceptualization of intentions as "we" intentions impact succession processes in the family and the family-owned business?* This paper adopts a very broad and inclusive definition of family and not simply one of a biological nuclear family of father, mother, and children. For the purposes of this paper "family" could be any emotionally bonded group (Carsrud, 2006). This would include start-up teams, same-sex couples, and even tribes or clans in traditional societies. The issue here is of identity and bonding, not genetics. The role of intentions in these emotionally bonded groups is the focus of this paper.

Brief overview of research on succession

A number of academic papers over the years have provided guidance on what should be the future foci of family business research, with a number of these focused on succession as the critical issue in the study of family firm. These include Danco (1982), Beckhard and Dyer (1991), Handler (1994), Rogers et al. (1996), Brockhaus (2004), and Sharma (2004). Most would agree that succession is an important topic if not the defining topic of the field. For example, research has looked at the predictors of satisfaction with the succession process (Sharma et al., 2003), while others have focused on the characteristics and behaviors of the potential successor (Shepherd and Zacharakis, 2000). Interestingly, these all reflect that although looking at family processes they are really focused on individual influences and intentions (Lumpkin et al., 2008).

However, Carsrud and Brännback (2012) called for moving beyond a simplistic view of general systems theory and a one-dimensional view of succession to look at the conflict of intentions within the family system (Brännback and Carsrud, 2012) as that may impact the success or failure of succession. Although not clearly stating a view of "we" intentions, they imply in their chapter that when this collective intent does exist, succession is far less problematic. This can be seen in Carsrud and Brännback (2011a) in which a child requested to enter the family firm and the CEO parent ultimately agreed. While the parent had control of the firm in this case, she came to an agreement with her son as to his entry to the firm. This illustrates how succession is inherently an issue of control, both accepting and relinquishing. Understanding how individual and "we-intentions" work can go a long way in predicting the future direction of the family business and the business-owning family. Clearly, when a family firm is involved, the concepts in effectuation (Sarasvathy, 2001) become important as part of the discussion, as well as social identity theory (Stryker, 1987).

Effectuation and succession behaviors in the family firm

Recently Barrett and Moores (2012), building on the work of Sarasvathy (2001, 2008), proposed that entrepreneurial behavior is more than just causally reasoned behavior where goals like succession are predetermined. Barrett and Moores (2012) propose that in fact actions within a family firm are more interactive with the aspirations of those involved and thus are full of contingent goals, which emerge over time. Intentions in this case are like aspirations. This is consistent with the role of goals as part of entrepreneurial motivation (Carsrud and Brännback, 2011). What is critical with this perspective on succession is that although a founder may have the goal to transfer the leadership/ownership of the firm they founded to a member of the second generation, in reality that transfer is contingent upon the aspirational goals of their children, their skills, abilities, and career choices. That is, the founder accepts the reality that succession is contingent on a number of factors beyond their control. The successful exhibition of their goal intentions is contingent upon the match with the goal intentions of their "potential" successors. If these two sets of intentions are in sync, then conflict is reduced and the potential for successful succession is enhanced. If they are not in sync, then the potential for conflict is increased and the risk of a failed succession is enhanced. This is most evident in the case of Frieda's Inc. (Carsrud and Brännback, 2011d) where the individual intentions of two female potential successors and the firm's female founder were mutually compatible, which could be perceived as a "we" intent.

Effectuation when applied to defining family business is best demonstrated by the work of Miller and Le Breton-Miller (2005). They categorized family firms by their contingent behaviors into firms that are focused on *continuity, community, connection,* and *command* (Barrett and Moores, 2012). For the purpose of this discussion on succession, family firms that are focused on *continuity* have members who have a shared vision of the future, or what we might consider a network with very tight boundaries (Centola, 2015). They exercise stewardship of resources and are group, rather than just individual, oriented. This clearly reflects the notion of strongly shared intentions, social values, and social norms. An example of continuity can be seen in Carsrud and Brännback (2011d) in which the tradition of a woman-owned and managed family firm in the specialty produce industry was part of the tradition that held both the family and their firm together. This view of women as more "we" oriented is consistent with the findings of Danes and Olson (2003) on the role of women in dealing with the tensions in a family firm and the firm's success. At this point a discussion of social norms is appropriate.

Social identity in family firms: the impact of social norms

A factor that influences both intentions and family business is social norms (Miller and Le Breton-Miller, 2011; Kowalewski et al., 2009; Gómez-Mejía et al., 2007). As Brännback and Carsrud (2012) point out, intentions in family firms are heavily influenced by the existing social norms of the business-owning family. That is, different social reference norms for firm-owning families will produce different outcomes. Following this logic, beliefs that are closely held as social norms of a family should also impact succession as well as firm performance, which is consistent with the networking studies of Centola (2015). Shepherd and Haynie (2009) demonstrated that identity conflict within a family firm was a critical process issue and most likely will occur with individuals who have access to influences outside their immediate family, such as education, foreign travel, marriage into another family, etc.

Family-based social norms are an underpinning assumption of Stewardship Theory (Davis et al., 1997; Miller et al., 2008). That is, there is an inherent assumption of "we" in the conceptualization of the management of a firm, and its assets and resources over generations. As Davis et al. (1997) note, stewardship in this case is identified with an organization's core values and culture. In a similar vein, Miller et al. (2008) see stewardship as in the long-term interest of the family unit (a form of "we"). Although stewardship theory implies both group and individual levels of analysis, it only implies intentions to actions at only one level.

As we have said earlier, family business, like entrepreneurship, occurs in social settings involving usually at least two persons, but more often small groups, which over time can become very large. Even the self-employed entrepreneur does not exist in solitude. They remain a part of a family or a part of a local community. No founder is going to take a mortgage out on their home without the approval of their spouse and not face some consequences from the larger group, i.e. the family. However, research and business practice very often only refer to the founder entrepreneur as if they alone are the ones making decisions. The classic article by Gartner (1988), "'Who is an entrepreneur?' is the wrong question", is a case in point—except in this case it is the entrepreneurial start-up team, not the founder, that is the correct question. Gartner's question is also addressed by Shaver and Carsrud (this volume) because it impacts how we study the entrepreneurial personality. Let us turn now to the research literature on intentions.

Intentions research

As mentioned earlier, for over two decades, research on entrepreneurial intent (e.g. Davidsson, 1991; Krueger, 1993; Krueger et al., 2000) has been dominated by variations on Ajzen's (1991) Theory of Planned Behavior (TPB). TPB (Ajzen, 1987) was an extension of the Theory of Reasoned Action (TRA) (Ajzen and Fishbein, 1980). Both models assume that intentions are driven by personal attitudes and social norms where TPB also includes personally perceived behavioral control. In subsequent entrepreneurial intentionality studies, perceived behavioral control has often been replaced by Bandura's concept of self-efficacy (Bandura, 1982). All variables are measured on the individual level, ignoring the collective.

Despite the fact that TPB in particular has proven robust across remarkably different implementations, both TRA and TPB have been criticized (Bagozzi and Warshaw, 1990; Bagozzi, 1992) for viewing action as one final performance. Bagozzi and Warshaw (1990) argue that intentions should be seen as a process of goal pursuit or a process where an individual is trying to act. This process is captured in the extension of TPB known as Theory of Trying (ToT). The critique has, with a few exceptions, gone largely unnoticed in entrepreneurship and family business research. Brännback et al. (2007) initially tested the notion of entrepreneurial intentions as goal-directed behavior and found it viable.

According to ToT, a process of trying to act is where a person may perceive something as desirable but may, for various reasons, find action at that very moment problematic. An example is the intention to start a firm or the intention to take over a family firm (succession). The latter is the situation in the Packard Marketing Group case (Carsrud and Brännback, 2011a) where the son had the intention to join the firm while the mother initially had no such intention. Only after trying was the son successful in changing the intention of his mother so that they came into sync. Interestingly, these are examples of individual intentions, consistent with how ToT was initially presented as a model for individual-level analyses.

However, Bagozzi (2000) conceptualized the idea of intentional social action in the area of consumer behavior (Xie et al., 2008). Bagozzi argues that it is highly relevant, but often neglected, to study groups (e.g. families, teams, organizations, and other social entities) to understand group consumer action. This is where the theory is grounded in both mental states (such as attitudes and belief, motivations and emotions) of the individuals constituting the group, and in jointly held "will and volitions." A body of literature in philosophy inspires this theory, which sees group action as collective intentions, shared intentions or we-intentions. The theory integrates ideas on social entities with action theory (Searle, 1983; Gilbert, 1992; Tuomela, 1995; Bagozzi, 2000). This paper conceptualizes family business intentions as collective intentions or "we-intentions" as developed by Bagozzi (2000).

The remainder of this paper is devoted to developing a framework for both modeling entrepreneurial behaviors and succession intentions in family business, using ToT as the basis. That is, the succession process is seen as a process of trying. Moreover, this paper conceptualizes intentions to enter a family firm as collective intentions or "we-intentions." Thus, this paper contributes to the literature of family business intention in particular but also into the entrepreneurial intentions literature in general by building on ToT and viewing trying as an intentional social action that can be applied to any variety of behaviors within the context of a family firm or an entrepreneurial start-up team.

Models of entrepreneurial intentions

Understanding why and when attitudes affect intentional social action has been studied in many areas for more than three decades, e.g. consumer choice (Ajzen and Driver, 1992; Bagozzi, 2000; Bagozzi et al., 2003), technology adoption (Davis et al., 1989; Bagozzi, 1992), entrepreneurship (Davidsson, 1991; Krueger, 1993, 2000; Krueger and Brazeal, 1994; Krueger et al., 2000; Brännback et al., 2007), family business (Brännback and Carsrud, 2012) and social psychology (Liska, 1984; Fazio

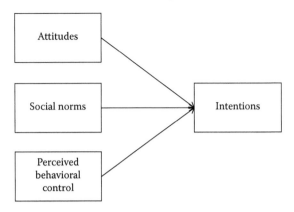

Figure 5.1a   Theory of Planned Behavior (Brännback et al., 2007)

and Williams, 1986; McBroom and Reed, 1992; Terry and Hogg, 1996; Gollwitzer and Brandstätter, 1997; Scheeran et al., 2005). Common to all of these studies is that they draw on a theoretical framework presented by Ajzen and Fishbein (1980). The initial model, Theory of Reasoned Action (TRA), assumed a linear relationship where attitudes and subjective or social norms predicted intentions (Fishbein and Ajzen, 1975; Ajzen and Fishbein, 1980).

The TRA model has since been modified with additional moderating variables (Fazio and Williams, 1986). Ajzen (1991) found that *perceived behavioral control* had a direct predicting effect of intentions. This model—the Theory of Planned Behavior (TPB) (Figure 5.1a)—has since dominated research on intentions. A modification of TPB has commonly been used in entrepreneurial intentions research. The fundamental thesis here is that attitudes impact behavior because attitudes impact intentions, and intentions are the strongest predictors of future behavior (Brännback et al., 2007).

While TPB has proven robust across remarkably different implementations (Brännback et al., 2007) the model has also been criticized because intentions are considered insufficient impetus for action (Bagozzi and Warshaw, 1990; Bagozzi, 1992, McBroom and Reed, 1992). Social action is a far more complex phenomenon (Bagozzi, 2000, 2005; Xie et al., 2008). Bagozzi and Warshaw (1990) argued that intentions ought to be conceptualized as goal-directed behavior, that an intention to act was preceded by a desire to act, which in turn was preceded by a desire for a goal (to act) (Bagozzi, 2005).

Additionally, it has been seen as problematic that TRA is limited to predicting volitional behavior and TPB is suitable for action under partial volitional control. In order to accommodate for possible contingencies, Bagozzi and Warshaw (1990) presented a refinement, the Theory of Trying (ToT) (Figure 5.1b), where action was assumed to depend on goal persistence, as well as to be preceded by a series of trials. However, ToT need not assume a fixed goal. This is consistent with effectuational thinking (Sarasvathy, 2008) that characterizes entrepreneurial activ-

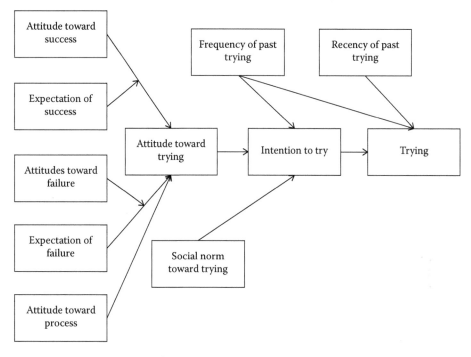

Figure 5.1b Theory of Trying (Bagozzi and Warshaw, 1990)

ity by assuming a goal flexibility that TPB does not. Thus, ToT offers an immediate advantage (Brännback et al., 2007).

ToT assumes that behavior is goal driven, and that performance of a problematic behavior may involve a series of trials. Certainly succession can be problematic. Therefore, the succession goal may be seen as either an end goal or as an intermediate goal (Carsrud and Brännback, 2011e; Carsrud et al., 2009). Moreover, action is influenced by an individual's subjective perception that there may be something in the way, thus affecting an individual's decision to ultimately act. According to the model, an individual develops an attitude towards trying, which then transforms into an intention to try and subsequently into action (trying).

The intention to try is also influenced by social norms towards trying. An attitude towards trying is influenced by a person's attitude and expectation towards succeeding or failing, as well as an attitude towards the entire process (of trying to perform something). In subsequent models (see, for example, Perugini and Conner, 2000; Bagozzi, 2000), these attitudes were seen as *desires*, where desires are the motivational state of mind where reasons to act become motivations to do so. Desires in turn are an integrative function of attitudes, social norms, and perceived behavioral control. Later studies show that goal desires, which are the link between one's goals and intentions, moderate the link between intentions and behavior (Prestwich et al., 2008).

Although TRA and TPB do not include the influence of past behavior, Bagozzi and Warshaw (1990) argue that past behavior improves the predictive power of attitudes and social norms for behavioral intentions and therefore they include this variable in ToT. Clearly, if a family firm has gone through many successful successions, those events should and will influence future successions. This can be seen in firms that have successfully managed to remain in family control for centuries. However, past behavior in the context of family business may also imply that a person has past experience of entrepreneurship (being close to the company), rather than having had hands-on experience of *succession*.

Bagozzi and Warshaw (1990) also make a distinction between frequency and recency of past *trying*. Perugini and Conner (2000) show that the past impacts both future desires and intentions. Fielding et al. (2008) also find that past behavior is a strong predictor of intentions. They also find that group norms and intergroup perceptions are significant predictors of intentions, which supports the argument that social identity theory concepts should be included in models of intentions, also proposed by Bagozzi (2005) and visible in Figure 5.4, which appears later in this paper. However, succession in family-owned firms is typically a once in a generation process for a family firm, thus recency may well be a 20-year-old event (Rogers et al., 1996).

More importantly to the discussion of succession intentions is that these critiques and suggested modifications to the models of intentions have not been applied in either entrepreneurship or family business research. With a few exceptions (Brännback et al., 2007), the dominating models for studying entrepreneurial intentionality studies have been based on TPB (Ajzen, 1987), and/or on Shapero's entrepreneurial event (Shapero, 1982). Both of these models have been shown to be powerful in *predicting* entrepreneurial activity (Krueger et al., 2000) (Figure 5.2). Recently, a model for integrating the two models has been presented (Schlaegel and Koenig, 2014). However, as pointed out by several researchers (Gollwitzer and Brandstätter, 1997; Bagozzi, 2005; Brännback et al., 2007; Carsrud and Brännback, 2011e), TPB is limited in explaining the intentions–behavior link when intentions become enacted. ToT offers an improvement by incorporating the idea of goal-

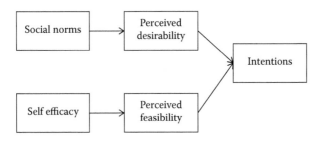

Source: Brännback et al., 2007.

Figure 5.2   The entrepreneurial event model for entrepreneurial intentions

directed behavior as well as making a distinction between goals, desires to act, intentions to act, and trying to act.

Regardless of which model is used for studying entrepreneurial or succession intentions, the level of analysis is always the *single* individual. This is the case in many large-scale surveys such as the Global Entrepreneurship Monitor (GEM) studies and the Panel Studies of Entrepreneurial Dynamics (PSED1 and PSED2), which purport to survey the founding entrepreneur. Still, with the exception of self-employed entrepreneurs, there is usually more than one person creating a venture and clearly family firms are usually comprised of both family members and employees. This means that if a venture is a joint effort there are also shared intentions. That is, both entrepreneurial and family business intentions may well be a collective concept that builds on intentional action of singular agents, but are not fully reducible to a single person's intentions (Tuomela, 1995; Gilbert, 1992; Searle, 1983; Bagozzi, 2000). Both venture creation and the operation of a family firm are seen as social action—social as in more than one person. In this case, intentions become *"we" intentions*, a plural subject concept as opposed to the singular subject concept of *"I" intentions*.

Thus, it is not only in considering venture creation where "we-intentions" become relevant. "We-intentions" become highly relevant in the context of family business and especially for understanding intentions related to succession, as we have shown in several case studies discussed in this chapter (Carsrud and Brännback, 2011a, 2011b, 2011c, 2011d). As mentioned earlier, there is more than one person that will have to intend to act on succession. The senior has to intend to pass on the business to a junior and the junior has to intend to enter into and take over the family business. Thus, within family businesses, intentions would become a plural subject concept. This is simply an area that the traditional "I intentions" approaches fail to address adequately. The next section explores the concept of "we-intentions", drawing on a literature base in philosophy (Searle, 1983; Gilbert, 1992; Tuomela, 1995; Velleman, 1997), and consumer behavior and marketing (Bagozzi, 2000, 2005). The paper will then demonstrate how the concept of "we-intentions" enhances the understanding of succession in family business.

"I" and "we-intentions"

Why focus on "we"? As noted earlier, Searle (1990) has argued that collective intentions cannot be simply derived from the intentions of critical individuals. So how do we move forward? Pacherie (2007) and Bratman (1993) offer a different perspective by framing intentions within the notion of plans. Social cognition research allows us to move toward productive modeling of collective intent (e.g. Theory of Trying) and how family firms, especially succession, represent the perfect "hunting ground" for scholars seeking to understand "we" intent.

This paper adopts Gilbert's (1992) view that "I" refers to the self, whereas "we" denotes the self and at least one or more person's sense of us (Bagozzi, 2000).

According to Gilbert (1992), members of a group such as a family (plural subjects) can experience a strong sense of sharing among the parties. Bagozzi (2000, p. 389) suggests that social identity and social categorization theories provide a theoretical base for understanding shared consciousness and a readiness towards group action. Bagozzi (2000) continues to state that "...members of a group achieve a social identity that is manifest in (1) a cognitive component made up of self-awareness of membership, (2) an affective component consisting of attachment or feelings of belongingness, and (3) an evaluative component inherent in collective self-esteem." This is quite similar to the conceptualization of stewardship proposed by Miller et al. (2008).

Social identity allows a person to develop a way of thinking about one's self, a perception of other "in-group" and "out-group" members and how one behaves in relationship to in-group and out-group members (e.g. favoritism or derogation in a family), a view consistent with seeing some networks as having strong barriers (Centola, 2015; Obschonka et al., 2012). This view of in-group and out-group was noted by Carsrud (2006) in perceptions of justice in a family firm. Group action is volitional and requires a degree of readiness to act among group members (Gilbert, 1992), i.e. mutual understandings to act on behalf of group goals. Gilbert (1992, p. 204; Bagozzi, 2000, p. 390) states that:

> ...individual wills of group members are bound to a group will 'simultaneously and interdependently' such that each expresses a *conditional commitment* of his will, understanding that only if the others express similar commitments are all of the wills jointly committed to accept a certain goal when the time comes.

This also corresponds with Tuomela's (1995, p. 2) definition of "we-intention" as "...a commitment of an individual to participate in joint action that involves an implicit or explicit agreement between the participants to engage in that joint action."

In this chapter it is important in making another distinction, which is rooted in Tuomela's (1995) conceptualization of a social group, a view shared by Searle (1983). According to Tuomela, social groups are not ontologically real entities, but it is the *relationships* among the group's members and the *processes* that are real. It is these that result in the formation of the group. Tuomela (1995) sees a social group as an authority system shared by its members. The social group creates a shared group-intention stating *we collectively will do x*. If the individual will is not transferred to the will of the group, there will not be a shared group-intention. It is also important to understand the distinction between an interpersonal perspective on groups and the plural subject concept presented by Gilbert (1992).

Bagozzi (2000, p. 391) offers the following illustration, which is highly appropriate for this discussion:

> When family decision making is conceived as a cycle of interactions between individual members such that each person is seen to give off and to receive attempts to influence

others, the perspective is an *interpersonal one*. Here family members act and react in coordinated ways, but no notion of mutual sharing or collective concepts are incorporated into the explanatory framework.. . .By contrast, when family decision making is seen as a *social process of joint formation of goals and intentions*, the perspectives is a *plural subject one* (emphasis added by the authors).

It is our conviction that successful succession in a family business is precisely such a social process of joint formation of goals and intentions, or at least it ought to be that.

As an example, this collective intention with respect to the transfer of leadership is certainly the case of the successful succession in the Frieda's Inc. case (Carsrud and Brännback, 2011d) in which open communication between two potential female successors and the female founder demonstrated the formation of "we-intentions". According to Tuomela (1995) "we-intentions" are subjective beliefs that need not necessarily be true, but are acted upon as if they were, a kind of within group altruism. It is important that group members are committed to do their own part, as well as helping others in the group to do their part. There is also an idea that the individual member does not believe he/she can achieve the goal driving the intention alone and that each member of a group intends that the group performs jointly (Bagozzi, 2000, 2005).

Building on the Theory of Trying developed a model for effortful decision making and enactment (Bagozzi et al., 2003, p. 276). A similar rationale was also offered by Gollwitzer and Brandstätter (1997), Perugini and Conner (2000) and Prestwich et al. (2008). Common to these models is the recognition of *goals as drivers of intentions*. For succession, the goal of a smooth and conflict-free transfer of leadership can become a powerful driver of both "I intentions" and "we-intentions". Gollwitzer and Brandstätter (1997) argue that the process starts with an awakening of desires, which then leads to the formation of goal intentions, which then develops into implementation intention and finally action intention. Similarly, the model by Bagozzi et al. (2003) starts with goal desires that form the basis of goal intention, which develops into implementation desires and then implementation intention and finally enactment (Figure 5.3). This is consistent with the view of the role of goals in entrepreneurial motivation (Carsrud and Brännback, 2011e). Although these models are *singular subject* conceptualizations, they are useful in understanding how "we-intentions" are formed as well.

At this point it may help to show how a subsequent development of the singular subject model of effortful decision making in consumer choice was transformed into a plural subject conceptualization of social action driven by "we-intentions". Moreover, this will show how the concept of "we-intentions" is relevant to entrepreneurial intentions and how collective desires, goals commitment and we-intentions is relevant in the context of family business succession in particular. This draws on Bagozzi's (2005, p. 105) conceptualization of social action in the context of consumer action and develops by analogy *a theory of succession intentions in family business*.

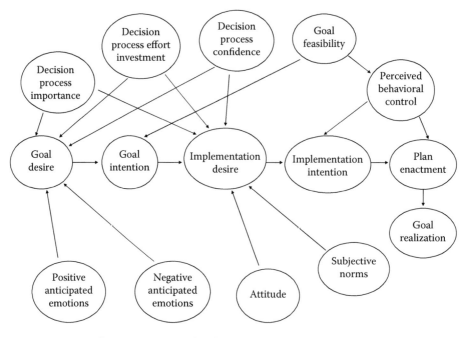

Source: Bagozzi et al., 2003, p. 276; Carsrud et al., 2009, p. 159.

Figure 5.3   Model for effortful decision making and enactment

A model for studying "we" intentions in family business

The key variables in the model of we-intentions, which form the basis for the theory of succession intentions in family business, is shown in Figure 5.4. To begin with, a collective desire for a common goal needs to be formed. This could be a shared understanding that the family business should continue to exist in the following generation when the current head decides to retire. This shared goal or desire then leads to the actual formation of a collective goal, to which the members of the family then commit. Bagozzi illustrates the collective goal formation as something occurring as a result of an internal crisis or external threat. Succession is potentially such a traumatic internal event, while an external threat may be the threat of a competitor to take over the family firm in a hostile fashion. The mutually agreed-upon desire thus offers a reason for forming a collective goal, which is followed by a collective desire to act. When subsequently the family collectively commits to act, the desire to act becomes a "we-intention" to act. Once a collective intention to act is formulated, mutual planning, or what Gollwitzer and Brandstätter (1997) call *implementation intention*, takes place. Planning is followed by a collective attempt to act—the formation of joint effort to enact the plan. Usually this means overcoming impediments, conflicts, or other constraints in the way of collectively acting and jointly reaching the goal.

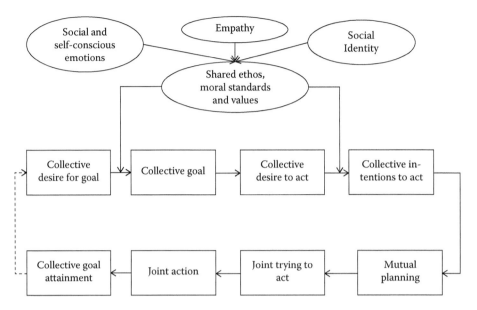

Source: Adapted from Bagozzi, 2005, p. 105.

Figure 5.4 Key variables in the theory of intentions of succession in family business.

This process will be moderated by shared ethos, moral standards, and values in two potential instances, that is when or whether collective goal desires are transformed into collective goal intention, as well as when or whether collective desire to act is transformed into collective intentions to act. The shared ethos, moral standards, and values are influenced by social identity (including group norms), empathy, and social and self-conscious emotions (pride, guilt, shame, embarrassment, jealousy, envy).

How does one get from "I" to "we" and how can one study "we" intentions? A rationale for this is outlined later, which is based on Bagozzi's (2005) model for socializing marketing, which in turn draws on insights from Gilbert (1992), Tuomela (1995), and Velleman (1997). To begin with, one has to move from "I" attitudes to "we" attitudes. Following Tuomela, a person has an intention (I_{we}) if the person believes that the other group members have I_{we} and believes those are mutually shared. As an example: members in a family have a mutually shared intention that Person M should succeed X as the CEO. It is necessary that M and X have this shared intention, but it helps if other family members also share this I_{we}. This clearly is the situation in the Frieda's case cited earlier (Carsrud and Brännback, 2011d). Bagozzi (2005) outlines a model based on three-person groups. Here for this purpose the model is restricted to two persons (Figure 5.5). Obviously, the three-person model will indeed be instrumental for studying intentions to create a venture by larger groups, but also in families with multiple siblings as potential successors.

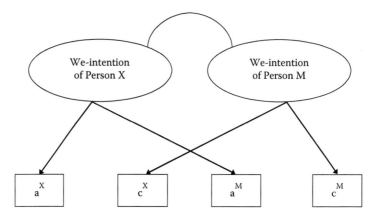

Figure 5.5   Conceptual model of we-intentions

Table 5.1   Estimating of "we" intentions

Item	Categories for respondents	
	by Person X	by Person M
Estimate of the strength of M's I_{we}		
a X's estimate of his/her own I_{we} to participate in succession	a^X	a^M
b M's estimate of X's I_{we} to participate in succession	b^X	b^M
Estimate of the strength of X's I_{we}		
c X's estimate of M's I_{we}	c^X	c^M
d M's estimate of his/her own I_{we} to participate in succession	d^X	d^M

Source: Adapted from Bagozzi, 2005, p. 107.

To estimate collective intentions, it will be necessary to estimate M's and X's I_{we}. One must then estimate X's intention to participate in succession, as well as X's estimate of M's I_{we}, and then estimate M's estimation of his/her I_{we} to participate in succession, as well as M's estimate of X's I_{we} (Table 5.1). Clearly, looking at we-intentions is far more complex than the reasonably simple study of individual intentions.

This means that one can estimate one's own I_{we} (a in Table 5.1), as well as the I_{we} of co-member c, and that I_{we} is mutually held (b, d), which results in 8 I_{we}.

This in turn can be further simplified as a 2x2 matrix as shown in Table 5.2. This is where X(HI) is the self-estimate by X that X has "we" intentions and M(HI) is the self-estimate by M that M has "we" intentions. Thus, $E_X M(HI)$

Table 5.2 Self and mutual I_{we}

	by Person X	by Person M
Self-expression of I_{we}	X(HI)	M(HI)
Belief of mutual I_{we}	$E_X M(HI)$	$E_M X(HI)$

Source: Adapted from Bagozzi, 2005, p. 108.

then becomes the estimate by X that M shares the intention, and $E_M X(HI)$ correspondingly that M shares the "we" intention with X. For further details, with respect to statistical analysis, see Bagozzi (2005). From this, it should be clear that group-level intentions are not simply looking at individual intentions, but also their communality with others' intentions. This kind of collective modeling is something few if any researchers in either entrepreneurship or family business have attempted. Yet, these collective intentions are critical to the success of team efforts both in a new venture and in the succession event in the life of a firm-owning family.

Measuring "we-intentions"

What also remains to be done is to develop scales and mechanisms that can adequately measure collective "we-intentions" with regard to succession. This measurement may be very different from the measure of "we-intentions" in the start-up of a new venture. Such measures may well be multi-dimensional in nature and most likely will not be a single-item measure, as is the case in the measurement of intentions in either TPB or TRA. Finally, the concept of "we-intentions" needs to be tested empirically in both family business and entrepreneurial contexts, something extensively explored by Elfving et al. (2009).

Clearly, a big drawback to studying "we-intentions" comes from the lack of existing measurement tools. Until such collective measures are created and validated, one can still use individual intention measures. For example, one could look at "we-intentions" in a potential start-up by looking at individual intentions and determining a median response or even a deviational score of the lowest intention to the highest. Obviously the less the deviation in intentions the more "we-intention" is exhibited. Simply asking as a percentage of intention to do something would be a start towards measuring the impact of individual intentions on we-intentions.

When looking at succession, the relative difference is between the intention of the current CEO to give up control of the firm and the intention of the would-be successor to take control of the firm. Once again, this could be done with a question asking the percentage of willingness (think intention) to give or take control. The better the match, the more "we-intentions" are exhibited.

Discussion, implications and future research

Hopefully, this paper has raised interest in moving beyond the TPB and TRA approaches to individual intentions. It should be clear that when looking at the collective behavior of groups, such as a start-up team of a new venture or a family undergoing the transition of the leadership of a family-owned and managed business, researchers must start looking seriously into the "we-intentions" conceptualization. This means far more complex analysis of group cognitions and behaviors than simply looking at demographic characteristics or external variables. Sometimes "we-intentions" extends beyond immediate family to include employees and key management who are not family, as in the case of Jacoby Construction, Inc. (Carsrud and Brännback, 2011c), where there was a history of building a strong family firm on the sound foundation of a collective succession.

This paper should also raise issues within the entrepreneurial research community concerning the very nature of reasoned and planned intentions. In the case of family business succession, there may be members of a family who are unaware of various consequences or implications of a succession plan and thus demonstrate "un-informed intent" with regard to their future behaviors. One may think that leading the family firm is easy work and then discovers that, between inheritance issues and family conflict, leading the family-owned and managed firm is anything but easy.

In fact, one could argue that no one is fully informed about the consequences of their intentions. As illustrated in the Packard case (Carsrud and Brännback, 2011a) the mother's intent to have no children in the firm had the unintended consequence of her son deciding he would change her mind simply because she never asked him about his desire to be in the firm. Likewise, most individual intentions are based on assumptions about what others want or about what are appropriate actions—often these are assumptions with a basis in social norms. Those assumptions may or may not accurately reflect reality, for example assuming a child wants to succeed in the leadership of the family firm without actually finding out if the assumption is correct. This was certainly the case of the succession crisis in the Los Angeles Dodges Major League Baseball team (Carsrud and Brännback, 2011b).

Unilateral collective intentions are where one may assume there is "we-intentions" but, in actuality, it is an imposed intention by the patriarch or matriarch of the family. This is often less driven by a collectively held social norm, and more likely driven by the goals and desires of the current leadership. This was in some respects the situation during the first succession transition in the Dodger's case (Carsrud and Brännback, 2011b). This view of unilateral collective intentions may well be prevalent in more traditional societies, something that should be researched.

References

Ajzen, I. (1987). Attitudes, traits and actions: Dispositional prediction of behavior in social psychology. *Advances in Experimental Social Psychology*, 20(1), 1–63.

Ajzen, I. (1991). Theory of Planned Behavior: Some unresolved issues. *Organizational Behavior & Human Decision Processes*, 50(2), 179–21.

Ajzen, I. and Driver, B. L. (1992). Application of the Theory of Planned Behavior to leisure choice. *Journal of Leisure Research*, 24(3), 207–24.

Ajzen, I. and Fishbein, M. (1980). *Understanding Attitudes and Predicting Social Behavior*. Englewood Cliffs, NJ: Prentice-Hall.

Bagozzi, R. P. (1992). Self-regulation of attitudes, intentions, and behavior. *Social Psychology Quarterly*, 55(2), 178–204.

Bagozzi, R. P. (2000). On the concept of intentional social action in consumer behavior. *Journal of Consumer Research*, 27(3), 388–96.

Bagozzi, R. P. (2005). Socializing marketing. *Journal of Research and Management*, 1(1), 101–10.

Bagozzi, R. P. and Warshaw P. R. (1990). Trying to consume. *Journal of Consumer Research*, 17(2), 127–40.

Bagozzi R. P., Dholakia, U. and Basuron, S. (2003). How effectful decisions get enacted: The motivating role of decision processes, desires and anticipated emotions. *Journal of Behavioral Decision Making*, 16(4), 273–95.

Bandura, A. (1982). Self-efficacy mechanisms in human agency. *American Psychologist*, 37(2), 122–47.

Barrett, M. A. and Moores, K. (2012). New theoretical perspectives on family business entrepreneurial behavior. In A. L. Carsrud and M. Brännback (eds), *Understanding Family Business: Undiscovered Approaches, Unique Perspectives, and Neglected Topics*. New York, NY: Springer, pp. 271–88.

Beckhard, R. and Dyer, W. G. (1991). Managing change in the family firm: Issues and strategies. In C. E. Arnoff and J. L. Ward, (eds), *Family Business Sourcebook*. Detroit, MI: Omnigraphics, pp. 126–34.

Brännback, M. and Carsrud, A. L. (2012). Intentions in the family business: The role of family norms. In A. L. Carsrud and M. Brännback (eds), *Understanding Family Business: Undiscovered Approaches, Unique Perspectives, and Neglected Topics*. New York, NY: Springer Verlag, pp. 27–38.

Brännback, M., Carsrud, A. L., Kickul, J., Krueger, N. F. and Elfving, J. (2007). "Trying" to be an entrepreneur? A "goal-specific" challenge to the intentions model. *Frontiers of Entrepreneurship Research*, 27(6), article 8.

Bratman, M. E. (1993). Shared intention. *Ethics*, 104, 97–113.

Brockhaus, R. H. (2004). Family business succession: Suggestions for future research. *Family Business Review*, 17, 165–77.

Carsrud, A. L. (2006). Commentary: "Are we family and are we treated as family? Non-family employee's perceptions of justice". It all depends on perceptions of family, fairness, and justice. *Entrepreneurship: Theory and Practice*, 30, 855–60.

Carsrud, A. L. and Brännback, M. (2011a). Case one: The Packard Marketing Group: Letting children into the business. In A. L. Carsrud and M. Brännback (eds), *Family Firms in Transition: Case Studies on Succession, Inheritance, and Governance*. New York, NY: Springer Briefs, pp. 9–14.

Carsrud, A. L. and Brännback, M. (2011b). Case four: Dodger Baseball – the end of family-owned Major League Baseball. In A. L. Carsrud and M. Brännback (eds), *Family Firms in Transition: Case Studies on Succession, Inheritance, and Governance*. New York, NY: Springer Briefs, pp. 33–58.

Carsrud, A. L. and Brännback, M. (2011c). Case six: Jacoby Construction, Inc. – Building a strong family firm on the sound foundation of succession. In A. L. Carsrud and M. Brännback (eds), *Family Firms in Transition: Case Studies on Succession, Inheritance, and Governance*. New York, NY: Springer Briefs, pp. 71–83.

Carsrud, A. L. and Brännback, M. (2011d). Case nine: Frieda's Inc. – Successful succession: Women do it right. In A. L. Carsrud and M. Brännback (eds), *Family Firms in Transition: Case Studies on Succession, Inheritance, and Governance*. New York, NY: Springer Briefs, pp. 111–20.

Carsrud, A. L. and Brännback, M. (2011e). Reflections on twenty years of research on entrepreneurial motivation: Have we learned anything at all? *Journal of Small Business Management*, 49(1), 9–26.

Carsrud, A. L. and Brännback, M. (2012). Where have we been and where we should be going in family business research? In A. L. Carsrud and M. Brännback (eds), *Understanding Family Business: Undiscovered Approaches, Unique Perspectives, and Neglected Topics*. New York, NY: Springer Verlag, pp. 1–8.

Carsrud, A. L., Brännback, M., Elfving, J. and Brandt, K. (2009). Motivations: The entrepreneurial mind and behavior. In A. L. Carsrud and M. Brännback (eds), *Understanding the Entrepreneurial Mind*. New York, NY: Springer, pp. 141–66.

Centola, D. (2015). The social origins of networks and diffusion. *American Journal of Sociology*, 120(5), 1295–338.

Chrisman, J. J., Chua, J. H. and Litz, R. (2003). A unified systems perspective of family firm performance: An extension and integration. *Journal of Business Venturing*, 18(4), 467–72.

Chua, J. H., Chrisman, J. J. and Sharma, P. (1999). Defining the family business by behavior. *Entrepreneurship: Theory & Practice*, 23, 19–36.

Danco, L. (1982). *Beyond Survival: A Business Owner's Guide to Success*. Reston, VA: Reston Publishing.

Danes, S. M. and Olson, P. D. (2003). Women's role involvement in family businesses, business tensions, and business success. *Family Business Review*, 16(1), 53–68.

Davidsson, P. (1991). Continued entrepreneurship, *Journal of Business Venturing*, 6(6), 405–29.

Davis, F. D., Bagozzi, R. P. and Warshaw, P. R. (1989). User acceptance of computer technology: A comparison of two theoretical models. *Management Science*, 35(9), 982–1003.

Davis, J. H., Schoorman, F. D. and Donaldson, L. (1997). Towards a stewardship theory of management. *Academy of Management Review*, 22(1), 20–47.

Elfving, J., Brännback, M. and Carsrud, A. L. (2009). Towards a contextual model of entrepreneurial intentions. In A. L. Carsrud and M. Brännback (eds). *Understanding the Entrepreneurial Mind: Opening the Black Box*. New York, NY: Springer, pp. 23–34.

Fazio, R. H. and Williams, C. J. (1986). Attitude accessibility as a moderator of the attitude–perception and attitude–behavior relations: An investigation of the 1984 presidential election. *Journal of Personality and Social Psychology*, 51(3), 504–14.

Fielding, K. S., Terry, D. J., Masser, B. M. and Hogg, M. A. (2008). Integrating social identity theory and the theory of planned behavior to explain decisions to engage in sustainable agricultural practices. *British Journal of Social Psychology*, 47(1), 23–48.

Fishbein, M. and Ajzen, I. (1975). *Belief, Attitude, Intention and Behavior: An Introduction to Theory and Research*. Reading, MA: Addison-Wesley.

Gartner, W. B. (1988). "Who is an entrepreneur?" is the wrong question. *American Journal of Small Business*, 12(1), 11–31.

Gilbert, M. (1992). *On Social Facts*, Princeton University Press, Princeton NJ.

Gollwitzer, P. M. and Brandstätter, V. (1997). Implementation intentions and effective goal pursuit. *Journal of Personality and Social Psychology*, 73(1), 186–99.

Gómez-Mejía, L. R., Takács Haynes, K., Nùñez-Nickel, M., Jacobson, K. J. L. and Moyano-Fuentes, J. (2007). Socioemotional wealth and business risk in family controlled firms. *Administrative Science Quarterly*, 52(1), 106–37.

Handler, W. C. (1994). Succession in family business: A review of the research. *Family Business Review*, 7, 133–57.

Kowalewski, O., Talavera, O. and Stetsyuk, I. (2009). Influence of family involvement in management and ownership on firm performance: Evidence from Poland. *Family Business Review*, 20(10), 1–15.

Krueger, N. (1993). The impact of prior entrepreneurial exposure on perceptions of new venture feasibility and desirability. *Entrepreneurship Theory & Practice*, 18(1), 521–30.

Krueger, N. (2000). The cognitive infrastructure of opportunity emergence. *Entrepreneurship Theory & Practice*, 24(3), 5–23.

Krueger, N. and Brazeal, D. (1994). Entrepreneurial potential and potential entrepreneurs. *Entrepreneurship Theory & Practice*, 18(1), 5–21.

Krueger, N., Reilly, M. and Carsrud, A. L. (2000). Competing models of entrepreneurial intentions. *Journal of Business Venturing* 15(5/6), 411–532.

Liska, A. E. (1984). A critical examination on the causal structure of the Fishbein/Ajzen attitude–behavior model. *Social Psychology Quarterly*, 47(1), 61–74.

Lumpkin, G. T., Martin, W. L. and Vaughn, M. (2008). Family orientation: individual–level influences on family firm outcomes. *Family Business Review*, 21, 127–38.

McBroom, W. H. and Reed, F. W. (1992). Toward a reconceptualization of attitude–behavior consistency. *Social Psychology Quarterly*, 55(2), 205–16.

Miller, D. and Le Breton-Miller, I. (2005). *Managing for the Long Run: Lessons in Competitive Advantage from Great Family Businesses*. Cambridge, MA: Harvard Business School Press.

Miller, D. and Le Breton-Miller, I. (2011). Governance, social identity, and entrepreneurial orientation in closely held public companies. *Entrepreneurship: Theory and Practice*. 1051–76.

Miller, D., Le Breton-Miller, I. and Scholnick, B. (2008). Stewardship vs. stagnation: An empirical comparison of small family and non-family businesses. *Journal of Management Studies*, 45(1), 51–78.

Obschonka, M., Goethner, M., Silbereisen, R. K. and Cantener, U. (2012). Social identity and the transition to entrepreneurship: The role of group identification with workplace peers. *Journal of Vocational Behavior*, 80(1), 137–47.

Pacherie, E. (2007). Is collective intentionality really primitive? In M. Beaney, C. Penco and M. Vignolo (eds), *Mental Processes: Representing and Inferring*. Cambridge: Cambridge Scholars Press, pp.153–75.

Perugini, M. and Conner, M. (2000). Predicting and understanding behavioral volitions: The interplay between goals and behaviors. *European Journal of Social Psychology*, 30(5), 705–31.

Prestwich, A., Perugini, M. and Hurling, R. (2008). Goal desires moderate intention–behaviour relations. *British Journal of Social Psychology*, 47(1), 49–71.

ProtoSociology (2003). Special issue on collective intentions, edited by R. Tuomela, pp.18–19.

Rogers, E. D., Carsrud, A. L. and Krueger, N. (1996). Chiefdoms and family firm regimes: Variations on the same anthropological theme. *Family Business Review*, 9(1), 15–28.

Romano, C. A., Tanewski, G. A. and Smyrnios, K. X. (2001). Capital structure decision making: A model for family business. *Journal of Business Venturing*, 16(3), 285–310.

Sarasvathy, S. D. (2001). Causation and effectuation: Toward a theoretical shift from economic inevitability to entrepreneurial contingency. *Academy of Management Review*, 26 (2), 243–88.

Sarasvathy, S. D. (2008). *Effectuation: Elements of Entrepreneurial Expertise*. Cheltenham, UK: Edward Edgar.

Scheeran, P., Webb, T. L. and Gollwitzer, P. M. (2005). The interplay between goal intentions and implementation intention. *Personality and Social Psychology Bulletin*, 31(1), 87–98.

Schlaegel, C. and Koenig, M. (2014). Determinants of entrepreneurial intent: A meta-analytic test and integration of competing models. *Entrepreneurship: Theory & Practice*, 38(2), 291–332.

Schulze, W. S., Lubatkin, M. H. and Dino, R. N. (2003). Toward a theory of agency and altruism in family firms. *Journal of Business Venturing*, 18(4), 473–90.

Searle, J. R. (1983). *Intentionality: An Essay in the Philosophy of Mind*. Cambridge, UK: Cambridge University Press.

Searle, J. R. (1990). Collective intentions and actions. In P. R. Cohen, J. Morgan and M. Pollack (eds), *Intentions in Communication*. Cambridge, MA: MIT Press, pp.401–15.

Shapero, A. (1982). Social dimensions of entrepreneurship. In C. Kent, D. Sexton and K. Vesper (eds), *The Encyclopedia of Entrepreneurship*. Englewood Cliffs, NJ: Prentice-Hall, pp.72–90.

Sharma, P. (2004). An overview of the field of family business studies: Current status and directions for the future. *Family Business Review*, 17, 1–36.

Sharma, P., Chrisman, J. J. and Chua, J. H. (2003). Predictors of satisfaction with the succession processes in family firms. *Journal of Business Venturing*, 18(5), 667–87.

Shepherd, D. A. and Haynie, J. M. (2009). Family business, identity conflict, and an expedited entrepreneurial process: A process of resolving identity conflict. *Entrepreneurship: Theory & Practice*, 33(6), 1245–54.

Shepherd, D. A. and Zacharakis, A. (2000). Structuring family business succession: An analysis of the future leader's decision making. *Entrepreneurship: Theory & Practice*, 24(4), 25–39.

Stavrou, E. T. (1999). Succession in family businesses: Exploring the effects of demographic factors on offspring intentions to join and take over the business. *Journal of Small Business Management*, 37(3), 43–61.

Stewart, A. (2003). Help one another, use one another: Towards an anthropology of family business. *Entrepreneurship Theory & Practice*, 4, 383–96.

Stryker, S. (1987). Identity theory: Development and extensions. In K. Yardley and T. Honess (eds), *Self and Identity*. New York, NY: Wiley, pp. 89–103.

Terry, D. J. and Hogg, M. A. (1996). Group norms and attitude-behaviour relationship: A role for group identification. *Personality and Social Psychology Bulletin*, 22(8), 776–93.

Tuomela, R. (1995). *The Importance of Us. A Philosophical Study of Basic Social Notions*. Stanford, CA: Stanford University Press.

Velleman, D. T. (1997). How to share an intention. *Philosophy and Phenomenological Research*, 57(1), 29–50.

Xie, C., Bagozzi, R. P. and Troye, S. V. (2008). Trying to prosume: Toward a theory of consumers as co-creators of value. *Journal of the Academy of Marketing Science*, 36(1), 109–22.

Zellweger, T., Sieger, P. and Hatter, F. (2011). Should I stay or should I go? Career choice intentions of students with family business background. *Journal of Business Venturing*, 26, 521–36.

6 Implementation intentions: the when, where, and how of entrepreneurial intentions' influence on behavior

Leon Schjoedt

Introduction

Entrepreneurial intention is considered a central construct in explaining behavior (Krueger et al., 2000). Intentions are instructions to one self to do something or achievement of a goal, like "I intend to do X" (Triandis, 1980). Much of the research on intentions is based on perhaps the most recognized intention models: Theory of Reason Action (TRA; Fishbein & Ajzen, 1975) and Theory of Planned Behavior (TPB; Ajzen, 1991, 2012). In these theories, intention is the key construct in the attitude–behavior relationship and intention is considered to be the immediate determinant of behavior; in effect, intentions mediate the effects of attitude on behavior. A substantial body of research provides support for this mediated relationship (Ajzen, 2012). Because TPB is a revised version of TRA (Ajzen, 1991, 2012), most recent research on intentions in entrepreneurship is based on TPB (Schlaegel & Koenig, 2014).

Despite the prevalence of research employing the TPB in entrepreneurship, a meta-analysis found that only three published studies had employed the full TPB (Schlaegel & Koenig, 2014). Further, the majority of entrepreneurship research is limited to explaining the formation of intentions (Kautonen et al., 2015; Kautonen et al., 2013). Research on the intention–behavior relationship in the entrepreneurship literature has not focused on intentions to launch a new business venture (e.g. Kolvereid, 1996a, 1996b) and has used focused samples (e.g. Goethner et al., 2012) or small samples (Kautonen et al., 2013). Only recently have entrepreneurship scholars (Kautonen et al., 2015) examined the link between intentions and behavior using large and not-focused samples to find that intentions accounted for 31 percent of variance in behavior; an amount similar to people in general (Armitage & Conner, 2001; Sheeran, 2002).

Meta-analyses support the predictive power of intentions on behavior. Based on a meta-analysis of ten meta-analyses of the intention–behavior relationship, including 422 correlational studies, Sheeran (2002) found that intention explains 28 percent of the variance in behavior, indicating that intentions are "good" predictors of behavior. As most meta-analyses are based on correlational studies, it

Table 6.1   Two x two matrix of the intention–behavior relationship

		Subsequent behavior	
		Did act	Did not act
Intention	To act	Inclined actors	Inclined abstainers
	Not to act	Disinclined actors	Disinclined abstainers

Source: Sheeran (2002).

cannot be ruled out that it is possible that a third unmeasured variable (Mauro, 1990), or "spuriousness" (Kenny, 1979), influences both intention and behavior or the intention–behavior relationship. Thus, these meta-analyses do not illustrate whether intentions cause behavior.

To assess whether changes in intentions predict changes in behavior, Webb and Sheeran (2006) conducted a meta-analysis of 47 experimental studies that demonstrated a medium-to-large change in intention leads to a small-to-medium change in behavior. This suggests that intentions do influence behavior; but then again that intentional control of behavior is substantially less than suggested in previous meta-analyses based on correlational research. Further, to examine the sources of consistency and discrepancy between intention and behavior, Orbell and Sheeran (1998) employed a 2x2 matrix (see Table 6.1): intention (intention to act vs. intention not to act) x behavior (did act vs. did not act). Their results showed that consistency in the intention–behavior relationship is attributable to "inclined actors" (people with intentions to act who subsequently act) and to "disinclined abstainers" (people with no intentions to act who do not act). On the other hand, discrepancies between intentions and behavior may be attributed to "inclined abstainers" (people with intentions to act who do not act) and to "disinclined actors" (people with no intentions to act who acted). More specifically, these researchers found that inclined abstainers, rather than disinclined actors, are primarily responsible for the magnitude of the intention–behavior relation. Sheeran (2002) confirmed this as he found the median proportion of inclined abstainers was 47 percent, whereas the median proportion of disinclined actors was 7 percent. These findings indicate that approximately half of people with intentions to act do not act upon those intentions.

Considering "intentions are the single best predictor of any planned behavior" (Krueger et al., 2000, p. 412) and entrepreneurship is about planned actions, the limited research (e.g. Kautonen et al., 2015; Kautonen et al., 2013) that addresses the intention–behavior relationship in entrepreneurship is surprising. It is also surprising that entrepreneurial intention seems to account for about 30 percent of variance in behavior (Kautonen et al., 2015). One reason for the limited effect intentions have on subsequent behavior indicates that research on entrepreneurial intention needs to go beyond predicting intentions and beyond merely assuming that intentions predict subsequent behavior. As this shows, there is a need for detailing how intentions influence subsequent behavior. The aim of this chapter is to assist entrepreneurship researchers by linking entrepreneurial intentions to behavior for future research on when, where, and how people enact their intentions to launch new ventures and become entrepreneurs.

This chapter is organized as follows: first, TPB is considered, including its empirical support, to illustrate the theory's inherent weakness, the link between intention and behavior. Second, implementation intention is considered as a way to explain when, where, and how intentions influence behavior. Lastly, after considering ideas for future research, concluding comments are provided.

Theory of Planned Behavior

Several social psychological models agree that the most important and proximal predictor of human behavior is intention. These models include TRA (Ajzen & Fishbein, 1980; Fishbein & Ajzen, 1975, 2010), attitude–behavior theory (Triandis, 1980), protection motivation theory (Rogers, 1983), and TPB (Ajzen, 1991, 2012). Considering that TPB is a widely applied intention model (Conner & Armitage, 1998) and is the most commonly used intention model in entrepreneurship research (Schlaegel & Koenig, 2014), the focus of this section is on TPB.

Predicting behavior

TPB is an expectancy-value model that details determinants of people's decision to perform a particular behavior (Ajzen, 1991, 2012). Ajzen (1991, 2015) points out that the purpose of TPB is to predict and explain behavior in specific contexts, such as entrepreneurship. He also notes that intentions are assumed to capture the motivational factors that influence behavior because intentions are considered indicators of how hard people are willing to try and how much effort they anticipate to exert to perform a given behavior. Ajzen further observes that behavior depends on the intention and behavioral control. TPB is based on a set of assumptions and mediated and direct relationships, which will be considered later to provide an appreciation of the model. TPB is considered a complete, parsimonious, and sufficient model of behavior in that any other influences not considered in TPB are held to have their impact via its various components (Ajzen, 1991, 2012). Despite these positive features, Ajzen (1991, 2012, 2015) observes that TPB may be revised to include additional antecedents of intentions if justified. Several such additions have been considered (e.g. belief salience, habit, self-efficacy, moral norms, affect; see Conner & Armitage, 1998, for a review).

Assumptions inherent in Theory of Planned Behaviour

It is assumed that TPB describes a causal process in which beliefs cause evaluations that influence intentions and behavior directly and indirectly. Despite this assumption, most intention research is correlational, preventing a test of this assumption (Conner & Armitage, 1998). Another not oft considered assumption is that TPB is built upon the principle of comparability (Ajzen, 1991, 2012). According to this principle, intentions are strongly related to behavior when intentions, behavioral control, and behavior are at the same level of specificity in relation to the action, target, context, and time frame (Fishbein & Ajzen, 1975, 2010).

Another important consideration inherent in TPB is time between an intention and the enactment of the intention. Ajzen (1991, 2012) points out that the time between intention and behavior should be short to have a strong relationship between intention and behavior. If the temporal continuity substantially affects the intention–behavior relationship, then TPB may have limited utility in predicting behavior from intentions. Using meta-analysis, Randall and Wolff (1994) examined the temporal continuity of TPB to find that the intention–behavior relationship does not significantly decline over time.

Beliefs: the indirect antecedent of intentions

Although many representations and examinations of TPB do not include beliefs, they are critical to appreciation of TPB. The beliefs are at times referred to as the indirect antecedents of intentions because evaluations mediate their influence on intentions (Ajzen, 1991, 2012). TPB includes three beliefs. One, behavioral beliefs refer to a person's salient belief about a behavior, which directly influences the person's attitude towards the behavior, and is a function of the person's perception of likely outcomes and attributes of a behavior. Two, normative beliefs are based on a person's perception of whether referents—persons or groups of people important to the person—think that the person should or should not engage in the behavior and whether the person complies with the salient referents' expected wishes. In short, normative beliefs constitute a person's perception of social pressures and motivation to comply with those social pressures. Three, control beliefs pertain to whether a person believes he or she has access to the resources and opportunities necessary to perform the behavior successfully. It is based upon a weighted summation of the person's perception that accessible and controllable factors facilitate or inhibit the behavior. These three factors include both internal factors (e.g. emotions, knowledge, skills, and abilities) and external factors (e.g. opportunities, threats, and dependency on others). As this shows, the concept of control beliefs is similar to Bandura's concept of self-efficacy—a person's belief that he or she has the capability to control behavioral performance and achieve what he or she intends to do (Bandura, 1997).

For each of these beliefs, it is important to observe that the belief is based upon an expectancy-value conceptualization (Peak, 1955)—the perceived outcome is based upon the perceived likelihood that performance will result in a particular outcome and evaluation of that outcome. These evaluations are summed over various salient consequences to form the person's belief. It is also noteworthy to observe that these beliefs are also affected by past behaviors and their outcomes (Fishbein & Ajzen,

2010). Specifically for control beliefs, it is noteworthy to observe that past experiences influence a person's self-efficacy (Bandura, 1997). It is these expectancy–value relationships for each of the three beliefs that influence the direct antecedent of intentions.

Evaluations: the direct antecedents of intentions

Attitude towards a behavior (ATB) refers to the overall evaluation of the behavior by a person. Applying the principle of compatibility means that the relevant attitudes are the attitudes toward performance of a behavior. Subjective norms (SN) are based upon a person's normative beliefs and, thus, refer to a person's beliefs about what other people important to the person think about whether the person should engage in the behavior. Perceived behavioral control (PBC) refers to a person's perception of the degree, from easy to difficult, that a behavior is under the control of the person. It is a direct consequence of a person's control beliefs and, thus, the degree of PBC depends upon whether the behavior requires resources, opportunities, or specialized knowledge, skills, and abilities. Because control beliefs are a direct and immediate antecedent of PBC, Ajzen (2002), as well as Fishbein and Cappella (2006), observe that PBC and self-efficacy (Bandura, 1997) are the same.

Intentions

According to TPB, intention represents a person's motivation to conscientiously enact a behavior, and it is a function of three direct determinants: ATB, SN, and PBC (Ajzen, 1991, 2012).

Intentions to act

The link between intention and behavior reflects that a person tends to enact a behavior the person intends to perform. Considering that PBC, or self-efficacy, influences both intentions and behavior directly in TPB, a person is more likely to engage in a behavior he or she has control over than engage in a behavior he or she has no or limited control over. Also, if intentions are held constant, as PBC increases, a behavior is more likely to be performed (Ajzen, 1991, 2012).

Feedback loops

An often overlooked but critical aspect of TPB is the feedback loops from behavior to cognition (Ajzen, 2012; Fishbein & Ajzen, 2010). Since self-efficacy is influenced by past experiences of performing a behavior (Bandura, 1997), self-efficacy is a critical factor in forming intentions and in enacting intentions.

Empirical support for the intention–behavior relationship

Despite the fact that intentions are considered the best and most proximal predictor of behavior (Ajzen, 1991; Krueger et al., 2000), Ajzen (2015) observes that TPB does not fully account for the variance in intentions and in behavior. This observation is consistent with results from meta-analyses (e.g. Armitage & Conner, 2001; Godin & Kok, 1996; Randall & Wolff, 1994; Schlaegel & Koenig, 2014; Sheeran, 2002; Sutton, 1998). For example, in his meta-analysis, Sutton (1998) finds that TPB accounts for 40–50 percent of variance in intentions and 19–38 percent of variance in behavior. He points to nine reasons why the amount of explained variance is expected to be lower, including that intentions may be provisional and intentions may change. Although variety of measurement artifacts affect estimates of the intention–behavior relationship (Sutton, 1998), the "gap" between intentions and behavior is not negligible (Sheeran, 2002). As noted earlier, Sheeran (2002) found in his meta-analysis of meta-analyses that intentions accounted for 28 percent of variance in behavior. Despite such a "large" effect size (Cohen, 1992), indicating that intentions are "good predictors" of behavior, most meta-analyses are based on correlational research. This means that the relationship may be affected by a third variable (Mauro, 1990), or spuriousness (Kenny, 1979). Thus, such meta-analyses do not illustrate whether intentions cause behavior.

An explanation for the less than expected effect size of intentions on behavior may be found in a meta-analysis by Webb and Sheeran (2006). These scholars shed light upon the causal relationship between intention and behavior. Specifically, Webb and Sheeran found that medium-to-large change in intention (d = 0.66; Cohen, 1992) causes a small-to-medium change in behavior of (d = 0.36; Cohen, 1992) suggesting that although intentions do influence behavior, the effect an intention has on behavior is more limited than suggested in other meta-analyses based on correlational research. It is worth noting that the small-to-medium change intentions caused in behavior means that intentions account for 3 percent of variance in behavior (d = 0.36 equals R^2 = 0.03). This is surprisingly small change in behavior.

Another explanation for the lower than expected effect size of intentions on behavior may be found in the observations provided by Sheeran (2002) in his meta-analysis of meta-analyses. He found that 47 percent of the people with intentions to act did not act upon those intentions. In the entrepreneurship literature, Kautonen et al. (2015) noted that 37 percent were inclined actors—people who had entrepreneurial intentions who also acted upon these intentions.

As this highlights, empirical research shows that intention causes behavior but only to a limited degree. While entrepreneurial intention is considered the most proximal and important predictor of behavior (e.g. Ajzen, 1991; Krueger et al., 2000), some questions become apparent: (1) why do only about half of the people with intentions to act subsequently take action; and (2) is intention truly the most proximal determinant of behavior or, phrased differently, is it possible to improve prediction of behavior? Answers to these questions may be found in the, perhaps, most notable advancement in explaining when, where, and how people enact their intentions. Beyond a few mentions in the entrepreneurship literature (Brännback et al., 2007; Carsrud & Brännback, 2011; Carsrud et al., 2017; Elfving et al., 2017; Kautonen et al., 2015; Krueger, 2017), a concept that holds potential to explain the when, where, and how intentions influence behavior, as well as enhance enact-ment of intentions, is the concept of implementation intentions (Gollwitzer, 1993, 1999).

Implementation intentions

Implementation intentions are if-then intentions, or plans, that mediate the rela-tionship between intentions and behavior. Although intentions may be defined as the instructions people give themselves to perform a particular behavior, e.g. "I intend to do X" (Triandis, 1980), implementation intentions take the form of if-then intentions, or plans, e.g. "if situation Y occurs, then I will do X" (Gollwitzer, 1993, 1999). While an intention pertains to the *what*, an implementation intention specifies the *when*, *where*, and *how* of enacting an intention. As such, implementa-tion intentions are subordinate to intentions or, phrased differently, an implemen-tation intention occurs subsequent to an intention but before behavior whereby it mediates the intention–behavior relationship.

A person forms implementation intentions by first identifying a response that will lead to enactment of a behavior or achievement of a goal—the *what* of an intention—and then anticipating an appropriate opportunity to initiate that particular response (Gollwitzer, 1993, 1999). The process of forming an imple-mentation intention is, therefore, a self-regulatory activity that links an antici-pated opportunity to a suitable response. In effect, implementation intentions are advance plans of how to act when an opportunity occurs. Research shows that intentions and implementation intentions are cognitively distinctive (Gilbert et al., 2009). Research also shows that implementation intentions substantially enhance the likelihood that intentions will be enacted (Gollwitzer & Sheeran, 2006).

Implementation intentions in the context of intentions and behavior

The preceding implies that intentions and implementation intentions take place in a larger process. Research on goals provides a model of action phases (Gollwitzer, 1990, 2012; Heckhausen, 1991; Heckhausen & Gollwitzer, 1987). The model of action phases may assist in contextualizing intentions and implementation inten-tions. The first phase is the pre-decision phase. This phase starts with the assump-tion that people have more wishes and desires—goals—that they can realize. The task in this phase is to deliberate about desirability and feasibility of their wishes and desires and to select the ones a person wishes to pursue. This phase agrees with TPB on intention formation (Gollwitzer, 1990, 2012).

Unlike TPB that links intention directly to behavior, the second phase, pre-action phase, of the model of action phases takes place between intention formation and behavior. The focus of the pre-action phase is to initiate behaviors by developing plans for the when, where, and how to take action to enact an intention. In other words, this is the implementation intention phase. This is especially the case when people are faced with complex or unfamiliar situations (Gollwitzer, 1990, 2012), such as those facing people with entrepreneurial intentions.

Initiation of behavior in accordance with the implementation intentions makes the beginning of the third phase, the action phase (Gollwitzer, 1990, 2012). This is where intentions are enacted in the face of contextual threats. This is where behavior results in performance (Bird et al., 2012).

The fourth and last phase of the model, the post-action phase, is where a person evaluates if his or her performance meets the goal, the wishes, and desires inherent in the intention (Gollwitzer, 1990, 2012). This is also the phase in which feedback takes place—feedback on the action and performance that feeds into perceived behavioral control (Ajzen, 1991, 2012) and self-efficacy (Bandura, 1997).

When intentions do not result in behavior and what to do about it

Like TPB, the model of action phases does not specify when intentions do not result in behavior and in performance. Unlike TPB, the model of action phases shows that implementation intentions are critical for people to enact their intentions. Three processes seem to prevent people from enacting their intentions. These processes also help distinguish between disinclined actors and inclined abstainers.

First, intention variability refers to the lack of ability to form an intention in the absence of particular abilities, resources, or opportunities (Ajzen, 1991, 2012). This is evident from a meta-analysis by Webb and Sheeran (2006). These scholars found that intentions had less impact on behavior when people lack control over a behavior. Forming implementation intentions helps overcome intention variability because people considering if-then scenarios also consider the when, where, and how to enact the intention in advance of action (Bayer & Gollwitzer, 2007).

Second, intention activation refers to the extent contextual demands alter the direction, intensity, or salience of an intention (Gollwitzer & Sheeran, 2006). This is particularly relevant for entrepreneurs, who have multiple, maybe even conflicting, intentions. When people have multiple intentions competing for their time and attention, only the most salient intentions hold potential to be enacted (Vancouver et al., 2010). An implementation intention helps overcome intention inaction because the if-then plan includes a clue to when an intention is to be enacted.

Third, in the absence of intention elaboration people may fail to enact the intentions. Intention elaboration refers to consideration of contextual opportunities and behavioral responses that are expected to lead to enactment of the intention (Abraham & Sheeran, 2004; Bagozzi & Kimmel, 1995). This is particularly an issue when people are faced with complex behaviors or action sequences (Abraham et al., 1998), like enacting entrepreneurial intentions. Forming implementation intentions helps overcome poorly elaborated intentions as people engage in if-then scenarios that assist in specifying the opportunities and responses deemed to be effective in enacting the intention (Prestwich et al., 2015).

How implementation intentions work

The effectiveness of implementation intentions, relative to merely forming intentions, is based on two processes (Gollwitzer, 1993, 1999; Gollwitzer & Sheeran, 2006). First, forming implementation intentions means people identify good opportunities to act. Forming implementation intentions increases the awareness of cues (the if-component of an implementation intention) that then become easier to detect (Aarts et al., 1999; Webb & Sheeran, 2004, 2007, 2008). In terms of entrepreneurial intentions, entrepreneurial implementation intentions may take the form of alertness to competitive imperfections in markets that may not be widely understood by those operating in a particular industry. Alertness is, by some, considered the essence of entrepreneurship (e.g. Kirzner, 1989).

Second, forming implementation intentions helps to automate the execution of behavior (the then-component of an implementation intention). The initiation of behavior in the presence of the cue becomes more automatic (requires less conscious effort) after the formation of an implementation intention, resulting in the initiation of a behavior becoming more immediate and efficient, with less need for conscious awareness (Bayer et al., 2009; Bargh, 1994; Brandstätter et al., 2001; Gollwitzer, 1993; Gollwitzer & Brandstätter, 1997; Moors & De Houwer, 2006; Webb & Sheeran, 2004, 2008). Further, research indicates that there is more to the underlying mechanisms in implementation intentions than a mere cue-behavior association. Papies et al. (2009) note that forming implementation intentions leads to richer mental representations of the intention–behavior relationship that, in turn, increases the likelihood that the intention is enacted.

For the automatic processes to be immediate, efficient, and without awareness (Bargh, 1994; Moors & De Houwer, 2006), people need to give up action control to a degree when forming an implementation intention. Action control is given up to the extent that a behavior is performed on the cue specified in the implementation intention which switches control of the intended behavior from the person to the specified cue that elicits the behavior (e.g. Gollwitzer & Sheeran, 2006). Several studies support the immediacy of (Orbell & Sheeran, 2000; Webb & Sheeran, 2004), efficiency of (Baumeister et al., 1998; Brandstätter et al., 2001; Webb & Sheeran, 2003), and automatic (Bayer et al., 2009; Bargh et al., 2001; Sheeran et al., 2005) action that stems from forming implementation intention.

Empirical support for implementation intentions

When people form implementation intentions, it facilitates identification of opportunities and cues to act that initiate behavior. Forming an implementation intention also facilitates more immediate, efficient, automatic, and effective behavior relative to merely forming an intention. The effect of implementation intentions

Table 6.2   Effect size estimates of the impact of implementation intentions on behaviors

Authors	Effect size estimate (d)	Number of studies
Gollwitzer & Sheeran (2006)	0.65	94
Koestner, Lekes, Powers, & Chicoine (2002)	0.54	13
Sheeran (2002)	0.70	15
Toli, Webb, & Hardy (2015)	0.63	27

Note: The effect size estimate, d, is the sample-weighted difference between means for an implementation intention condition versus a control condition divided by the within-group standard deviations. $d = 0.20$ is a "small" effect size; $d = 0.50$ is a "medium" effect size; and $d = 0.80$ is a "large" effect size (Cohen, 1992).

on behavior has been the subject of numerous meta-analyses. These meta-analyses have examined the effects of implementation intentions on a range of behaviors. Table 6.2 provides an overview of the effect size estimates provided by these meta-analyses. The effect size estimates (d), ranging from 0.54 to 0.70, found in the meta-analyses reveal that implementation intentions have a medium-to-large effect size on behavior (Cohen, 1992). One meta-analysis (Gollwitzer & Sheeran, 2006) stands out due to the number of studies included (and to the inclusion of both published and unpublished research, and studies based on experimental and correlational designs, and on self-reported and objective data). In this meta-analysis that is based on 94 studies and a total of 8,461 participants, Gollwitzer and Sheeran (2006) found a medium-to-large effect size ($d = 0.65$) for the effect of implementation intentions on behavior. As the effect sizes show, implementation intentions have a substantial impact on behavior that is above and beyond that of intentions only.

Even though the effect size of implementation intentions on behavior is substantial, there are two factors that are of particular interest in the implementation intention–behavior relationship with respect to entrepreneurial intentions as they may moderate the effect of implementation intentions on behavior. First, when facing few obstacles and enacting a behavior is easy, intentions facilitate action because there is little benefit from forming implementation intentions. This is supported by research showing implementation intentions are more effective for intentions based on difficult goals (Gollwitzer & Brändstatter, 1997; Koestner et al., 2002; Webb & Sheeran, 2003). Thus, self-regulation moderates the effect of implementation intentions on behavior.

Second, the quality of implementation intentions moderates the effect of implementation intentions on behavior. Studies show that forming higher quality implementation intentions is related to higher levels of performance (e.g. De Vet et al., 2011). Further, research shows that forming implementation intentions is more effective when people are poor planners (Allan et al., 2013). Therefore, it is imperative that participants not only form implementation intentions, but form implementation intentions that specify opportunity, cue to act, and intended action and link these together. This provides an argument for development of business plans in entrepreneurship education that emphasizes if-then scenarios in a similar manner to scenario planning (and analysis) in strategic management (e.g. Linneman, 1980; Schwartz, 1996).

Implementation intentions in entrepreneurship: ideas for future research

Predicting entrepreneurial intentions has been the focus of intentions research in the entrepreneurship literature. This has, in no small part, been due to TPB (Ajzen, 1991, 2012) dominating the intentions research in entrepreneurship (Schlaegel & Koenig, 2014). Even though TPB posits that intention is the most proximal antecedent of behavior, Webb and Sheeran (2006) found in their meta-analysis that intentions only cause 3 percent variance in behavior. Ajzen (2015) has recently acknowledged the imperfect relationships among the relationships inherent in TPB, the imperfect relationship between intentions and behavior, and the very limited causal effect intentions have on behavior raises concerns. Similar to Ajzen (1991, 2012), Krueger et al. (2000) observed that entrepreneurial intentions are the most proximal and best predictor of entrepreneurial action. This forms an assumption in the entrepreneurship literature that predicting entrepreneurial intentions suffices as entrepreneurial intention is a proxy for behavior that leads to launching new ventures.

Kautonen et al. (2015) conducted a longitudinal study examining if entrepreneurial intentions were associated with subsequent entrepreneurial action. These researchers found that intentions explain 31 percent of variance in behavior, which is in line with meta-analyses examining the intention–behavior relationship (e.g. Sheeran, 2002). Even though this means that intentions are good predictors of behavior, it does not reveal whether intentions cause behavior.

In their meta-analysis, Webb and Sheeran (2006) examine the causal relationship between intentions and behavior. They found a medium-to-large change in intention causes a small-to-medium change in behavior. This suggests that intentions do influence behavior but the causal effect of intention on behavior is more limited than suggested in meta-analyses based on correlational studies. Their results revealed that intentions cause only 3 percent of variance in behavior. With these considerations in mind, it cannot be said that entrepreneurial intentions may be the most proximal and best predictor of entrepreneurial action despite such claims (e.g. Ajzen, 1991, 2012; Krueger et al., 2000). Thus, there is potential to advance the entrepreneurship literature if future research (1) tests the relationship between implementation intentions and behavior and (2) examines the causal impact that implementation intentions have on behavior in the context of entrepreneurial intentions to determine if intentions or implementation intentions are the most proximal and best predictor of behavior that result in new venture creation.

Further, Kautonen et al. (2015) found that 37 percent were inclined actors (they had acted upon their entrepreneurial intentions) and 63 percent were inclined abstainers (they had not acted upon their entrepreneurial intentions). This is more than the median proportion of inclined abstainers of 47 percent found in a meta-analysis by Sheeran (2002). Even though the intentions included in the meta-analysis include various intentions, including less complex intentions than entrepreneurial intentions, entrepreneurial intentions research does not account for why so many do not act on their entrepreneurial intentions. Nor does this body of research examine disinclined actors—people who do not have entrepreneurial intentions yet still take actions to launch a new venture.

Implementation intentions may explain why inclined abstainers do not enact their entrepreneurial intentions; why disinclined actors become entrepreneurs; and when, where, and how inclined actors take action to launch their new ventures. Inclined abstainers who do not form implementation intentions may not be aware when to take action as they are not aware of the opportunity to act, the cue to begin action, and what to do when faced with an appropriate opportunity. The disinclined actors may have implicitly formed implementation intentions. As actors engage in a hobby or activity that make them alert to opportunities and cues, and they then act when cued, inclined actors may form implementation intentions that make them alert to opportunities and cues to act that they then act upon to create their new ventures.

Considering that implementation intentions consist of if-then plans, planning becomes a central issue in entrepreneurship. Like intentions, implementation intentions are cognitive, unless discussed with other people (Bird et al., 2012). Based on the quote by E. M. Forster (1927) "How can I tell what I think till I see what I say?", and implementation intentions are cognitive, development of a business plan focusing on if-then plans holds potential to enhance immediacy, efficiency, clue and opportunity awareness, and effectiveness of enacting intentions. It may be fruitful if future entrepreneurship research examines how business plans, developed based on implementation intentions, increase the number of inclined actors and decrease the percentage of inclined abstainers in enacting their entrepreneurial intentions.

Further, as research shows that forming implementation intentions is more effective when people are poor planners (Allan et al., 2013), people who intend to become entrepreneurs for the first time may find that implementation intentions enhance their self-efficacy and potential to act (Bandura, 1997; Webb & Sheeran, 2008). It is therefore imperative that people who are poor planners and seeking counsel or training in relation to their entrepreneurial intentions be assisted with forming implementation intentions that specify opportunity, cue to act, intended action, and link them together. Consequently, implementation intentions hold potential to make entrepreneurship education and training more effective. Future research holds potential to shed light on the effects of implementation intentions by examining how training sessions affect the use of implementation intentions and the subsequent entrepreneurial actions in longitudinal research.

In this chapter consideration of moderators of the effect of implementation intentions was limited to two factors, self-regulation and quality of implementation intentions. Future research on moderators of the effect of implementation intentions also holds potential to enhance our understanding of why some, but not others, enact their entrepreneurial intentions. This could include research on the complexity of implementation intentions.

Perhaps the first step in advancing the entrepreneurship literature on intentions is for scholars to move beyond the assumption inherent in entrepreneurial intentions research that intention is the most proximal and best predictor of entrepreneurial behavior (e.g. Ajzen, 1991, 2012; Krueger et al., 2000). A second step is for scholars to advance the literature by examining the effect of implementation intentions on enacting entrepreneurial intentions.

Concluding comments

Entrepreneurial intention research is based on an assumption that intentions are the most proximal and best predictor of behavior (e.g. Ajzen, 1991, 2012; Krueger et al., 2000). Consequently, most research has focused on predicting intentions because intentions are presumed to be a proxy for behavior. Research on the effect of entrepreneurial intentions on behavior (Kautonen et al., 2015) is consistent with meta-analytical results based on correlational research designs (e.g. Sheeran, 2002). However, meta-analysis on the causal effect intentions have on behavior shows that intentions have very limited direct causal effect on behavior (Webb & Sheeran, 2006). Evidence shows that implementation intentions (if-then plans of when, where, and how to enact intentions) have potential to enhance enactment of intentions (Gollwitzer & Sheeran, 2006).

There is therefore a need for entrepreneurship scholars to examine implementation intentions in future research to improve our understanding of when, where, and how people enact their entrepreneurial intentions. Research on implementation intentions also holds potential to explain why people with no entrepreneurial intentions become entrepreneurs (disinclined actors)—an overlooked group in entrepreneurship research. As this chapter shows, consideration of implementation intentions and its effect on behavior holds the potential to substantially advance the entrepreneurship literature because it addresses the when, where, and how of entrepreneurial action—key issues in entrepreneurship research (Shane & Venkataraman, 2000).

It should be noted that the focus of this chapter is linking intentions to behavior by implementation intentions. However, there are other reasons for people not enacting their intentions. In their review, Gollwitzer and Sheeran (2006) observe that people may become derailed from enacting their intentions, may not disengage from engaging in behavior that is unproductive, or may overextend themselves in their behavior and thus prevent themselves from enacting intentions that may be more productive. Together with failure to initiate the enactment of their intentions, these three reasons for people failing to enact their intentions, especially in face of multiple competing intentions as is the case for people with entrepreneurial intentions, may be overcome by developing implementation intentions. As this chapter shows, inclusion of implementation intentions holds potential to account for the intention–behavior relationship in entrepreneurship research, and why some (inclined actors and disinclined actors), but not others (inclined abstainers and disinclined abstainers) enact their entrepreneurial intentions.

References

Aarts, H., Dijksterhuis, A. & Midden, C. (1999). To plan or not to plan? Goal achievement or interrupting the performance of mundane behaviors. *European Journal of Social Psychology*, 29, 971–9.

Abraham, C. & Sheeran, P. (2004). Implications of goal theories for the theories of reasoned action and planned behaviour. *Current Psychology*, 22, 218–33.

Abraham, C., Sheeran, P. & Johnson, M. (1998). From health beliefs to self-regulation: Theoretical advances in the psychology of action control. *Psychology and Health*, 13, 569–92.

Ajzen, I. (1991). Theory of planned behavior: Some unresolved issues. *Organizational Behavior & Human Decision Processes*, 50(2), 179–211.

Ajzen, I. (2002). Residual effects of past on later behavior: Habituation and reasoned action perspectives. *Personality and Social Psychology Review*, 6(2), 107–22.

Ajzen, I. (2012). The Theory of Planned Behavior. In P. A. M. Lange, A. W. Kruglanski & E. T. Higgins (Eds), *Handbook of Theories of Social Psychology* (Vol. 1). London, UK: SAGE, pp. 438–59.

Ajzen, I. (2015). The Theory of Planned Behaviour is alive and well, and not ready to retire: A commentary on Sniehotta, Presseau, and Araújo-Soares. *Health Psychology Review*, 9(2), 131–7.

Ajzen, I. & Fishbein, M. (1980). *Understanding Attitudes and Predicting Social Behavior*. Englewood Cliffs, NJ: Prentice-Hall.

Allan, J. L., Sniehotta, F. F. and Johnston, M. (2013). The best laid plans: Planning skill determines the effectiveness of action plans and implementation intentions. *Annals of Behavioral Medicine*, 46, 114–20.

Armitage, C. J. & Conner, M. (2001). Efficacy of the theory of planned behaviour: A meta-analytic review. *British Journal of Social Psychology*, 40(4), 471–99.

Bagozzi, R. P. & Kimmel, S. K. (1995). A comparison of leading theories for the prediction of goal-directed behavior. *British Journal of Social Psychology*, 34, 437–61.

Bandura, A. (1997). *Self-Efficacy: The Exercise of Control*. New York, NY: W. H. Freeman.

Bargh, J. A. (1994). The four horsemen of automaticity: Awareness, efficiency, intention, and control in social interaction. In R. S. Wyer, and T. K. Srull (Eds), *Handbook of Social Cognition* (2nd edn.). Hillsdale, NJ: Erlbaum, pp. 1–40.

Bargh, J. A., Gollwitzer, P. M., Lee-Chai, A., Barndollar, K. & Trötschel, R. (2001). The automated will: Nonconscious activation and pursuit of behavioral goals. *Journal of Personality and Social Psychology*, 81, 1014–27.

Baumeister, R. F., Bratlavsky, E., Muraven, M. & Tice, D. M. (1998). Egodepletion: Is the active self a limited resource? *Journal of Personality and Social Psychology*, 74, 1252–65.

Bayer, U. C. & Gollwitzer, P. M. (2007). Boosting scholastic test scores by willpower: The role of implementation intentions. *Self and Identity*, 6, 1–19.

Bayer, U. C., Achtziger, A., Gollwitzer, P. M. and Moskowitz, G. B. (2009). Responding to subliminal cues: Do if-then plans facilitate action preparation and initiation without conscious intent? *Social Cognition*, 27, 183–201.

Bird, B. J., Schjoedt, L. & Baum, J. R. (2012). Entrepreneurs' behavior: Elucidation and measurement. *Entrepreneurship Theory & Practice*, 36(5), 889–913.

Brandstätter, V., Lengfelder, A. & Gollwitzer, P. M. (2001). Implementation intentions and efficient action initiation. *Journal of Personality and Social Psychology*, 81, 946–60.

Brännback, M., Krueger, N., Carsrud, A. & Elfving, J. (2007). *Trying to be an entrepreneur? A "goal-specific" challenge to the intentions model*. Paper presented at the Babson College Entrepreneurship Research Conference, Madrid, Spain, June 6–9.

Carsrud, A. & Brännback, M. (2011). Entrepreneurial motivations: What do we still need to know? *Journal of Small Business Management*, 49(1), 9–26.

Carsrud, A., Brännback, M., Elfving, J. & Brandt, K. (2017). Motivations: The entrepreneurial mind and behavior. In M. Brännback & A. L. Carsrud (Eds), *Revisiting the Entrepreneurial Mind: Inside the Black Box: An Expanded Edition*. New York, NY: Springer, pp. 185–209.

Cohen, J. (1992). A power primer. *Psychological Bulletin*, 112, 155–9.

Conner, M. & Armitage, C. J. (1998). Extending the theory of planned behavior: A review and avenues for further research. *Journal of Applied Social Psychology*, 28(15), 1429–64.

De Vet, E., Oenema, A. and Brug, J. (2011). More or better: Do the number and specificity of implementation intentions matter in increasing physical activity? *Psychology of Sport and Exercise*, 12, 471–7.

Elfving, J., Brännback, M. & Carsrud, A. (2017). Motivations matter in entrepreneurial behavior: Depends on the context. In M. Brännback & A. L. Carsrud (Eds), *Revisiting the Entrepreneurial Mind: Inside the Black Box: An Expanded Edition*. New York, NY: Springer, pp. 83–9.

Fishbein, M. & Ajzen, I. (1975). *Belief, Attitude, Intention, and Behavior: An Introduction to Theory and Research*. Reading, MA: Addison-Wesley.

Fishbein, M. & Ajzen, I. (2010). *Predicting and Changing Behavior: The Reasoned Action Approach*. New York, NY: Psychology Press.

Fishbein, M. & Cappella, J. N. (2006). The role of theory in developing effective health communications. *Journal of Communication*, 56(s1), S1–S17.

Forster, E. M. (1927). *Aspects of the Novel*. London: Edward Arnold.

Gilbert, S. J., Gollwitzer, P. M., Cohen, A. L., Oettingen, G. & Burgess, P. W. (2009). Separable brain systems supporting cued versus self-initiated realization of delayed intentions. *Journal of Experimental Psychology: Learning, Memory, and Cognition*, 35, 905–15.

Godin, G. & Kok, G. (1996). The theory of planned behavior: A review of its applications to health-related behaviors. *American Journal of Health Promotion*, 11, 87–98.

Goethner, M., Obschonka, M., Silbereisen, R. K. & Cantner, U. (2012). Scientists' transition to academic entrepreneurship: Economic and psychological determinants. *Journal of Economic Psychology*, 33(3), 628–41.

Gollwitzer, P. M. (1990). Action phases and mind-sets. In E. T. Higgins & R. M. Sorrentino (Eds), *The Handbook of Motivation and Cognition: Foundations of Social Behavior* (Vol. 2). New York, NT: Guilford Press, pp. 53–92.

Gollwitzer, P. M. (1993). Goal achievement: The role of intentions. *European Review of Social Psychology*, 4, 141–85.

Gollwitzer, P. M. (1999). Implementation intentions: Strong effects of simple plans. *American Psychologist*, 54(7), 493–503.

Gollwitzer, P. M. (2012). Mindset theory of action phases. In P. Van Lange, A. W. Kruglanski & E. T. Higgins (Eds), *Handbook of Theories of Social Psychology*. (Vol. 1). London: SAGE, pp. 526–45.

Gollwitzer, P. M. & Brandstätter, V. (1997). Implementation intentions and effective goal pursuit. *Journal of Personality and Social Psychology*, 73, 186–99.

Gollwitzer, P. M. & Sheeran, P. (2006). Implementation intentions and goal achievement: A meta-analysis of effects and processes. *Advances in Experimental Social Psychology*, 38, 69–119.

Heckhausen, H. (1991). *Motivation and Action*. Heidelberg: Springer-Verlag.

Heckhausen, H. & Gollwitzer, P. M. (1987). Thought contents and cognitive functioning in motivational versus volitional states of mind. *Motivation and Emotion*, 11, 101–20.

Kautonen, T., van Gelderen, M. & Fink, M. (2015). Robustness of the theory of planned behavior in predicting entrepreneurial intentions and actions. *Entrepreneurship Theory & Practice*, 655–74.

Kautonen, T., van Gelderen, M. & Tornikoski, E. T. (2013). Predicting entrepreneurial behaviour: A test of the theory of planned behaviour. *Applied Economics*, 45(6), 697–707.

Kenny, D. A. (1979). *Correlation and Causality*. New York, NY: Wiley.

Kirzner, I. M. (1989). *Discovery, Capitalism, and Distributive Justice*. Oxford: Basil Blackwell.

Koestner, R., Lekes, N., Powers, T. A. and Chicoine, E. (2002). Attaining personal goals: Self-concordance plus implementation intentions equals success. *Journal of Personality and Social Psychology*, 83, 231–44.

Kolvereid, L. (1996a). Prediction of employment status choice intentions. *Entrepreneurship Theory & Practice*, 20(3), 47–57.

Kolvereid, L. (1996b). Organizational employment versus self-employment: Reasons for career choice intentions. *Entrepreneurship Theory & Practice*, 21, 23–31.

Krueger, N. (2017). Entrepreneurial intentions are dead: Long live entrepreneurial intentions. In M. Brännback & A. L. Carsrud (Eds), *Revisiting the Entrepreneurial Mind: Inside the Black Box: An Expanded Edition*. New York, NY: Springer, pp. 13–34.

Krueger, N. F., Reilly, M. D. & Carsrud, A. L. (2000). Competing models of entrepreneurial intentions. *Journal of Business Venturing*, 15(5–6), 411–32.

Linneman, R. E. (1980). *Shirt-Sleeve Approach to Long-Range Planning for the Smaller, Growing Corporation*. Englewood Cliffs, NJ: Prentice-Hall.

Mauro, R. (1990). Understanding L. O. V. E (left out variables error): A method for estimating the effects of omitted variables. *Psychological Bulletin*, 108, 314–29.

Moors, A. & De Houwer, J. (2006). Automaticity: A theoretical and conceptual analysis. *Psychological Bulletin*, 132, 297–326.

Orbell, S. & Sheeran, P. (1998). "Inclined abstainers": A problem for predicting health-related behavior. *British Journal of Social Psychology*, 37, 151–65.

Orbell, S. & Sheeran, P. (2000). Motivational and volitional processes in action initiation: A field study of the role of implementation intentions. *Journal of Applied Social Psychology*, 30, 780–97.

Papies, E. K., Aarts, H. & de Vries, N. K. (2009). Planning is for doing: Implementation intentions go beyond the mere creation of goal-directed associations. *Journal of Experimental Social Psychology*, 45, 1148–151.

Peak, H. (1955). Attitude and motivation. In M. R. Jones (ed.), *Nebraska Symposium on Motivation* (Vol. 3). Lincoln, NE: University of Nebraska Press, pp. 149–88.

Prestwich, A., Sheeran, P., Webb, T. L. & Gollwitzer, P. M. (2015). Implementation intentions. In M. Conner & P. Norman (Eds), *Predicting Health Behavior* (3rd edn.). New York, NY: McGraw-Hill, pp. 321–57.

Randall, D. M. & Wolff, J. A. (1994). The time interval in the intention–behavior relationship: meta-analysis. *British Journal of Social Psychology*, 33, 405–18.

Rogers, R. W. (1983). Cognitive and physiological processes in fear appeals and attitude change: A revised theory of protection motivation. In J. T. Cacioppo & R. E. Petty (Eds), *Social Psychophysiology: A Sourcebook*. New York, NY: Guilford Press, pp. 153–76.

Schlaegel, C. & Koenig, M. (2014). Determinants of entrepreneurial intent: A meta-analytic test and integration of competing models. *Entrepreneurship Theory & Practice*, 38(2), 291–32.

Schwartz. P. (1996). *The Art of the Long View: Paths to Strategic Insight for Yourself and Your Company*. Sydney: Prospect Publishing.

Shane, S. & Venkataraman, S. (2000). The promise of entrepreneurship as a field of research. *Academy of Management Review*, 25(1), 217–26.

Sheeran, P. (2002). Intention–behaviour relations: A conceptual and empirical overview. *European Review of Social Psychology*, 12(1), 1–36.

Sheeran, P., Webb, T. L. & Gollwitzer, P. M. (2005). The interplay between goal intentions and implementation intentions. *Personality and Social Psychology Bulletin*, 31, 87–98.

Sutton, S. (1998). Predicting and explaining intentions and behavior: How well are we doing? *Journal of Applied Social Psychology*, 28(15), 1317–38.

Toli, A., Webb, T. L. & Hardy, G. E. (2015). Does forming implementation intentions help people with mental health problems to achieve goals? A meta-analysis of experimental studies with clinical and analogue samples. *British Journal of Clinical Psychology*, 55(1), 69–90.

Triandis, H. C. (1980). Values, attitudes, and interpersonal behavior. In H. E. Howe Jr. & M. Page (Eds), *Nebraska Symposium of Motivation* (Vol. 27). Lincoln, NE: University of Nebraska Press, pp. 195–259.

Vancouver, J. B., Weinhardt, J. M. & Schmidt, A. M. (2010). A formal, computational theory of multiple-goal pursuit: Integrating goal-choice and goal-striving processes. *Journal of Applied Psychology*, 95, 985–1008.

Webb, T. L. & Sheeran, P. (2003). Can implementation intentions help to overcome ego-depletion? *Journal of Experimental Social Psychology*, 39, 279–86.

Webb, T. L. & Sheeran, P. (2004). Identifying good opportunities to act: Implementation intentions and cue discrimination. *European Journal of Social Psychology*, 34, 407–19.

Webb, T. L. & Sheeran, P. (2006). Does changing behavioral intentions engender behavior change? A meta-analysis of the experimental evidence. *Psychological Bulletin*, 132, 249–68.

Webb, T. L. & Sheeran, P. (2008). Mechanisms of implementation intention effects: The role of goal intentions, self-efficacy, and accessibility of plan components. *British Journal of Social Psychology*, 47, 373–95.

7 Revisiting entrepreneurial motivation and opportunity recognition

Ronit Yitshaki and Fredric Kropp

Introduction: Entrepreneurial motivations

Motivation is a core concept within the psychological literature and can be traced back to early work by Freud more than 100 years ago. It first appeared in the entrepreneurship literature in the 1980s, but fell out of favor as more focus was placed on attitude–intentions–behavior research (Carsrud et al., 2009; Carsrud & Brännback, 2011). Entrepreneurial motivations can be explicated in many ways, including drive and incentive theories (Carsrud & Brännback, 2011), personal and career theories (Buttner & Moore, 1997; Hall & Chandler, 2005), social theories (Amit & Muller, 1995; Robichaud et al., 2010), and psychological and personality theories (Piperopoulos & Dimov, 2015). However, research in entrepreneurial motivation often suffers from narrow theoretical articulation and a lack of integration of the psychological, cognitive, and affective aspects. Recent research identifies that, in addition to cognitive components (Grégoire et al., 2011), entrepreneurial motivation contains affective elements such as passion (Cardon et al., 2009; Murnieks et al., 2014), compassion (Miller et al., 2012), and founder's self and social identities (Fauchart & Gruber, 2011; Powell & Baker, 2014; Yitshaki & Kropp, 2016a).

Entrepreneurial agency addresses the question "why, when, and how some people and not others discover and exploit these opportunities" (Shane & Venkataraman, 2000, p. 218). However, motivation theories are fragmented (Carsrud & Brännback, 2011). Entrepreneurial motivation reflects a desire for *self-starting*, the desire to create something new, based on internal impetus rather than external demands (Frese & Gielnik, 2014). In trying to understand entrepreneurial motivations, theories are often divided into two categories: (1) theories that focus on personality and traits, and (2) theories that focus on cognitive processes. In the first category, the need for achievement and self-efficacy are among the most dominant aspects that explain venture creation and success (Rauch & Frese, 2007). The second category includes process-oriented cognitive models that focus on attitudes and beliefs (Segal et al., 2005). Shane et al. (2003) suggest that entrepreneurial motivation consists of a combination of personality, affect, and task-specific aspects that impact opportunity recognition and exploitation processes. These scholars argue that entrepreneurs integrate motivations within cognitive processes such as knowledge, skills, and abilities.

Although these theories make sense on a stand-alone basis, in some ways they are in opposition. There is a growing need to understand entrepreneurial motivations in a broader sense that captures earlier theories and integrates them with more recent research. Whether it is looking at motivation through the lens of personality and traits or through a cognitive lens, both often neglect affective motivations. We propose that entrepreneurial motivations are intertwined processes in which both affect and cognition shape opportunity recognition. Before describing the cognitive and affective components in detail and their relation to opportunity recognition, we first discuss opportunity recognition to provide a foundation for further discussion. This is followed by a theoretical review of the paths between motivation and opportunity recognition led by cognitive and affective motivations and the role of context. We conclude with a process model and suggestions for future research.

Opportunity recognition

Opportunity research (OR) is a well-established construct in entrepreneurship research. Most of the research has examined the cognitive aspects of OR, such as the role of learning (Corbett, 2007), socio-cognitive processes (De Koning & Muzyka, 1999), entrepreneurial alertness (Gaglio & Katz, 2001), pattern recognition (Baron, 2006; Baron & Ensley, 2006; Lumpkin & Lichtenstein, 2005), self-efficacy and self-belief (Krueger & Dickson, 1994), the role of human and social capital (Bhagavatula et al., 2010), and gender differences (DeTienne & Chandler, 2007). Ardichvili et al. (2003) found that entrepreneurial alertness, prior knowledge, social knowledge, personality traits including optimism and self-efficacy, and the type of opportunity can all have a role in shaping OR. In addition, other studies examined ontological issues (Ardichvili & Cardozo, 2000; Vaghely & Julien, 2010).

There are many definitions of OR, most of which contain overlapping elements. Despite its importance, the definitions of opportunity and opportunity-related processes are fragmented. In the broadest sense, Stevenson & Jarillo (1991) think of an opportunity as something that is feasible and desirable, and conceptualize it as the core of entrepreneurship. In line with the cognitive approach, Grégoire et al. (2010) take a more analytical approach to OR, which involves making sense of new information about new situations to ascertain whether or not the opportunity is worth pursuing. Hansen et al. (2011) describe that the elements of OR include examining the possibility of bringing a new product to market, developing a perception of how to create benefits, solving a problem or creating a service innovation. Opportunity-related processes include scanning or being alert to recognizing an idea and transforming it into a business concept (Hansen et al., 2011). George et al. (2016) identified six important aspects of OR: prior knowledge, social capital, cognition/personality traits, environmental conditions, alertness, and systematic search.

Opportunities can be viewed as discovered or created (Alvarez & Barney, 2007). Discovered opportunities are considered more objective than created opportunities as they can be *discovered* through systematic scanning of the environment. There are numerous ways entrepreneurs can discover opportunities, including heightened awareness, being more alert to the environment, and through social capital ties. Antithetically, created opportunities could not be *created* without the experiential knowledge of the entrepreneurs; they are endogenous, based on the entrepreneur's exploration processes and are considered more subjective (Alvarez & Barney, 2007).

Suddaby et al. (2015) describe two different mechanisms by which opportunities can be created—imprinting and reflexivity. Imprinted opportunities are embedded within the social, political, and economic environment; OR is based on elements of the environment, especially in sensitive periods of environmental transitions and uncertainty (Marquis & Tilcsik, 2013). Entrepreneurial cognitions and organizational heuristics are also core to entrepreneurial processes and performance (Bingham et al., 2007). In contrast, reflexivity mechanisms are generated by subjective and interpretive reflection of entrepreneurs who use their thoughts, imagination and feelings to create social realities (Suddaby et al., 2015).

Although OR is a core concept in the entrepreneurial literature, it has not been well integrated with entrepreneurial motivations (Short et al., 2010). In the next section, we discuss different aspects of entrepreneurial motivation and develop a process model that relates the cognitive and affective components to entrepreneurial motivations.

Entrepreneurial motivation as a multidimensional construct

Table 7.1 summarizes the multi-dimensional constructs of entrepreneurial motivation, including the core concepts, the theoretical perspectives, key papers and whether they are conceptual or empirical.

As shown in Table 7.1, there are different meanings and approaches for motivation. In general, these meanings are not integrated. A literature review of recent studies shows that entrepreneurial motivations contain psychological, cognitive, and affective aspects. As can be seen from Table 7.1, there is an overlap between the individual, team motivation, and organizational processes. Surprisingly, most of the motivational constructs refer to the economic context, neglecting non-economic contexts such as motivations for social entrepreneurship.

Cognitive-based motivations

A key challenge in entrepreneurship research is understanding entrepreneurial motivations and their impact on entrepreneurial processes and actions. Cognitive explanations, such as the entrepreneurial intention–behavior link, have been studied extensively (e.g. Krueger & Carsrud, 1993; Boyd & Vozikis, 1994; Kreuger et

Table 7.1 Entrepreneurial motivation as a multidimensional construct

Motivational construct	Core concepts	Main theoretical perspectives	Scope of analysis (individual/processes)	Conceptual (C) / Empirical (E)	Key papers for example
Motivations	Push (extrinsic) and pull motivations (intrinsic)	Self-oriented motivations; Self-oriented motivations	Individual	C; E (social entrepreneurship)	Carsrud & Brännback, 2011; Yitshaki & Kropp, 2016b
Entrepreneurial identity	Individual level (founder's identity); Entrepreneurs multiple identities	Identity theory; Identity hierarchy; Centrality vs. salient	Who I am (subjective meaning); Similarities to and differences from others	C/E	Murnieks & Mosakowski, 2007; Shepherd & Haynie, 2009; Powel & Baker, 2014
	Self-concept or self-identity	Self-identity theory; Identity work perspective	Individual	E (social and high-tech entrepreneurs)	Yitshaki & Kropp, 2016b
	Role identity	Role identity; Structural identity theory; Career transition perspective	Who am I?; How should I act?	C/E	Alvesson et al., 2008; Cardon et al, 2009; Hoang & Gimeno, 2010
	Social identity	Social psychology; Social cognitive perspective; social identity theory; Founder's identity	Who am I? How do I make decisions?	E	Fauchart & Gruber, 2011; Alsos et al., 2016
	Individual → organizational and institutional level	Institutional theory; Self-categorization theory; Social cognitive perspective; Social psychology; Self-discrepancy theory	Who are we and what do we do?; Identity synergy and synchronization between different levels	C/E	Ramarajan, 2014; Fisher et al., 2016; Hogg & Terry, 2000; Navis & Glynn, 2011
	Identity work	Self-identity theory; Social identity theory	Individual	C/E	Watson, 2008, 2009; Gill & Larson, 2014
	Organizational identity work	Organizational stigma theory; Institutional theory	Organizational identity	E	Tracey & Phillips, 2016

Table 7.1 (continued)

Motivational construct	Core concepts	Main theoretical perspectives	Scope of analysis (individual/processes)	Conceptual (C) / Empirical (E)	Key papers for example
Passion	Intrinsic drive; Harmonious vs. obsessive passion	Self-perception; Self-regulation	Processes	C	Cardon et al., 2009
	Passion – role identity (inventing, founding, developing)	Role identity; Theory of emotions	Processes	C/E	Cardon et al., 2009; Cardon et al., 2013
	Identity → passion	Identity theory; Psychological perspectives (affect)	Individuals	E	Murnieks et al., 2014
	Motivation → passion	Self-perception theory; Theory of emotions; Self-regulation theory	Individuals' efforts	E	Gielnik et al., 2015
		Intrinsic and extrinsic motivations; Self-determination theory	Individuals	C	Vallerand et al., 2007
	Individual → team level	Complementarity theory; Identity elasticity	Teams	C	Klotz et al., 2014; Cardon et al., 2017
Compassion	Individual level	Perspective taking; Career calling; Entrepreneurial intention theory; Social worth; Cognitive appraisal theory	Other oriented emotional-based feelings	C/E	Miller et al., 2012; Hall & Chandler, 2005; Grant & Gino, 2010; Rynes et al., 2012; Hockerts, 2015

				C/E	
	Organizational level	Self-expansion perspective; Psychology-driven theories; Cognitive appraisal theory; Sense-making; Relational frame theory; Psychological flexibility perspective	Interpersonal helping behavior; Status distance and prosocial behavior	C/E	Doyle et al., 2016; Dutton et al., 2014; Shepherd & Williams, 2014; Shepherd, 2015; Atkins & Parker, 2012
Opportunity recognition	Motivations and cognitive factors	Entrepreneurship theory	Individual/process	C	Shane et al., 2003
	Professional identity → opportunity recognition	Theory of structural alignment	Individual – cognitive processes	E	Grégoire et al., 2010
	Role identity → opportunity recognition	Emotion-as-information theory	Opportunity evaluation and exploitation	E	Grichnik et al., 2010
		Role identity theory	Opportunity evaluation and selection	E	Mathias & Williams, 2014
		Appraisal tendency framework	Opportunity evaluation	E	Foo, 2011
	Individual → organizational level	Entrepreneurship theory	Individual/processes: dual-identity (hybrid) social ventures	C	Busenitz et al., 2016
		Entrepreneurship theory	Definitions/processes	C	Hansen et al., 2011
	Opportunity assessment and entry decisions	Entrepreneurship theory	Individual/ organizational (funding strategy)	C	Shepherd et al., 2015

al., 2000). Entrepreneurial cognition is defined as "the knowledge structures that people use to make assessments, judgments or decisions involving opportunity evaluation and venture creation and growth" (Mitchell et al., 2002, p.97). Hence, entrepreneurial cognition is related to heuristics-based logic, alertness to new opportunities within the environment, entrepreneurial expertise, and effectuation processes (Mitchell et al., 2007). The social–cognitive theory of entrepreneurship acknowledges dynamic processes of interaction between environment, cognition, and action.

Tang et al. (2012) identify that alertness has three complementary dimensions: scanning and searching for new information, connecting previously disparate information, and evaluating whether the new information represents an opportunity. Specific human capital, acquiring new knowledge and cognitive capabilities to combine new knowledge with existing knowledge also are associated with opportunity identification (Corbett, 2007). Similarly, prior knowledge and experiences as entrepreneurs are associated with OR. Paradoxically, too much experience and knowledge can result in cognitive biases that limit the ability to find opportunities with wealth-creation potential (Ucbasaran et al., 2009).

Entrepreneurial cognition explains entrepreneurial motivations as part of an entrepreneur's "mental representations of self, of others, of events and contexts, and of other mental states and constructs" (Grégoire et al., 2011, p.1445). In this worldview, motivation is shaped by mental constructs and interpretations that lead to actions. Cognitive-based motivations to engage in entrepreneurial activity are based on prior knowledge (Shepherd & DeTienne, 2005; Grégoire et al., 2011).

In summary, with few exceptions (e.g. Yitshaki and Kropp, 2016a, 2016b) most of the research on entrepreneurial motivations and OR has examined cognitive aspects. Social cognitive explanations of entrepreneurial motivation neglect the possibility that entrepreneurial cognitions are intertwined with emotions (Lazarus & Folkman, 1984; Frese & Gielnik, 2014). In addition, the research that has examined the affective side has not integrated it well with the cognitive side. A recent study by Edelman and Yli-Renko (2010) suggests that opportunity perceptions mediate objective characteristics of the environment and efforts to launch a new venture. Accordingly, cognitive-based processes of OR are interpreted subjectively and are intertwined with affective processes.

Affect-based motivations

Much of existing research on entrepreneurial affect focuses on positive and negative affect (Baron, 2008; Hmieleski & Baron, 2009), and personality traits, such as regulatory focus (Hmieleski & Baron, 2008). Entrepreneurial motivations also consist of affective factors such as personal initiative and passion (Frese & Gielnik, 2014). Affect has a positive effect on cognitive performance (Baron et al., 2012). In addition, existing literature addresses the role of affect in enhancing creativity, alertness, and active search of new opportunities (Baron, 2008). However, with few exceptions (e.g. Murnieks et al., 2014; Powell & Baker, 2014; Yitshaki & Kropp, 2016a, 2016b) the role of affect in entrepreneurial motivation is under-examined. In particular, the literature does not examine how emotional motivations, such as affect, passion, identity, and compassion, influence entrepreneurial cognitions. We argue that passion, identity, and compassion serve as an affective–cognitive aspect of entrepreneurial motivations. There is limited understanding about how these constructs are related, both to themselves and OR. This understanding aligns with recent calls to include emotions and affect in management theory in general (Ashkanasy et al., 2017; Ashkanasy & Humphrey, 2011), and in the entrepreneurship theory specifically (Baron, 2008).

Passion

Shane et al. (2003) describe that passion contains an affective dimension that can motivate entrepreneurs. Passion typically evokes sustained strong feelings that motivate people to devote time and energy to an activity (Vallerand, 2012). In the entrepreneurial domain, passion has a strong influence on new venture formation and performance (Cardon, 2008; Cardon et al., 2009). Cardon et al. (2009, p. 517) define passion as "consciously accessible, intense positive feelings experienced by engagement in entrepreneurial activities associated with roles that are meaningful and salient to the self-identity of the entrepreneur".

Passion is considered a strong entrepreneurial motivation (Frese & Gielnik, 2014). Passion evokes a "positive inclination toward entrepreneurial activities" (Murnieks et al., 2014, p. 5) and can shape goal-related cognitions, entrepreneurial behavior, and entrepreneurial effectiveness (Cardon et al., 2009). High levels of passion lead to setting challenging goals associated with goal commitment (Frese & Gielnik, 2014). Passion can help entrepreneurs cope with failure and uncertainties that require frequent emotional and cognitive adjustments (Grichnika et al., 2010) and to not abandon their efforts. It can also play a role in developing social networks (Ho & Pollack, 2014), enhance a sense of enthusiasm and emotional energy required to perform entrepreneurial activities (Baum & Locke, 2004; Murnieks et al., 2014), and increase the likelihood of success (Foo, 2011).

The study of entrepreneurial passion is still in a relatively nascent stage. Numerous questions exist about how passion, identity, and motivation influence one another in the entrepreneurial context. Entrepreneurship is an intense, dynamic, stressful context that requires individuals to operate in uncertain environments. These environments present unique challenges to identity and the self-concept, which in turn influence passion. For example, Cardon et al. (2012) argue that, although intuitively reasonable, entrepreneurial passion and identity have not been shown to be empirically related in the entrepreneurial context. Many, we believe, mistakenly view entrepreneurial identity as an integral dimension of entrepreneurial passion (Vallerand et al., 2007; Cardon et al., 2012) rather than as a separate construct that is related to passion.

Although the studies described previously help explain and measure the importance of different types of entrepreneurial passion (Cardon et al., 2013), they do not empirically show how entrepreneurs perceive and manage the relations between their passion and identities. We argue that the relation between entrepreneurial passion and identity can be explained as a process in which passion nourishes identity construction by way of a double loop feedback between entrepreneurial micro-identities and passion. Simply stated, entrepreneurial passion and identity reinforce each other.

Identity

Identity has been a mainstay of the psychology literature for decades. Symbolic interactionism is an integral part of identity theory. Symbolic interactionism has three core principles:

> (1) that people act toward things, including each other, on the basis of the meanings they have for them; (2) that these meanings are derived through social interaction with others; and (3) that these meanings are managed and transformed through an interpretive process that people use to make sense of and handle the objects that constitute their social worlds. (Snow, 2001, p. 367)

Identity provides a set of meanings associated with roles in the social structure (Stryker, 1980). Roles contain a set of internalized meanings (Stets & Serpe, 2013) and can be organized at individual, role, and group levels. Individual or person identities differentiate an individual as a unique person (Burke & Stets, 2009). Stets & Burke (2000, p. 225) describe self-identity as the "categorization of the self as an occupant of a role, and the incorporation, into the self, of the meanings and expectations associated with that role and its performance". The three roles can be intertwined and not easily separated from each other (Stets & Serpe, 2013).

In an attempt to help define themselves, people try to develop coherent identities (Watson, 2008). These personal identities help create, support, and sustain self-concept (Snow & Anderson, 1987). In the entrepreneurial context, entrepreneurs subjectively construct and reconstruct their self-identity—it is a dynamic process (Anderson, 2000; Lindgren & Packendorff, 2009; Var der Haar & Hosking, 2004). An entrepreneur has a subjective interpretation around what it means to be an entrepreneur that shapes and supports self-identity (Watson, 2008).

Entrepreneurial identities are important to motivation. Like motivations, identities can have affective and cognitive components. One aspect of entrepreneurial identity is the *founder's identity*, which Powell & Baker (2014, p. 1417) define as "the set of identities that is chronically salient to a founder in her/his day-to-day work". Another aspect of entrepreneurial identity is role identity, which can include being an innovator, taking risks, being action oriented, being an organizer, facilitator, and communicator (Mitchell, 1997; Murnieks & Mosakowski, 2007). Role identities are precursors of entrepreneurial passion (see Vallerand et al., 2007; Cardon et al., 2012), and strongly condition how entrepreneurs recognize new opportunities (Mathias and Williams, 2014) and shape how opportunities are pursued. A founder's social identity and role identity influence entrepreneurs and help them become who they want to be (Fauchart & Gruber, 2011; Powell & Baker, 2014; Alsos et al., 2016).

Entrepreneurs can have conflicting or contradictory identities. For example, they view themselves as being like other people (*sameness*) and being different from other people (*otherness*) (Anderson & Warren, 2011). Another example of contradictory needs is *belonging*, the need for inclusiveness; that is, having social identity by being a part of a particular social group, and *distinctiveness*, the need to differentiate one's self-identity (Shepherd & Haynie, 2009). Powell & Baker (2014) discuss optimal distinctiveness, which involves multiple salient identities and a balance between the need for inclusiveness and the need to differentiate one's self-identity (Anderson & Warren, 2011; Bjursell & Melin, 2011; Shepherd & Haynie, 2009).

In summary, we can gain insight from sociological and psychological theories of identity to better understand how entrepreneurship develops and why entrepreneurs are motivated to create and build their ventures. As indicated earlier, passion and identity are linked and may be contextual. As an example, the relationships may vary across types of entrepreneurs, e.g. social and high-tech entrepreneurs. In some contexts, such as social entrepreneurship, compassion may also be strongly linked with passion and identity.

Compassion

Dutton et al. (2014, p. 277) describe compassion as "an interpersonal process involving the noticing, feeling, sensemaking and acting that alleviates the suffering of another person". In essence, noticing others' suffering (cognitive), feelings regarding others (affective), and responding (behavioral) are three integral components of compassion (Dutton et al., 2006; Kanov et al., 2004). Compassion creates an emotional energy that elicits feelings and distress that instill a desire to reduce suffering through prosocial behavior (Miller et al., 2012). Compassion is an antecedent of prosocial behavior that can explain the relationship between entrepreneurial motivations and behavior to alleviate suffering (Miller et al., 2012; Grimes et al., 2013; Kroeger & Weber, 2014; Muller et al., 2014).

Although it is possible to subdivide compassion into multiple categories, one important distinction is between self-compassion and other-regarding compassion. Self-compassion involves being touched and open to one's own suffering, not disconnecting from it, and trying to heal oneself with kindness (Neff, 2003a). Self-compassion contains three basic components:

1) extending kindness and understanding to oneself rather than harsh self-criticism and judgment; 2) seeing one's experience as part of the larger human experience rather than as separating and isolating; and 3) mindfulness and holding one's painful thoughts and

feelings in balanced awareness rather than over-identifying with them. (Neff, 2003b, p. 234)

Though the self-compassion aspects are distinct, they are interactive and synergistic (Neff, 2003a).

In contrast, other-regarding compassion occurs when a person notices another person's suffering, feels empathic concern, and responds to the suffering (Lilius et al., 2011). Other-regarding compassion can be based on an awareness of suffering, albeit a sudden awareness or one that develops over time, or be aligned with an individual's basic value structure. Consistent with Batson and Coke's (1981) empathy–altruism model, empathic concern results in an altruistic or selfless desire to help the person in need (Schroeder et al., 1988). The action that arises from other-regarding compassion can be viewed as the fortunate helping the less fortunate (Dutton et al., 2006; Shepherd & Williams, 2014). Self-compassion differs from other-regarding compassion because the genesis of self-compassion is awareness of one's own suffering, a desire to heal oneself and increase well-being (Kanov et al., 2004). Self-compassion is an inner process that involves a desire to concurrently alleviate one's own suffering and to alleviate others' suffering. Notwithstanding the source of compassion, both self-compassion and other-regarding compassion can be an antecedent to motivation. Compassion is important in different entrepreneurial contexts both social and commercial (Austin et al., 2006; Lee & Venkataraman, 2006).

In summary, affective aspects such as passion, identity, and compassion can serve as entrepreneurial motivations. While the literature pays much attention to OR as a cognitive process (Hansen et al., 2011; George et al., 2016), there is some evidence that entrepreneurs are also motivated by affective processes (Yitshaki & Kropp, 2016a, 2016b). Opportunities can be viewed as a combination of subjective and cognitive perceptions. These perceptions are what spur entrepreneurs into action through cognitive processes, social interaction, and the mobilization of resources (Edelman & Yli-Renko, 2010).

Entrepreneurial motivations and context

With few exceptions, the role of context on entrepreneurial motivations has not been well-explored. This is especially true for differences between cognitive and affective motivations among entrepreneurs in different contexts. By context, we are referring to different types of entrepreneurial activities, e.g. high-tech and social entrepreneurs. However, a growing evidence identifies that entrepreneurial cognition is contextually bound (Elfving et al., 2009; Brännback & Carsrud, 2016). In one of the first empirical studies that examined passion across different types of entrepreneurial activities, Yitshaki and Kropp (2016b) identified that passion is contextually based. Using life-story interviews of 45 high-tech and social entrepreneurs, the authors found that high-tech entrepreneurs think of passion as being composed of a strong challenge to lead a meaningful activity and to leave a fingerprint. For social entrepreneurs, passion is characterized more in terms of enthusiasm and excitement and a desire to make a mark. In both cases, passion was an important component of motivation and an antecedent of opportunity recognition.

We argue that OR, whether discovered or created, may be contextually dependent. Generally, environmental conditions and organizational aspects play a role in resource availability and norms that encourage entrepreneurial activities (Gartner, 1985; Wiklund & Shepherd, 2003). Certain technologies may be based on discovered opportunities, others may be based on both creation and discovery (Zahra, 2008). Similarly, the generation of opportunities depends on contextual and social influences rather than the insights of a single individual (Dimov, 2007).

Entrepreneurial cognitions and affect are also contextually bounded; however, less attention has been paid on how contextual norms and behaviors lead to different OR patterns among entrepreneurs (Brännback & Carsrud, 2016). New opportunities may be recognized based on imprinting mechanisms and existing core concepts derived from the social structure (Giddens, 1984; Short et al., 2010). It is therefore important to understand how those core concepts influence entrepreneurial cognitive and affective process as well as OR.

Discussion

With few exceptions (e.g. Murnieks et al., 2014; Powel & Baker, 2014; Yitshaki & Kropp, 2016a, 2016b), research in entrepreneurial motivational over the last 20 years has tended to focus on the cognitive side of motivation. Cognitive-based motivations imply that opportunities are recognized based on systematic search; however, opportunities might be discovered or created based on social awareness that developed through life events or by chance. Thus understanding OR through cognitive processes ignores important affective motivations.

Understanding the affective side of entrepreneurial motivation provides insights into OR. First, some entrepreneurs are motivated by affect. For example, social entrepreneurs are affectively motivated by their life events (Yitshaki & Kropp, 2016b). Second, affect helps shape cognitions (Edelman & Yli-Renko, 2010; Frese & Gielnik, 2014). Third, affect leads to OR because entrepreneurs are motivated by their passion and identities (Shane, Lock and Collins, 2003; Murnieks et al., 2014) and compassion (Shepherd, 2015). Entrepreneurial motivations can be associated with *created* opportunities, based on reflexivity, and with discovered opportunities, based on imprinting (Suddaby et al., 2015). Figure 7.1 summarizes the key motivational constructs, each developed within its core concept rather than across different motivational constructs.

The proposed process model suggests an integrative approach to entrepreneurial motivations, viewing it as a multi-dimensional construct that consists of a mix of

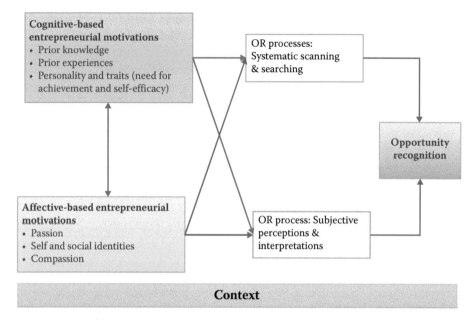

Figure 7.1   Entrepreneurial motivation as a multidimensional construct

cognitive–affective processes. Different motivational constructs can lead to different types of OR. While there is a growing call to understand entrepreneurial motivations as a combination of cognitive and affective processes (Frese & Gielnik, 2014), the current literature is fragmented, untied to the OR literature. By ignoring the affective aspects of entrepreneurial motivation, our understanding of OR is limited and can be biased by cognitive-based approaches. Further research is needed to clarify how entrepreneurial cognition and affect relate to motivation and OR. We discuss possible future research next.

Future research directions

Cognitive-based motivations and future possible questions

Current theories suggest that entrepreneurial cognition is related to entrepreneurial attitudes and beliefs, prior knowledge and experiences, and systematic search for opportunities. Possible research questions can focus on the ways in which entrepreneurial passion and identities influence how entrepreneurs synchronize new information about new opportunities. How do entrepreneurial traits, such as need for achievement and self-efficacy, interact with an entrepreneur's prior knowledge? How do cognitive-based entrepreneurial motivations interact with affective-based motivations regarding new opportunities in different contexts? How do entrepreneurs synchronize cognitive- and affective-based motivations? Do prior knowledge and experiences lead to discovered opportunities based on imprinting mechanisms?

Affect-based motivations and future possible questions

The current literature suggests that passion is a motivational construct. While there is evidence about the interrelations between passion and identities, less is known about how these constructs are associated with OR. There are many possible research questions that can explore these associations. For example, how do entrepreneurial passion and identities influence OR patterns? Do different types of passion create different types of motivations for different types of entrepreneurs? Do passion and identities shape entrepreneurial OR based on reflexive processes? Future research can also examine how founders' role identities influence OR among different entrepreneurs in different contexts. How do entrepreneurs' social identities interact with their prior knowledge and OR?

Compassion is an under-examined motivational construct in the entrepreneurial context (Shepherd, 2015). Possible research questions regarding compassion include the following. What is the role of compassion in explaining entrepreneurial motivations and OR in economic and non-economic contexts? Does compassion matter for SMEs and high-tech entrepreneurs? What are the interrelations between entrepreneurial identities, passion, and compassion?

Possible research questions can relate to the degree to which cognitive structural alignment between prior knowledge and OR (Grégoire et al., 2010) is aligned with entrepreneurial passion and identities. How do affect-based motivations differ from cognitive-based motivations with regard to created or discovered opportunities? Finally, how does compassion lead to OR in different contexts?

Although entrepreneurial firms operate in different contexts, such as social entrepreneurship, SMEs and high-tech entrepreneurs, cognitive- and affect-based motivations across contexts are not well understood. Entrepreneurial cognition may vary through lens of context, as each context operates based on different cognitive maps (Brännback & Carsrud, 2016). Therefore, another possible research stream would be a comparison between different contextual cognitions and OR.

These research questions suggest that both qualitative and quantitative methods can illuminate the possible connections between cognitive- and affect-based entrepreneurial motivations. Finally, as entrepreneurial activity also occurs at the team and organizational levels, researchers are encouraged to use multilevel analysis to examine the research questions. In closing, the relation between cognitive and affective elements of motivation and OR represent a rich area for further research.

References

Alsos, G. A., Clausen, T. H., Hytti, U. & Solvoll, S. (2016). Entrepreneurs' social identity and the preference of causal and effectual behaviours in start-up processes. *Entrepreneurship & Regional Development*, 28(3–4), 234–58.

Alvarez, S. A. & Barney, J. B. (2007). Discovery and creation: Alternative theories of entrepreneurial action. *Strategic Entrepreneurship Journal*, 1(1–2), 11–26.

Alvesson, M., Lee Ashcraft, K. & Thomas, R. (2008). Identity matters: Reflections on the construction of identity scholarship in organization studies. *Organization*, 15(1), 5–28.

Amit, R. & Muller, E. (1995). Push and pull entrepreneurship. *Journal of Small Business and Entrepreneurship*, 12(4), 64–80.

Anderson, A. R. (2000). The protean entrepreneur: The entrepreneurial process as fitting self and circumstance. *Journal of Enterprising Culture*, 8(3), 201–34.

Anderson, A. R. & Warren, L. (2011). The entrepreneur as hero and jester: Enacting the entrepreneurial discourse. *International Small Business Journal*, 29, 589–609.

Ardichvili, A. & Cardozo, R. N. (2000). A model of the entrepreneurial opportunity recognition process. *Journal of Enterprising Culture*, 8(02), 103–19.

Ardichvili, A., Cardozo, R. & Ray, S. (2003). A theory of entrepreneurial opportunity identification and development. *Journal of Business Venturing*, 18, 105–23.

Ashkanasy, N. M. & Humphrey, R. H. (2011). Current emotion research in organizational behavior. *Emotion Review*, 3(2), 214–24.

Ashkanasy, N., Humphrey, R. & Huy, Q. (2017). Integrating emotions and affect in theories of management. *Academy of Management Review*, 42(2), 175–89.

Atkins, P. W. & Parker, S. K. (2012). Understanding individual compassion in organizations: The role of appraisals and psychological flexibility. *Academy of Management Review*, 37, 524–46.

Austin, J., Stevenson, H. & Wei-Skillern, J. (2006). Social and commercial entrepreneurship: same, different, or both?. *Entrepreneurship Theory & Practice*, 30(1), 1–22.

Baron, R. A. (2006). Opportunity recognition as pattern recognition: How entrepreneurs "connect the dots" to identify new business opportunities. *The Academy of Management Perspectives*, 20, 104–19.

Baron, R. A. (2008). The role of affect in the entrepreneurial process. *Academy of Management Review*, 33(2), 328–40.

Baron, R. A. & Ensley, M. D. (2006). Opportunity recognition as the detection of meaningful patterns: Evidence from comparisons of novice and experienced entrepreneurs. *Management Science*, 52(9), 1331–44.

Baron R. A., Hmieleski K. M. & Henry R. A. (2012). Entrepreneurs' dispositional positive affect: The potential benefits and potential costs of being "up." *Journal of Business Venturing*, 27(3), 310–24.

Batson, C. D. & Coke, J. S. (1981). Empathy: A source of altruistic motivation for helping? In J. P. Rushton & R. M. Sorrentino (Eds), *Altruism and Helping Behavior: Social, Personality, and Developmental Perspectives*. Hillsdale, NJ: Erlbaum, pp. 167–87.

Baum, J. R. & Locke, E. A. (2004). The relationship of entrepreneurial traits, skill, and motivation to subsequent venture growth. *Journal of Applied Psychology*, 89, 587–98.

Bhagavatula, S., Elfring, T., Van Tilburg, A. & Van De Bunt, G. G. (2010). How social and human capital influence opportunity recognition and resource mobilization in India's handloom industry. *Journal of Business Venturing*, 25(3), 245–60.

Bingham, C. B., Eisenhardt, K. M. & Furr, N. R. (2007). What makes a process a capability? Heuristics, strategy, and effective capture of opportunities. *Strategic Entrepreneurship Journal*, 1(1–2), 27–47.

Bjursell, C. & Melin, L. (2011). Proactive and reactive plots: Narratives in entrepreneurial identity construction. *International Journal of Gender and Entrepreneurship*, 3, 218–35.

Boyd, N. G. & Vozikis, G. S. (1994). The influence of self-efficacy on the development of entrepreneurial intentions and actions. *Entrepreneurship Theory & Practice*, 18, 63–77.

Brännback, M. & Carsrud, A. L. (2016). Understanding entrepreneurial cognitions through the lenses of context. In F. Welter & W. B. Gartner (Eds). *A Research Agenda of Entrepreneurship and Context*. Cheltenham, UK: Edward Elgar, pp. 16–27.

Burke, P. J. & Stets, J. E. (2009). *Identity Theory*. New York, NY: Oxford University Press.

Busenitz, L. W., Sharfman, M. P., Townsend, D. M. & Harkins, J. A. (2016). The emergence of dual-identity social entrepreneurship: Its boundaries and limitations. *Journal of Social Entrepreneurship*, 7(1), 25–48.

Buttner, E. H. & Moore D. P. (1997). Women's organizational exodus to entrepreneurship: Self-reported motivations and correlates with success. *Journal of Small Business Management*, 35(1), 34–46.

Cardon, M. S. (2008). Is passion contagious? The transference of entrepreneurial passion to employees. *Human Resource Management Review*, 18, 77–86.

Cardon, M. S., Foo, M. D., Shepherd, D. & Wiklund, J. (2012). Exploring the heart: Entrepreneurial emotion is a hot topic. *Entrepreneurship Theory & Practice*, 36, 1–10.

Cardon, M. S. Grégoire A., Stevens, C. E. & Patel, P. C. (2013). Measuring entrepreneurial passion: Conceptual foundations and scale validation. *Journal of Business Venturing*, 28(3), 373–96.

Cardon, M. S., Post, C. & Forster, W. R. (2017). Team entrepreneurial passion: Its emergence and influence in new venture teams. *Academy of Management Review*, 42(2), 283–305.

Cardon, M. S., Vincent, J., Singh J. & Drnovsek, M. (2009). The nature and experience of entrepreneurial passion. *Academy of Management Review*, 34, 511–32.

Carsrud, A. L & Brännback, M. (2011). Entrepreneurial motivations: What do we still need to know? *Journal of Small Business Management*, 39(1), 9–26.

Carsrud, A. L., Brännback, M., Elfving, J. & Brandt, K. (2009). Motivations: The entrepreneurial mind and behavior. In A. L. Carsrud & M. Brännback (Eds), *Understanding the Entrepreneurial Mind: Opening the Black Box*. New York, NY: Springer, pp. 141–66.

Corbett, A. C. (2007). Learning asymmetries and the discovery of entrepreneurial opportunities. *Journal of Business Venturing*, 22(1), 97–118.

De Koning, A. & Muzyka, D. (1999). *Conceptualizing Opportunity Recognition as a Socio-Cognitive Process*. Stockholm, Sweden: Centre for Advanced Studies in Leadership.

DeTienne, D. R. & Chandler, G. N. (2007). The role of gender in opportunity identification. *Entrepreneurship Theory & Practice*, 31(3), 365–86.

Dimov, D. (2007). Beyond the single-person, single-insight attribution in understanding entrepreneurial opportunities. *Entrepreneurship Theory & Practice*, 5, 713–31.

Doyle, S., Lount, R., Wilk, S. & Pettit, N. (2016). Helping others most when they're not too close: Status distance as a determinant of interpersonal helping in organizations. *Academy of Management Discoveries*, 2(2), 155–74.

Dutton, J. E., Workman, K. M. & Hardin, A. E. (2014). Compassion at work. *Annual Review of Organizational Psychology and Organizational Behavior*, 1, 277–304.

Dutton, J. E., Worline, M. C., Frost, P. J. & Lilius, J. (2006). Explaining compassion organizing. *Administrative Science Quarterly*, 51, 59–96.

Edelman, L. & Yli-Renko, H. (2010). The impact of environment and entrepreneurial perceptions on venture-creation efforts: Bridging the discovery and creation views of entrepreneurship. *Entrepreneurship Theory & Practice*, 34(5), 833–56.

Elfving, J., Brännback, M. & Carsrud, A. L. (2009). Toward a contextual model of entrepreneurial intentions. In A. L. Carsrud & M. Brännback (Eds), *Understanding the Entrepreneurial Mind: Opening the Black Box*. New York, NY: Springer, pp. 23–34.

Fauchart, E. & Gruber, M. (2011). Darwinians, communitarians, and missionaries: The role of founder identity in entrepreneurship. *Academy of Management Journal*, 54, 935–57.

Fisher, G., Kotha, S. & Lahiri, A. (2016). Changing with the times: An integrated view of identity, legitimacy and new venture life cycles. *Academy of Management Review*, 41(3), 383–409.

Foo, M. D. (2011). Emotions and entrepreneurial opportunity evaluation. *Entrepreneurship Theory & Practice*, 35, 375–93.

Frese, M. & Gielnik, M. M. (2014). The psychology of entrepreneurship. *Annual Review of Organizational Psychology and Organizational Behavior*, 1(1), 413–38.

Gaglio, C. M. & Katz, J. A. (2001). The psychological basis of opportunity identification: Entrepreneurial alertness. *Small Business Economics*, 16(2), 95–111.

Gartner, W. B. (1985). A conceptual framework for describing the phenomenon of new venture creation. *Academy of Management Review*, 10(4), 696–706.

George, N. M., Parida, V., Lahti, T. & Wincent, J. (2016). A systematic literature review of entrepreneurial opportunity recognition: Insights on influencing factors. *International Entrepreneurship and Management Journal*, 12(2), 309–50.

Giddens, A. (1984). *The Constitution of Society: Outline of the Theory of Structuration*. Berkeley, CA: University of California Press.

Gielnik, M. M., Spitzmuller, M., Schmitt, A., Klemann, D. K. & Frese, M. (2015). "I put in effort, therefore I am passionate": Investigating the path from effort to passion in entrepreneurship. *Academy of Management Journal*, 58(4), 1012–31.

Gill, R. & Larson, G. S. (2014). Making the ideal (local) entrepreneur: place and the regional development of high-tech entrepreneurial identity. *Human Relations*, 67(5), 519–42.

Grant, A. M. & Gino, F. (2010). A little thanks goes a long way: Explaining why gratitude expressions motivate prosocial behavior. *Journal of Personality and Social Psychology*, 98(6), 946–55.

Grégoire, D. A., Barr, P. S. & Shepherd, D. A. (2010). Cognitive processes of opportunity recognition: The role of structural alignment. *Organization Science*, 21, 413–31.

Grégoire, D. A., Corbett, A. & McMullen, J. (2011). The cognitive perspective in entrepreneurship: An agenda for future research. *Journal of Management Studies*, 48(6), 1443–77.

Grichnik, D., Smeja, A. & Welpe, I. (2010). The importance of being emotional: How do emotions affect entrepreneurial opportunity evaluation and exploitation? *Journal of Economic Behavior & Organization*, 76(1), 15–29.

Grimes, M. G., McMullen, J. S., Vogus, T. J. & Miller, T. L. (2013). Studying the origins of social entrepreneurship: Compassion and the role of embedded agency. *Academy of Management Review*, 38, 460–63.

Hall, D. T. & Chandler, D. (2005). Psychological success: When the career is a calling. *Journal of Organizational Behavior*, 26, 155–76.

Hansen, D. J., Shrader, R. & Monllor, J. (2011). Defragmenting definitions of entrepreneurial opportunity. *Journal of Small Business Management*, 49(2), 283–304.

Hmieleski, K. M. & Baron, R. A. (2008). Regulatory focus and new venture performance: A study of entrepreneurial opportunity exploitation under conditions of risk versus uncertainty. *Strategic Entrepreneurship Journal*, 2(4), 285–99.

Hmieleski, K. M. & Baron, R. A. (2009). Entrepreneurs' optimism and new venture performance: A social cognitive perspective. *Academy of Management Journal*, 52(3), 473–88.

Ho, V. T. & Pollack, J. M. (2014). Passion isn't always a good thing: Examining entrepreneurs' network centrality and financial performance with a dualistic model of passion. *Journal of Management Studies*, 51(3), 433–59.

Hoang, H. & Gimeno, J. (2010). Becoming a founder: How founder role identity affects entrepreneurial transitions and persistence in founding. *Journal of Business Venturing*, 25(1), 41–53.

Hockerts, K. (2015). Determinants of social entrepreneurial intentions. *Entrepreneurship Theory & Practice*. doi:10.1111/etap.1217

Hogg, M,A., Terry, D. J. (2000). Social identity and self-categorization processes in organizational contexts. *Academy of Management Review*, 25(1): 121–40.

Kanov, J. M., Maitlis, S., Worline, M. C., Dutton, J. E., Peter, J. F. & Jacoba, L. (2004). Compassion in organizational life. *American Behavioral Scientist*, 47, 808–27.

Klotz, A. C., Hmieleski, K. M., Bradley, B. H. & Busenitz, L. W. (2014). New venture teams: A review of the literature and roadmap for future research. *Journal of Management*, 40(1), 226–55.

Kroeger, A. & Weber, C. (2014). Developing a conceptual framework for comparing social value creation. *Academy of Management Review*, 39, 513–40.

Krueger, N. & Carsrud, A. L. (1993). Entrepreneurial intentions: Applying the theory of planned behavior. *Entrepreneurship and Regional Development*, 5, 315–30.

Krueger, N. & Dickson, P. R. (1994). How believing in ourselves increases risk taking: Perceived self-efficacy and opportunity recognition. *Decision Sciences*, 25(3), 385–400.

Krueger, N. F., Reilly, M. D. & Carsrud, A. L. (2000). Competing models of entrepreneurial intentions. *Journal of Business Venturing*, 15(5), 411–32.

Lazarus, R. S. & Folkman, S. (1984). *Stress, Appraisal, and Coping*. New York, NY: Springer.

Lee, J. H. & Venkataraman, S. (2006). Aspirations, market offerings, and the pursuit of entrepreneurial opportunities. *Journal of Business Venturing*, 21, 107–23.

Lilius, J. M., Kanov, J., Dutton, J., Worline, M. C. & Maitlis, S. (2011). Compassion revealed: What we know about compassion at work (and where we need to know more). In K. Cameron & G. Spreitzer (Eds), *Handbook of Positive Organizational Scholarship*. New York, NY: Oxford University Press, pp. 273–87.

Lindgren, M. & Packendorff, J. (2009). Social constructionism and entrepreneurship: Basic assumptions and consequences for theory and research. *International Journal of Entrepreneurial Behaviour & Research*, 15(1), 25–47.

Lumpkin, G. T. & Lichtenstein, B. B. (2005). The role of organizational learning in the opportunity-recognition process. *Entrepreneurship Theory & Practice*, 29(4), 451–72.

Marquis, C. & Tilcsik, A. (2013). Imprinting: Toward a multilevel theory. *Academy of Management Annals*, 7(1), 195–245.

Mathias, B. D. & Williams, D. W. (2014). The impact of role identities on entrepreneurs' evaluation and selection of opportunities. *Journal of Management*, doi:10.1177/0149206314544747

Miller, T. L., Grimes, M. G., McMullen, J. S. & Vogus, T. J. (2012). Venturing for others with heart and head: How compassion encourages social entrepreneurship. *Academy of Management Review*, 37, 616–40.

Mitchell, R. K. (1997). Oral history and expert scripts: Demystifying the entrepreneurial experience. *International Journal of Entrepreneurial Behaviour and Research*, 3, 122–139.

Mitchell, R. K., Busenitz, L. W., Bird, B., Marie Gaglio, C., McMullen, J. S., Morse, E. A. & Smith, J. B. (2007). The central question in entrepreneurial cognition research. *Entrepreneurship Theory & Practice*, 31(1), 1–27.

Mitchell, R. K., Busenitz, L. W., Lant, T., McDougall, P. P., Morse, E. A. & Smith, B. (2002). Entrepreneurial cognition theory: Rethinking the people side of entrepreneurship research. *Entrepreneurship Theory & Practice*, 27(2), 93–104.

Muller, A. R., Pfarrer, M. D. & Little, L. M. (2014). A theory of collective empathy in corporate philanthropy decisions. *Academy of Management Review*, 39, 1–21.

Murnieks, C. Y. & Mosakowski, E. M. (2007). Who am I? Looking inside the "entrepreneurial identity". Babson College Entrepreneurship Research Conference (BCERC) 2007; Frontiers of Entrepreneurship Research 2007. Available at SSRN: https://ssrn.com/abstract=1064901

Murnieks, C. Y., Mosakowski, E. & Cardon, M. S. (2014). Pathways of passion: Identity centrality, passion, and behavior among entrepreneurs. *Journal of Management*, 40, 1583–606.

Navis, C. & Glynn, M. A. (2011). Legitimate distinctiveness and the entrepreneurial identity: Influence on investor judgments of new venture plausibility. *Academy of Management Review*, 36(3), 479–99.

Neff, K. D. (2003a). Self-compassion: An alternative conceptualization of a healthy attitude toward oneself. *Self and Identity*, 2(2), 85–101.

Neff, K. D. (2003b). The development and validation of a scale to measure self-compassion. *Self and Identity*, 2(3), 223–50.

Piperopoulos, P. & Dimov, D. (2015). Burst bubbles or build steam? Entrepreneurship education, entrepreneurial self-efficacy, and entrepreneurial intentions. *Journal of Small Business Management*, 53(4), 970–85.

Powell, E. E. & Baker, T. (2014). It's what you make of it: founder identity and enacting strategic responses to adversity. *Academy of Management Journal*, 57, 1406–33.

Ramarajan, L. (2014). Past, present and future research on multiple identities: Toward an intrapersonal network approach. *Academy of Management Annals*, 8(1), 589–659.

Rauch, A. & Frese, M. (2007). Born to be an entrepreneur? Revisiting the personality approach to entrepreneurship. In J. R. Baum, M. Frese & R. A. Baron (Eds), *The Psychology of Entrepreneurship*. Mahwah, NJ: Erlbaum, pp. 41–65.

Robichaud, Y., Le Brasseur, R. & Nagarajan, K. V. (2010). Necessity and opportunity-driven entrepreneurs in Canada: An investigation into their characteristics and an appraisal of the role of gender. *Journal of Applied Business and Economics*, 11(1), 59–79.

Rynes, S. L., Bartunek, J. M., Dutton, J. E. & Margolis, J. D. (2012). Care and compassion through an organizational lens: Opening up new possibilities. *Academy of Management Review*, 37(4), 503–23.

Schroeder, D. A., Dovidio, J. F., Sibicky, M. E., Matthews, L. L. & Allen, J. L. (1988). Empathic concern and helping behavior: Egoism or altruism? *Journal of Experimental Social Psychology*, 24(4), 333–53.

Segal, G., Borgia, D. & Schoenfeld, J. (2005). The motivation to become an entrepreneur. *International Journal of Entrepreneurial Behavior & Research*, 11(1), 42–57.

Shane, S. & Venkataraman, S. (2000). The promise of entrepreneurship as a field of research. *Academy of Management Review*, 25(1), 217–26.

Shane, S., Locke, E. A. & Collins, C. J. (2003). Entrepreneurial motivation. *Human Resource Management Review*, 13, 257–79.

Shepherd, D. A. (2015). Party On! A call for entrepreneurship research that is more interactive, activity based, cognitively hot, compassionate, and prosocial. *Journal of Business Venturing*, 30, 489–507.

Shepherd, D. A. & Haynie, M. J. (2009). Birds of a feather don't always flock together: Identity management in entrepreneurship. *Journal of Business Venturing*, 24, 316–37.

Shepherd, D. A. & DeTienne, D. R. (2005). Prior knowledge, potential financial reward, and opportunity identification. *Entrepreneurship Theory & Practice*, 29(1), 91–112.

Shepherd, D. A. & Williams, T. A. (2014). Local venturing as compassion organizing in the aftermath of a natural disaster: The role of localness and community in reducing suffering. *Journal of Management Studies*, 51(6), 952–94.

Shepherd, D. A., Williams, T. A. & Patzelt, H. (2015). Thinking about entrepreneurial decision making review and research agenda. *Journal of Management*, 41(1), 11–46.

Short, J. C., Ketchen Jr, D. J., Shook, C. L. & Ireland, R. D. (2010). The concept of "opportunity" in entrepreneurship research: Past accomplishments and future challenges. *Journal of Management*, 36(1), 40–65.

Snow, D. A. (2001). Extending and broadening Blumer's Conceptualization of Symbolic Interactionism. *Symbolic Interaction*, 24(3), 367–77.

Snow, D. A. & Anderson. L. (1987). Identity work among the homeless: The verbal construction and avowal of personal identities. *American Journal of Sociology*, 92, 1336–71.

Stets, J. E. & Burke. P. J. (2000). Identity theory and social identity theory. *Social Psychology Quarterly*, 63(3), 224–37.

Stets, J. E. & Serpe, R. T. (2013). Social identity. In J. DeLamata & A. Ward (Eds), *Handbook of Social Psychology, Handbooks of Sociology and Social Research*. Dordrecht: Springer Science + Business Media, pp. 31–60.

Stevenson, H. & Jarillo, J. C. (1991). A new entrepreneurial paradigm. In A. Etzioni & P. R. Lawrence (Eds), *Socio-Economics: Towards a New Synthesis*. Cambridge, MA: M. E. Sharp, pp. 185–208.

Stryker, S. (1980). *Symbolic Interactionism: A Social Structural Version*. Menlo Park, CA: Benjamin/Cummings Publishing.

Suddaby, R., Bruton, G. D. & Si, S. X. (2015). Entrepreneurship through a qualitative lens: Insights on the construction and/or discovery of entrepreneurial opportunity. *Journal of Business Venturing*, 30(1), 1–10.

Tang, J., Kacmar, K. M. M. & Busenitz, L. (2012). Entrepreneurial alertness in the pursuit of new opportunities. *Journal of Business Venturing*, 27(1), 77–94.

Tracey, P. & Phillips, N. (2016). Managing the consequences of organizational stigmatization: Identity work in a social enterprise. *Academy of Management Journal*, 59(3), 740–65.

Ucbasaran, D., Westhead, P. & Wright, M. (2009). The extent and nature of opportunity identification by experienced entrepreneurs. *Journal of Business Venturing*, 24(2), 99–115.

Vaghely, I. P. & Julien, P. A. (2010). Are opportunities recognized or constructed? An information perspective on entrepreneurial opportunity identification. *Journal of Business Venturing*, 25(1), 73–86.

Vallerand, R. J. (2012). From motivation to passion: In search of the motivational processes involved in a meaningful life. *Canadian Psychology/Psychologie Canadienne*, 53(1), 42–52.

Vallerand, R. J., Salvy, S. J., Mageau, G. A., Elliot, A. J., Denis, P. L., Grouzet, F. M. & Blanchard, C. (2007). On the role of passion in performance. *Journal of Personality*, 75, 505–34.

Var der Haar, D. & Hosking, D. M. (2004). Evaluating appreciative inquiry: A relational constructionist perspective. *Human Relations*, 57, 1017–36.

Watson, T. J. (2008). Managing identity: Identity work, personal predicaments and structural circumstances. *Organization*, 15(1), 121–43.

Watson, T. J. (2009). Entrepreneurial action, identity work and the use of multiple discursive resources: The case of a rapidly changing family business. *International Small Business Journal*, 27(3), 251–74.

Wiklund, J. & Shepherd, D. (2003). Aspiring for, and achieving growth: The moderating role of resources and opportunities. *Journal of Management Studies*, 40, 1919–41.

Yitshaki, R. & Kropp, F. (2016a). Entrepreneurial passions and identities in different contexts: A comparison between high-tech and social entrepreneurs. *Entrepreneurship & Regional Development*, 28 (3–4), 206–33.

Yitshaki, R. & Kropp, F. (2016b). Motivations and opportunity recognition of social entrepreneurs. *Journal of Small Business Management*, 54(2), 546–65.

Zahra, S. A. (2008). The virtuous cycle of discovery and creation of entrepreneurial opportunities. *Strategic Entrepreneurship Journal*, 2, 243–57.

8   On the use of configurational analysis in entrepreneurial research

József Mezei and Shahrokh Nikou

Introduction

Literature informs us that entrepreneurship researchers tend to focus on understanding the antecedents of entrepreneurial intentions (Bird, 1988; Boyd & Vozikis, 1994; Carr & Sequeira, 2007; Krueger, 1993; Krueger & Carsrud, 1993; Krueger et al., 2000; Liñán & Chen, 2009). However, our understanding of what makes people decide to start new business ventures is still limited (Carsrud & Brännback, 2011), and in this article we aim to demonstrate that research in this area is still highly justified and necessary.

Over the last 25 years, the Theory of Planned Behaviour (TPB) (Ajzen, 1991), an extension of Theory of Reasoned Action (TRA) developed by Ajzen & Fishbein (1980), has been the single most used theoretical framework to inspire entrepreneurial intention research. In addition to TPB, other theoretical models integrating attitude and behaviour theory, self-efficacy and social learning theory have been used to understand behaviour and entrepreneurial intention (Peterman & Kennedy, 2003). Notwithstanding the widespread acknowledgments of the merits and its applicability, TPB suffers from several troubling weaknesses as noted in recent critiques (Sniehotta et al., 2014). Some contributions, including Sniehotta et al. (2014), have recently raised serious concerns and have urged researchers to move on and employ novel and innovative theoretical frameworks and avoid using TPB due to its static explanatory nature, which does not help to understand the evidenced effects of behaviour on cognition and future behaviour (McEachan et al., 2011).

To address related methodological concerns, in this article we aim to offer an alternative approach to TBA-guided regression analysis-based literature by making use of a different methodological approach, specifically a configurational comparative method, namely Fuzzy-set Qualitative Comparative Analysis (hereinafter referred to as FsQCA). FsQCA has been introduced by Ragin (2000) and, since its conception, has widely been used in both variable-oriented and case-oriented studies. FsQCA is essentially a variant of the Qualitative Comparative Analysis introduced by Ragin (1987). In recent years, scholars have increasingly turned their attention to FsQCA to perform various types of studies (Krogslund et al., 2015). Proponents of this approach further argue that a set-theoretic technique such as FsQCA can offer distinct advantages in causal-oriented investigations, e.g. entrepreneurial intention research. To account for asymmetric relationships between variables, this article employs such approach in the context of entrepreneurship. Our aim is to complement the insights and knowledge we often gain from the mainstream regression-based methods in entrepreneurship research. One of the definitive feature of FsQCA is that it helps to understand better the causal conditions and asymmetric relationships between variables affecting an outcome.

In this chapter, we aim to achieve the following objectives:

- To elaborate on FsQCA and to highlight the rationale for embracing this method in entrepreneurship intention research.
- To provide a proof of concept and extend FsQCA to show that it can be used effectively as the basis of classification tasks to complement configurational analysis in entrepreneurial research.
- To apply the FsQCA method and the proposed extension in the context of entrepreneurial intention research by exemplifying an empirical study executed in eight countries.

The article also provides a literature review and presents related contributions in the domains of entrepreneurial research and configurational analysis. It then presents the FsQCA method, its rationale to be used in understanding entrepreneurial intention, and a new approach to utilize FsQCA as the basis of binary classifications tasks. The article continues with describing details of data collection and data analysis to demonstrate the usefulness of FsQCA in entrepreneurial intention research. It concludes with a discussion, conclusion and future research directions.

Literature review

In this section we present a brief literature review on entrepreneurial intention research, with the main focus on current challenges. Afterwards, we discuss configurational analysis, its potential use in entrepreneurship research, and how a particular method, i.e. FsQCA, can help to generate novel insights in the domain.

Entrepreneurial intention state-of-the-art

Entrepreneurial intention is a multidisciplinary and consolidated area of research within the field of entrepreneurship. Identifying the antecedent factors that constitute and reinforce entrepreneurial motivations, attitudes, behaviours and intentions to start a new business venture have primarily been the major concerns over the last 30 years in entrepreneurship research (Beynon et al., 2016; Carsrud & Brännback, 2011; Zhao et al., 2005). For example, Souitaris et al. (2007), drawing on TPB, argue that the intentions towards a new business are primarily made of inspirations provided by entrepreneurship education. By testing an exogenous variable (education) and its influence on the attitude and the intention towards behaviour (self-employment), the authors confirmed that the attitude–intention link can be investigated through TBA using correlational methods such as regression analysis. However, as we stated earlier, entrepreneurship is a multifaceted phenomenon rapidly changing over time, and thus conventional regression-based analyses or related statistical techniques cannot fully capture the underlying nuances and show the causal patterns of the factors stimulating entrepreneurial intentions. Consequently, it is hard to understand whether related factors are necessary or sufficient conditions for entrepreneurial intention as an outcome to occur (e.g. to become an entrepreneur). Relying on conventional methodological approaches, scholars have investigated the effect of various factors such as locus of control (Hansemark, 1998), subjective norms (the degree to which one perceives social pressure to perform or not a behaviour) (Ajzen, 1991), perceptions that are influenced by normative beliefs (Meek et al., 2010), or perceived behavioural control (non-volitional elements inherent in behaviours) (Krueger & Carsrud, 1993; Sommer & Haug, 2011).

However, regardless of (i) what antecedent (independent) variables (e.g. contextual factors, cognitive elements and personal characteristics) are considered and (ii) whether constructs have a direct or mediating effect on one's intention to become an entrepreneur, what we actually observe from the existing findings is a set of linear and symmetric relationships between the independent and dependent variables.

To support this reasoning, we rely on several prior studies that have addressed methodological pitfalls and drawbacks in entrepreneurial intentions research. For example, Krueger (2009) puts forward that the construct of intention appears to be deeply fundamental to human decision making and proposes future studies to focus on the connection between intent and other theories and models in relation to decision making under risk and uncertainty. Krueger further states that this view provides opportunities to develop integrative and more sophisticated theoretical models of the entrepreneurial processes, linking intention-based models with prospect theory (Kahneman & Tversky, 1979) or effectuation theory (Sarasvathy, 2009). On that account, McDougall and Oviatt (2000) argue that entrepreneurial intention research lacks a unifying and clear methodological direction and this represents a weakness in a field of study that, by definition, is concerned with behaviour as well as value-creating processes. Of the same opinion, Coviello and Jones (2004) recommend researchers to strive for minimizing the tendency toward methodological simplicity and make their methodological decisions with greater coherency and thoroughness. The authors claim that research on entrepreneurial intent is fundamentally geared towards capturing data in a logical positivist manner, emphasizing inferential statistics, and testing hypotheses in order to measure and predict reality through sets of predetermined variables and constructs. Some authors, such as Chandler and Lyon (2001) investigated issues of research design and construct measurement in entrepreneurship research, and showed that most empirical studies follow trends towards multivariate, multiple source datasets and an emphasis on the reliability and validity issues.

All in all, because entrepreneurship is a multifaceted phenomenon and to account for causal conditions contributing to an outcome, we suggest using a different methodological approach – a set-theoretical configurational analysis that enables going one step beyond a pure investigation of the individual factors that affect intentions.

Configurational analysis and entrepreneurship research

Over the last decades, we have witnessed that entrepreneurship research has increasingly continued to grow both in volume and density perspectives. Methodological decision, selection and coherency have become increasingly salient issues in the field of entrepreneurship research and it is unclear whether the methodologies and measurements employed are sufficiently robust to foster paradigmatic growth and maturation (Chandler & Lyon, 2001). Some authors argue that it is useful to pause and evaluate existing research methodologies and examine whether they have kept pace with the development of the entrepreneurship paradigm (Chandler & Lyon, 2001). The authors further suggested considering the methodological requirements of research models that posit causal relationships. On that account, we claim that more research designs that find a better balance, increase model specification and provide correspondingly greater understanding of the links in the causal chain of relationships are needed.

We acknowledge that the empirical and practical insights provided by conventional correlational approaches (such as regression analysis) are stunning and the alleged benefits have been extolled. Nevertheless, our vivid understanding on interdependencies, conjunctive paths and the causal relationships between antecedent variables is evidently limited. Many studies primarily focus and contribute only to the symmetric relationships between a set of antecedent variables, such as situational factors (e.g. social norms; see, for example Kwong & Thompson, 2016) or individual factors (e.g. self-efficacy; Baron et al., 2016). What has perhaps not been paid sufficient attention to and remains relatively untested is *how variables combine to cause a certain outcome* (Ragin, 1987, 2000; Mas-Tur et al., 2015). Recently, Sniehotta et al. (2014) argue that research designs employing traditional theories, such as TRA and TPB, should be replaced by more innovative methodological rigor that provides greater flexibility with regard to model specification.

As we pointed out, the most widely used quantitative methods in business, marketing and specifically entrepreneurial research are based on tools relying on the notions and assumptions of mathematical statistics. Consequently, researchers are constrained when aiming to translate results of quantitative analysis into causal explanations of a phenomenon (Ragin, 1987). In order to overcome various limitations of statistical models, one alternative approach is offered by Qualitative Comparative Analysis (QCA), one of the most widely used configurational analysis techniques (Grofman & Schneider, 2009).

On a general level, four main differences can be identified between QCA and statistical approaches. First, as was mentioned earlier, QCA allows for uncovering asymmetric causal relationships, both in terms of necessity and sufficiency. The necessary and sufficient configurations leading to an outcome can help research- ers discover insights about the underlying phenomenon from different perspec- tives, offering the basis for a causal understanding. Second, instead of obtaining the results in terms of relationship between individual constructs and the outcome, we obtain more complex explanations regarding the governing rules of the underlying processes. Third, configurational techniques, and specifically QCA, are based on the crucial assumption that several distinct causal explanations can exist simultane- ously leading to the same outcome. This notion of equifinality is in strong contrast to traditional statistical techniques. Last, in line with the general aim of qualitative research and as a consequence of the previous point, causal explanations that cover only a small number of cases, although they would not be identified as significant solutions with statistical approaches, can represent important theoretical insights characterizing a subset of the underlying population.

The main consequence of this stance is that a variable may only affect the outcome given the presence or absence of additional variable(s) (El Sawy et al., 2010; Fiss, 2007). As one of the configuration theory-based methods, QCA (Ragin, 1987) estimates the causal contribution of different possible configurations with respect to a specific outcome variable. According to this approach, a phenomenon is best represented and analysed as clusters of interconnected elements, rather than as a set of compo- nents that can be understood in isolation (Ragin, 2008). The main variants of QCA include Crisp-Set QCA, multi-valued QCA and Fuzzy-set QCA (FsQCA) (Schneider & Wagemann, 2007). In this article, we will specifically apply FsQCA because it is one of the most general extensions of the original QCA with numerous existing software implementations, offering the chance for researchers in the field on entrepreneurship to potentially apply the discussed approach in future research problems.

There exists in the literature a handful of studies that have recently started to apply different versions of QCA in entrepreneurship research (Beynon et al., 2016; Mas- Tur et al., 2015; Muñoz & Kibler, 2016; Roig-Tierno et al., 2015). For example, Roig-Tierno et al. (2015), by making use of Crisp QCA, argue that combinations of use of infrastructures such as incubators, technology centres and universities can positively affect entrepreneurial intentions and business growth and there is no single causal configuration completely explaining this growth. Moreover, Muñoz & Kibler (2016) have recently used FsQCA in an in-depth analysis of how causal condi- tions contribute to an outcome, specifically on the local institutional complexity and social entrepreneurship. Their results show that there are asymmetric relationships between variables and, in particular, in four configuration paths – the perceived influence capacity of local authorities is the most dominant institutional factor.

FsQCA as a predictive model

The traditional utilization of any version of QCA lies in performing an explanatory analysis in terms of uncovering configurations of variables that lead to a given outcome. In other words, the aim is to discover rules that explain the processes governing the underlying phenomenon. In this section, we first summarize the most important modelling aspects of the general use of FsQCA. Afterwards, we present a new approach to applying the output rules of FsQCA as the basis of tackling typical classification tasks present in data mining and business analytics literature.

Summary of FsQCA

In the following, we summarize the main steps of the FsQCA methodology in a way that can help researchers in the entrepreneurship domain to utilize the approach in further research problems. In our discussion, we assume that the methodology is applied for larger datasets, e.g. empirical data collected in surveys, rather than the original setting of smaller number of cases. This means that we do not assume extensive knowledge available regarding each data point, while still following the main logic of FsQCA. The description of the steps will be exemplified with the research problem we investigate in this article.

The use of the methodology requires the specification of an outcome variable and several attributes (variables). In our particular context, outcome is entrepreneurial intention, while the attributes include gender, family business background, perceived behaviour control, social norms, social capital and self-efficacy. After the data is collected, a transformation of the data values into the [0, 1] interval has to be specified – termed as data calibration. The typical recommendation is to use the values 1, 0.5 and 0 as maximum, intermediate and minimum, while the other values are calibrated on the basis of a linear function. For example, if a variable is measured on a seven-item scale (remembering that the values are now averages of several items), the membership values for 1, 4, and 7 are 0, 0.5, and 1, respectively, and the memberships for other value are assigned in keeping with the assumption of a linear membership function. However, calibration can be performed using different breaking points or non-linear calibration values, potentially altering the final output of the modelling.

Afterwards, all the possible configurations of logical combination of the attributes present in the dataset are identified. As a result of this, we obtain the number of data-points characterized by each configuration. In order to keep only the relevant information in the main derivation of solutions, cut-off values are specified and configurations appearing less frequently than the threshold value are excluded from the set of relevant configurations. This reduced set of logical combinations is then evaluated using the measure of consistency, assessing the extent to which a given combination is a sufficient condition for the outcome to occur. The original recommendation by Ragin and Fiss (2008) is to specify consistency cut-off value as 0.8, but this can be increased or decreased based on the problem context and the dataset. The consistency for a logical combination of the attributes is calculated as:

$$\text{Consistency} = \frac{\Sigma_i \min(\text{support of the rule, membership of outcome})}{\Sigma_i \text{the extent to which case } i \text{ supports the rule}} \qquad (8.1)$$

Table 8.1   Comparison of regression-based and FsQCA approaches

	Regression	FsQCA
Key assumptions	Symmetric and linear relationship	No assumptions
Relationship measurement	In terms of R^2	Causal explanations through configurations
Relationship strength	p value	Consistency
Assessing individual attributes	Effect of attributes assessed individually	Effect of attributes in terms of logical combinations
Theory building	Generalization of hypotheses assuming symmetry	Generalization of configurations allowing for asymmetry

Source: Adapted from Liu et al., 2017.

By applying a logical procedure, namely the Quine–McCluskey minimization procedure, three different solution sets can be identified: parsimonious, intermediate and complex. For our purpose in the large sample size FsQCA, complex solutions offer the most important alternative because parsimonious solutions in general represent oversimplified solutions, while intermediate solutions require extensive knowledge of the cases and extensive existing knowledge of the relationship between individual attributes and the outcome variable (Ragin, 2008). Complex solutions are obtained by taking the logical union of the remaining logical combinations and simplifying these by applying traditional logical operations. Although in contrast to regression analysis, in FsQCA we do not have a measure specifying individual importance of attributes within a configuration, following Fiss (2011), and they can be divided into core and peripheral conditions with respect to a specific configuration. Core conditions have to appear in both complex and parsimonious solutions, while peripheral conditions are not necessarily present in configuration in the parsimonious solution set.

To show the rationale for embracing the FsQCA method in entrepreneurship intention research and to highlight the most important differences between regression-based analysis and FsQCA, the main differences are presented in Table 8.1.

Prediction based on FsQCA output configurations

As we discussed earlier, different versions of QCA are utilized to identify configurations of some variables that lead to an outcome. By applying different measures capturing the relationship of configurations and outcome variables, one can capture *necessity* and *sufficiency*. In the following we will look at how these two notions can naturally translate to the context of traditional classification tasks and be utilized as such in binary classification problems.

In order to present the proposal, first we recall some basic notions from the field of classification. Our general setting is the task of assigning one of two classes

Table 8.2   Confusion matrix of a binary classification problem

Real/Predicted	Negative	Positive
Negative	True Negative (TN)	False Positive (FP)
Positive	Positive False Negative (FN)	True Positive (TP)

to each data point. In our case, it will translate to assigning every respondent a binary proxy specifying their intention to become entrepreneurs. The calibration of survey results into fuzzy sets naturally allows for this binary classification because it is used in the FsQCA analysis: respondents with calibrated intention value higher (lower) than 0.5 are assigned the positive (negative) intention label. The general task of unsupervised learning consists of building a model based on cases with known class assignment to be used for predicting the class of new observations. Supervised learning has numerous applications in business, and specifically in marketing, for example in service personalization, market basket analysis or targeted advertising.

The evaluation of binary classification methods usually relies on the confusion or contingency matrix, as seen in Table 8.2. The table describes the four possible cases that can occur as the result of a binary classification exemplified by our case on entrepreneurial intention (positive and negative output reflecting intention and the lack of intention, respectively):

1. True Positive (TP): the prediction correctly classifies the observation as positive;
2. True Negative (TN): the prediction correctly classifies the observation as negative;
3. False Positive (FP): the prediction incorrectly classifies a negative observation as positive;
4. False Negative (FN): the prediction incorrectly classifies a positive observation as negative.

Using this terminology, several measures can be defined to assess classification performance based on the main goal of the modelling process. The most widely used measure is accuracy, the ratio of correctly classified cases, formally calculated as:

$$ACC = \frac{TP + TN}{TP + TN + FN + FP} \tag{8.2}$$

While this is a straightforward and intuitive measure, it can offer a wrong indication regarding performance. For example, if one of the two classes is overrepresented in the data, i.e. the proportion of cases belonging to one class is very high, assigning each new observation to this larger class can result in high accuracy, but at the same time misclassifying all the cases belonging to the smaller class.

In order to apply the output of FsQCA as the basis of binary classification, we need to specify a procedure to estimate the class for a data point. Let us denote the configurations identified as belonging to the set of complex solutions as c_1, $c_2, \ldots, c_m$. The first intuitive idea to assign a class to a new observation d would be to check first to what extent any of the complex solutions characterize the observation in terms of fuzzy membership. If there is at least one rule with sufficiently high membership value, we assign the positive class, otherwise the negative class to the observation. The threshold on the membership can be derived using traditional data mining techniques aimed at maximizing accuracy, AUC or other performance measures (Witten et al., 2016). The problem in this basic approach lies in the nature of complex solutions – they are derived with the goal of identifying sufficient configurations, meaning that a high membership of the configuration guarantees (with associated consistency level) high output variable value. However, the converse of this statement is not true – high output value can happen even when the configuration membership is low for an observation. The only situation when this does not happen is the case of a sufficient and necessary configuration, which rarely occurs in real datasets. In other words, in terms of the confusion matrix specified later, this observation implies that whatever the choice of the threshold value, one can expect a significant number of false negatives – cases where the output is present but a sufficient configuration has low membership value.

To improve this basic approach, one can make use of an important feature of FsQCA, and configurational approaches in general: not only we can derive several rules explaining what configurations of attributes lead to entrepreneurial intention, but we can perform the same process to identify rules explaining the behaviour of individuals without entrepreneurial intention. This is an important benefit of FsQCA over other approaches, specifically because in general the configurations leading to the lack of an output of interest cannot simply be characterized as the ones obtained by simply negating the ones leading to the output itself. In general, there is no necessary logical or functional relationship between the two solution sets. Accordingly, we can derive two solution sets consisting of several configurations:

$C = \{c_1, c_2, \ldots, c_m\}$ for the output, and $S = \{s_1, s_2, \ldots, s_n\}$ for the negation of output.

Using these sets, we can calculate the maximum memberships for the observation d in S and C as the maximum of membership associated to the individual solutions as S_d and C_d, respectively. Finally, if $C_d \geq S_d$, we assign the positive class to the observation, otherwise we assign the negative class. Moreover, as the results of FsQCA are known to be very sensitive to the initial choice of the frequency and consistency cut-off values, one of the bottlenecks of using this approach (Krogslund et al., 2015), we can perform the same process for various initial specifications of those parameters. This iterative selection of complex solution sets resulting in the best classification performance can decrease the sensitivity with respect to parameter initialization.

We can summarize the approach in the following pseudo code:

1. **procedure** FsQCA for binary classification (dataset, feasible intervals for frequency ($[f_l, f_u]$) and consistency cut-off values ($[c_l, c_u]$))
2. Calibrate the variables in the dataset
3. Set c_{opt} and f_{opt} as 1 for optimal cut-off values, and p for optimal classification performance as 0
4. **for** $f \in [f_l, f_u]$ do
5. **for** $c \in [c_l, c_u]$ do
6. Derive solutions sets C, S with cut-off values f and c
7. Calculate maximum memberships C_d and S_d
8. Assign class to observations based on the higher membership value
9. Evaluate the parameter selection
10. If performance is better than current optimal update c_{opt}, f_{opt} and p
11. **end for**
12. **end for**
13. **return** the optimal cut-off values and final classification performance achieved
14. **end procedure**

We note here that although the main use of FsQCA lies in identifying the configurations consistent enough with the output, our proposed prediction approach can supplement the main analysis in case an actionable output is required and also to offer an indication regarding optimal cut-off values. However, as we will see in the numerical analysis, in this work we did not attempt to use state-of-the-art developments in data mining and machine learning to optimize parameter selection or to improve data calibration as our main goal was to present a new methodological possibility to build on the output of FsQCA.

Case study

In this section, we apply and evaluate the procedure described in the previous section to a dataset based on a survey aimed at understanding the most important determinants of entrepreneurial intention. We start with data collection and present the reliability and the validity results, followed by the traditional FsQCA analysis. Afterwards, we present the results on the prediction performance of the developed approach, and compare it to traditional classification procedures.

Data collection and descriptive analysis

Data were collected using pen and paper-based survey questionnaires. In addition to general questions, several background questions (demographic information) in relation to the respondents' experience working on a business owned by a family member were asked. It has been pointed out that students are the young generation who are most likely to be active in developing new business ideas through the latest

Table 8.3   List of countries and participants

Country	Spain	Turkey	Canada	Chile	China	Finland	Germany	USA	Total
N	201	474	221	292	278	156	220	96	2038

technologies (Compeau et al., 2012; Lu et al., 2010). Our study population consists of the undergraduate students at urban institutes of higher education in Canada, Chile, China, Finland, Germany, Spain, Turkey and the USA. The questionnaire was distributed to 2282 potential respondents at selected universities in these countries in 2011. In the study, 2038 complete and usable responses were analysed (see Table 8.3). University students face important career decisions during their undergraduate and graduate educational programs, and prior research has found they have a broad spectrum of intentions and attitudes toward the entrepreneurial career path (Krueger, 1993; Peterman & Kennedy, 2003; Wilson et al., 2007; Zhao et al., 2005).

In total, 2038 valid and complete responses were collected. Of the respondents, 797 (39.1 per cent) were female and 1241 (60.9 per cent) male. The respondents' average age was 25 years. More than 31 per cent of the respondents (N=635) have a job in addition to going to school, 136 respondents (6.7 per cent) operated their own businesses at the time of the survey, and 748 (36.7 per cent) indicated that they had worked in a business owned by a member of their family. Table 8.3 shows the countries with the number of participants.

Reliability and validity

To examine the adequacy of the measurement model and reliability of the data, Cronbach's Alpha was computed. The recommended threshold for α was 0.70, and the result shows that α values were all over the recommended threshold, indicating that the measures have all acceptable reliability. Moreover, the psychometric properties of the measures were tested through the average variance extracted (AVE) index (Fornell & Larcker, 1981) and composite reliability (CR). The results show that all the AVE and CR values were above the recommended values of 0.5 and 0.7, respectively (Bagozzi & Edwards, 1998; see Table 8.4).

Results of FsQCA analysis

Before proceeding with the sufficiency analysis, first we analysed whether there were any attributes that could be identified as necessary for entrepreneurial intention (Ragin, 2006). The relevance of necessity relationships can be assessed using consistency, with values higher than 0.9 indicating important relationships (Schneider & Wagemann, 2007). Table 8.5 shows that there were two attributes that could be seen as necessary for entrepreneurial intention: social norms and self-efficacy. These results imply that in a large number of cases specified by the coverage value, intention can only be present if the conditions self-efficacy and social norms are

Table 8.4   Discriminant assessment with square root of average variance extracted[a]

	α	CR[b]	AVE[c]	INT[d]	PBC[e]	SN[f]	SC[g]	EFFI[h]
Intention	0.942	0.940	0.726	**0.852**				
Perceived behaviour control	0.723	0.752	0.602	0.140	**0.834**			
Social norms	0.871	0.873	0.775	0.546	0.465	**0.880**		
Social capital	0.813	0.814	0.594	0.274	0.019	0.288	**0.771**	
Self-efficacy	0.924	0.921	0.592	0.327	0.132	0.354	0.151	**0.769**

Notes: [a]The values in bold are the highest discriminant values; [b]composite reliability; [c]average variance extracted; [d]intention; [e]perceived behaviour control; [f]social norms; [g]social capital, [h]self-efficacy.

Table 8.5   Checking the necessity of causal conditions

Condition	Consistency	Coverage
Gender	0.37	0.46
Family business background	0.60	0.46
Social norms	0.92	0.69
Social capital	0.75	0.80
Perceived behavioural control	0.76	0.86
Self-efficacy	0.94	0.64

satisfied. Although this observation offers useful insights, this does not mean that high values of these two attributes automatically imply high level of intention; that could be measured by sufficiency, assessed in the main part of FsQCA analysis.

In this section, we provide FsQCA analysis results which were identified based on the causal configuration of six conditions: gender (GEN), family business background (FBB), social norms (SN), social capital (SC), perceived behavioural control (PBC) and self-efficacy (EFFI) leading to the occurrence of the outcome, i.e. entrepreneurial intention. It is necessary to mention that in the results in Table 8.6 we use the following notations: black circles (●) to indicate the presence of a condition and blank circles (O) to indicate its absence. Blank spaces indicate "do not care"; in other words the causal condition may be either absent or present (Ragin & Fiss, 2008). Large circles show the core conditions and small ones indicate the peripheral conditions (Fiss, 2011). The frequency cut-off was set to 7 and the lowest acceptable level of solution consistency threshold was set to 0.90, which is above the minimum recommended cut-off value (0.80) suggested by Ragin (2006, 2008). The FsQCA analysis revealed five solutions leading to entrepreneurial intention. The first three solutions were dominated by male respondents and, interestingly, self-efficacy appears to have positive impact in four out of five solutions. As can be seen from Table 8.6, solution five is the most important configuration leading to

Table 8.6   Complex solution for entrepreneurial intention[a]

Solution	GEN[b]	FBB[c]	SN[d]	SC[e]	PBC[f]	EFFI[g]	Raw coverage	Unique coverage	Consistency
1	○				●	●	0.47	0.05	0.87
2	○	●		●	○	○	0.16	0.01	0.85
3	○	○		●		●	0.19	0.02	0.85
4		○		○	●	●	0.25	0.01	0.88
5			●	●	●	●	0.64	0.16	0.90

Notes: [a]Black circles indicate the presence of a condition, and blank circles indicate its absence. Large circles indicate core conditions and small circles show peripheral conditions. Blank spaces indicate "*do not care*". [b]Gender; [c]family business background; [d]social norms; [e]social capital; [f]perceived behaviour control; [g]self-efficacy.

the outcome as it has the highest coverage 0.64. This means that this rule explains the behaviour of almost 2/3 of all the respondents.

Solution one shows a combination of causal conditions that include perceived behavioural control (PBC) and self-efficacy (EFFI), and this solution is applicable only to male respondents. In this configuration, perceived behavioural control is a core condition. Solution two is an interesting outcome. In this solution, a combination of causal conditions of social capital and the absence (lack) of perceived behavioural control and self-efficacy led to the outcome. It is important to mention that this solution is applicable, again, to male respondents and only to those who experienced working in a business owned by a family member. Another interesting issue to address is that social norms had no impact on the decision making of respondents to start a new business venture. In this solution, social capital and self-efficacy were the core conditions. Nevertheless, this solution covers only 1/5 of all the respondents. Solution three shows a combination of causal conditions that included the presence of social capital (SC) and self-efficacy (EFFI). It is important to notice that this solution was applicable only to male respondents who did not have any experience working in a business which was owned by a family member. With regard to coverage value, this solution is the second lowest in Table 8.6, and social capital, family business background and gender (male) were the core conditions.

Solution four illustrates a combination of causal conditions that include the presence of perceived behavioural control and self-efficacy together with the absence (lack) of social capital. Interestingly, this solution is only applicable to those respondents that had no experience working in a business owned by a family member. Gender in this solution has no impact; in other words this solution is applicable to both female and male respondents. Perceived behavioural control in this solution was a core condition. The raw coverage for this solution is 0.25, meaning it covers 1/4 of all the respondents. The most important solution obtained based on the FsQCA analysis is solution five. In this solution, gender has no impact and the coverage value is 0.64, i.e. covering almost 2/3 of all the respondents. This solution shows a combination of causal conditions that included the presence of social norms, social capital, perceived behavioural control and self-efficacy. In this solution, the social capital and perceived behavioural control were the core conditions. It is worth mentioning at this point the presence of the social norms for the first time and its impact on the entrepreneurial intent. Based on the solutions depicted in Table 8.6, social norms have appeared only once, but in the most important solution.

Combining these results (see Table 8.6) with the necessity analysis, one can make an important observation. While necessity analysis revealed that two conditions (attributes), namely social norms (SN) and self-efficacy (EFFI) can be seen as necessary for the outcome (i.e. entrepreneurial intention) to occur, among the five solutions obtained from FsQCA analysis, we found that social norms (SN) only appeared in one configuration, i.e. solution five; whereas self-efficacy (EFFI), either its presence or absence, appeared in all solutions. This finding carries direct implications regarding the importance of this attribute on entrepreneurial intention research. In terms of the coverage values, the FsQCA results show an overall solution coverage score of 0.75 which means that the five configurations of causal conditions explain 75 per cent of the overall performance of business. The overall solution consistency was 0.85.

Prediction performance

In order to complement this analysis with a more prediction oriented approach, in the following we will apply the procedure presented in the previous section. In this article, we only perform in-sample analysis. Although this cannot guarantee generalizability from a statistical point of view, as we mentioned previously, our main goal is to present a first attempt on using FsQCA as a basis of classification. From this perspective, we aim to show that the obtained results are close to the ones achieved by traditional classification algorithms, showing the potential of the classification procedure assisting in obtaining more actionable results beyond the rules, and assisting in cut-off value selection.

In order to evaluate classification performance, we note here that in some cases it is more important to correctly identify members of one of the classes rather than achieving good overall accuracy. For example, in marketing, high individual advertisement cost would imply that one wants to avoid having false positive cases because it would mean that resources are spent on cases with no potential. In contrast, for example in medical context, one wants to avoid false negatives because it means identifying a person as healthy although he or she is not healthy. Corresponding to these cases, one can specify the measure of true positive rate (TPR, also called sensitivity or recall) measuring the proportion of correctly identified positive cases as:

$$TPR = \frac{TP}{TP + FN} \qquad (8.3)$$

Table 8.7   Classification performance for different cut-off values

	Accuracy	Specificity	Sensitivity
Maximum	0.73	0.82	0.77
Mean	0.72	0.73	0.70
Minimum	0.70	0.67	0.58

Table 8.8   Classification performance with traditional approaches

	Accuracy	Specificity	Sensitivity
SVM	0.75	0.79	0.72
CT	0.76	0.77	0.76

and the measure of true negative rate (TNR, also called specificity) measuring the proportion of correctly identified negative cases as:

$$TNR = \frac{TN}{TN + FP} \qquad (8.4)$$

In order to assess the performance of the proposed approach, we performed the classification tasks with two of the most widely used data mining techniques, namely Support Vector Machines (SVM) (Cortes & Vapnik, 1995) and Classification Trees (CT) (Breiman et al., 1984). In the experiments, according to the proposal, we tested several different cut-off value combinations, separately specified for deriving sufficient configurations for positive and negative outcome. The frequency cut-off was allowed to be in the set 5, 6, 7, while consistency cut-off was used with values 0.84, 0.85, 0.86. This resulted in $3^4 = 81$ performed experiments. The results are shown in Table 8.7, with the performance of the traditional classification algorithms presented in Table 8.8.

Although one could apply a larger set of feasible values, we can identify several important points already based on this limited experiment. First, the best accuracy value achieved with our procedure offers a result close to the ones using traditional approaches. While this observation should be confirmed with further experiments, this is a good indication that classification on top of FsQCA results can be an informative complement to the traditional analysis. Second, we can confirm the literature on the role of parameter setting in terms of classification performance, especially when we look at sensitivity and specificity values; even with the used narrow cut-off ranges, there can be significant differences in terms of identifying negative and positive cases correctly. When we looked at the 81 resulting complex solution sets obtained for the positive output, we found several that do not share a single common configuration. This extreme behaviour with respect to the choice of cut-off values close to each other and all of them falling below the original recommended range highlights the importance of developing new procedures, such as in this article, for identifying optimal parameters, otherwise one can obtain very misleading and incorrect results. Third, the maximum specificity and sensitivity values obtained with the new approach exceed the ones from the traditional classification algorithms. This shows that the right choice of cut-off values can help identify configurations that satisfy context-dependent needs of system users by aiming to maximize either positive or negative classification rates.

Discussion, conclusions and future research

Entrepreneurial intention is a rapidly evolving field of research and the volume and number of studies that use entrepreneurial intention as a research design continues to grow. Despite the large number of publications and their diversity in entrepreneurial intention research, the present spectrum shows that methodology is becoming an increasingly salient issue in this domain. As the paradigm develops, we have seen attempts recently to move away from the use of simple descriptive statistics and regression analysis towards more sophisticated and complex research designs, such as the one used in this article, i.e. configurational methods (FsQCA) (Beynon et al., 2016).

In this article, we discussed recent developments in the domain and reasoned why configurational approaches, particularly Qualitative Comparative Analysis (QCA) and specifically its extensions using Fuzzy-sets (FsQCA) can offer important tools in discovering new and relevant insights. We do not reason for a complete methodological shift, but only point out the benefits of QCA in offering causal explanations in terms of configurations of characterizing attributes to understand entrepreneurial intention. The relevance and potential of the methodology are exemplified using an extensive dataset collected from eight countries. The results illustrate the type of novel insights that can be generated in order to complement research studies in the entrepreneurial intention research using traditional statistical approaches.

From the methodological perspective, we introduced a new approach utilizing FsQCA in a novel way in the classical data mining problem of binary classification. We showed that the overall accuracy level of the present approach is comparable to traditional classification algorithms, and we can obtain very good results in terms of particular performance measures. Additionally, we illustrated how significantly cut-off parameter selection can alter the final solution set of FsQCA, highlighting a crucial step to consider when performing configurational analysis (Ragin, 2008).

Our contribution raises a number of potential future research issues. First, the study will hopefully facilitate the use of configurational techniques in entrepreneurial intention research beyond the existing level because we have shown the potential of the approach in generating new insights. Second, the proposed classification approach needs more validation by applying it to various datasets, focusing on out-of-sample analysis combined potentially with various cross-validation techniques. Finally, on the general methodological level, our study attempted to draw attention to the crucial problem of parameter selection in FsQCA, and hopefully will generate further discussion and new proposals to tackle this problem in a rigorous way, moving from the application of general frequency and consistency cut-off values towards more systematic parameter selection in order to strengthen the robustness of results.

References

Ajzen, I. (1991). The Theory of Planned Behaviour. *Organizational Behaviour and Human Decision Processes*, 50 (2), 179–211.

Ajzen, I. & Fishbein, M. (1980). *Understanding Attitudes and Predicting Social Behaviour*. Upper Saddle River, NJ: Prentice-Hall.

Bagozzi, R. P. & Edwards, E. A. (1998). Goal setting and goal pursuit in the regulation of body weight. *Psychology and Health*, 13 (4), 593–621.

Baron, R. A., Mueller, B. A. & Wolfe, M. T. (2016). Self-efficacy and entrepreneurs' adoption of unattainable goals: The restraining effects of self-control. *Journal of Business Venturing*, 31 (1), 55–71.

Beynon, M. J., Jones, P. & Pickernell, D. (2016). Country-based comparison analysis using FsQCA investigating entrepreneurial attitudes and activity. *Journal of Business Research*, 69 (4), 1271–6.

Bird, B. (1988). Implementing entrepreneurial ideas: The case for intention. *Academy of Management Review*, 13 (3), 442–53.

Boyd, N. G. & Vozikis, G. S. (1994). The influence of self-efficacy on the development of entrepreneurial intentions and actions. *Entrepreneurship Theory & Practice*, 18, 63–77.

Breiman, L., Friedman, J., Stone, C. J. & Olshen, R. A. (1984). *Classification and Regression Trees*. Boca Raton, FL: CRC Press.

Carr, J. C. & Sequeira, J. M. (2007). Prior family business exposure as intergenerational influence and entrepreneurial intent: A theory of planned behavior approach. *Journal of Business Research*, 60 (10), 1090–98.

Carsrud, A. L. & Brännback, M. (2011). Entrepreneurial motivations: what do we still need to know? *Journal of Small Business Management*, 49 (1), 9–26.

Chandler, G. N. & Lyon, D. W. (2001). Issues of research design and construct measurement in entrepreneurship research: The past decade. *Entrepreneurship Theory & Practice*, 25 (4), 101–14.

Compeau, D., Marcolin, B., Kelley, H. & Higgins, C. (2012). Research commentary – generalizability of information systems research using student subjects – a reflection on our practices and recommendations for future research. *Information Systems Research*, 23 (4), 1093–109.

Cortes, C. & Vapnik, V. (1995). Support-vector networks. *Machine Learning*, 20 (3), 273–97.

Coviello, N. E. & Jones, M. V. (2004). Methodological issues in international entrepreneurship research. *Journal of Business Venturing*, 19 (4), 485–508.

El Sawy, O. A., Malhotra, A., Park, Y. & Pavlou, P. A. (2010). Research commentary-seeking the configurations of digital eco dynamics: It takes three to tango. *Information Systems Research*, 21 (4), 835–48.

Fiss, P. C. (2007). A set-theoretic approach to organizational configurations. *Academy of Management Review*, 32 (4), 1180–98.

Fiss, P. C. (2011). Building better causal theories: A fuzzy set approach to typologies in organization research. *Academy of Management Journal*, 54 (2), 393–420.

Fornell, C. & Larcker, D. F. (1981). Evaluating structural equation models with unobservable variables and measurement error. *Journal of Marketing Research*, 18 (1), 39–50.

Grofman, B. & Schneider, C. Q. (2009). An introduction to crisp set QCA, with a comparison to binary logistic regression. *Political Research Quarterly*, 62 (4), 662–72.

Hansemark, O. C. (1998). The effects of an entrepreneurship programme on need for achievement and locus of control of reinforcement. *International Journal of Entrepreneurial Behavior & Research*, 4 (1), 28–50.

Kahneman, D. & Tversky, A. (1979). Prospect theory: An analysis of decision under risk. *Econometrica: Journal of the Econometric Society*, 263–91.

Krogslund, C., Choi, D. D. & Poertner, M. (2015). Fuzzy sets on shaky ground: Parameter sensitivity and confirmation bias in FsQCA. *Political Analysis*, 23 (1), 21–41.

Krueger, N. F. (1993). The impact of prior entrepreneurial exposure on perceptions of new venture feasibility and desirability. *Entrepreneurship Theory & Practice*, 18 (1), 5–22.

Krueger, N. F. (2009). Entrepreneurial intentions are dead: Long live entrepreneurial intentions. In A. L. Carsrud and M. Brännback (eds), *Understanding the Entrepreneurial Mind*. Berlin: Springer, pp. 51–72.

Krueger, N. F. & Carsrud, A. L. (1993). Entrepreneurial intentions: Applying the theory of planned behaviour. *Entrepreneurship & Regional Development*, 5 (4), 315–30.

Krueger, N. F., Reilly, M. D. & Carsrud, A. L. (2000). Competing models of entrepreneurial intentions. *Journal of Business Venturing*, 15 (5), 411–32.

Kwong, C. & Thompson, P. (2016). The when and why: Student entrepreneurial aspirations. *Journal of Small Business Management*, 54 (1), 299–318.

Liñán, F. & Chen, Y.-W. (2009). Development and cross-cultural application of a specific instrument to measure entrepreneurial intentions. *Entrepreneurship Theory & Practice*, 33 (3), 593–617.

Liu, Y., Mezei, J., Kostakos, V. & Li, H. (2017). Applying configurational analysis to IS behavioural research: a methodological alternative for modelling combinatorial complexities. *Information Systems Journal*, 27 (1), 59–89.

Lu, H. P., Lin, J. C. C., Hsiao, K. L. & Cheng, L. T. (2010). Information sharing behaviour on blogs in Taiwan: Effects of interactivities and gender differences. *Journal of Information Science*, 36 (3), 401–16.

Mas-Tur, A., Pinazo, P., Tur-Porcar, A. M. & Sánchez-Masferrer, M. (2015). What to avoid to succeed as an entrepreneur. *Journal of Business Research*, 68 (11), 2279–84.

McDougall, P. P. & Oviatt, B. M. (2000). International entrepreneurship: The intersection of two research paths. *Academy of Management Journal*, 43 (5), 902–906.

McEachan, R. R. C., Conner, M., Taylor, N. J. & Lawton, R. J. (2011). Prospective prediction of health-related behaviours with the Theory of Planned Behaviour: A meta-analysis. *Health Psychology Review*, 5 (2), 97–144.

Meek, W. R., Pacheco, D. F. & York, J. G. (2010). The impact of social norms on entrepreneurial action: Evidence from the environmental entrepreneurship context. *Journal of Business Venturing*, 25 (5), 493–509.

Muñoz, P. & Kibler, E. (2016). Institutional complexity and social entrepreneurship: A fuzzy-set approach. *Journal of Business Research*, 69 (4), 1314–18.

Peterman, N. E. & Kennedy, J. (2003). Enterprise education: Influencing students' perceptions of entrepreneurship. *Entrepreneurship Theory & Practice*, 28 (2), 129–44.

Ragin, C. C. (1987). *The Comparative Method: Moving Beyond Qualitative and Quantitative Strategies*. Berkeley. CA: University of California Press.

Ragin, C. C. (2000). *Fuzzy-Set Social Science*. Chicago, IL: University of Chicago Press.

Ragin, C. C. (2006). Set relations in social research: Evaluating their consistency and coverage. *Political Analysis*, 14 (3), 291–310.

Ragin, C. C. (2008). *Redesigning Social Inquiry: Fuzzy Sets and Beyond* (Vol. 240). Wiley Online Library.

Ragin, C. C. & Fiss, P. C. (2008). Net effects analysis versus configurational analysis: An empirical demonstration. In C. C. Ragin (ed.), *Redesigning Social Inquiry: Fuzzy Sets and Beyond* (Vol. 240). Wiley Online Library, pp. 190–212.

Roig-Tierno, N., Alc'azar, J. & Ribeiro-Navarrete, S. (2015). Use of infrastructures to support innovative entrepreneurship and business growth. *Journal of Business Research*, 68 (11), 2290–94.

Sarasvathy, S. D. (2009). *Effectuation: Elements of Entrepreneurial Expertise*. Cheltenham, UK: Edward Elgar.

Schneider, C. Q. & Wagemann, C. (2007). *Qualitative Comparative Analysis (QCA) and Fuzzy Sets*. Leverkusen, Germany: Barbara Budrich.

Sniehotta, F. F., Presseau, J. & Araújo-Soares, V. (2014). Time to retire the theory of planned behaviour. *Health Psychology Review*, 8 (1), 1–7.

Sommer, L. & Haug, M. (2011). Intention as a cognitive antecedent to international entrepreneurship – understanding the moderating roles of knowledge and experience. *International Entrepreneurship and Management Journal*, 7 (1), 111–42.

Souitaris, V., Zerbinati, S. & Al-Laham, A. (2007). Do entrepreneurship programmes raise entrepreneurial intention of science and engineering students? The effect of learning, inspiration and resources. *Journal of Business Venturing*, 22 (4), 566–91.

Wilson, F., Kickul, J. & Marlino, D. (2007). Gender, entrepreneurial self-efficacy, and entrepreneurial career intentions: Implications for entrepreneurship education. *Entrepreneurship Theory & Practice*, 31 (3), 387–406.

Witten, I. H., Frank, E., Hall, M. A. & Pal, C. J. (2016). *Data Mining: Practical Machine Learning Tools and Techniques*. Burlington, MA: Morgan Kaufmann.

Zhao, H., Seibert, S. E. & Hills, G. E. (2005). The mediating role of self-efficacy in the development of entrepreneurial intentions. *Journal of Applied Psychology*, 90 (6), 1265.

9 Cognition to culture: a still-missing link in the development of an entrepreneurial resource

Patricia G. Greene and Candida G. Brush

Introduction

Organizational culture is a resource that can help or hinder organizational growth and/or success because it guides both structure and function of a business; ultimately serving as a source of competitive advantage (Brush et al., 2001; Barney, 1991). While culture is sometimes directly acknowledged in the entrepreneurship research, the manner in which it is addressed is far more likely considered at the micro level as the creation of an "entrepreneurial culture" in an existing firm (Shepherd et al., 2010) or at the macro level, as the development of an entrepreneurial climate for a geographic region (Kelley et al., 2016). What continues to be missing is a deeper dive into the question of how the organizational culture of a new venture is created – and perhaps how it should be created.

Given that organizational culture is based on a system of shared values and beliefs, we propose a more carefully articulated pathway of the cognitive relationship between the values and beliefs of the founder(s) and the eventual culture of the founded organization. We are guided by a foundational definition of entrepreneurial cognition as ". . .the knowledge structures that people use to make assessments, judgements, or decisions involving opportunity evaluation, venture capital, and growth" (Mitchell et al., 2002, p. 97), and consider the question of whether and/ or when individuals use these behaviors consciously. Thus far, research studies on cognitive factors have largely focused on topics of intentions (Krueger & Carsrud, 1993; Manolova et al., 2012), opportunity identification (Krueger & Dickson, 1994; Krueger et al., 2000), and motives and goals or aspirations (Hessels et al., 2008); how each of these play a role in the entrepreneurial process is central to all these topics. In particular, this body of work shows how the perceptions, expectations, and values of the founder(s) influence the kind of business and its growth patterns over time. However, what is still needed in the literature is research that examines how aspects of the entrepreneur's identity are manifested inside the new organization, the processes by which this occurs, and the structure and organizational practices it may lead to for all members. More specifically, in this exploratory chapter we push still further to go beyond our current understanding of the pathway between individual identity, entrepreneurial identity, and organizational identity in order to explore organizational culture predicated as a key component of that organizational identity. We begin with a brief overview of individual level identity theories, consider how entrepreneurial identity is defined and constructed, and then move to a consideration of organizational identity. We conclude this part of the paper with an overview of approaches to organizational culture creation, specified within the context of a new business. We propose a preliminary conceptual framework and propositions regarding the pathway for culture creation in new ventures and conclude with suggestions for future research as well as the impact on entrepreneurship education and practice.

The subject of identity

We start with the identity of the individual. While identity is a topic of inquiry in many social science disciplines, conceptual differences are readily evident both across and within these disciplines (Stryker & Burke, 2000; Greene & Brush, 2017). Typically, the discussion builds from personal identity (Ashforth & Mael, 1989), Social Identity Theory (SIT) (Tajfel, 1982), and Identity Theory (Stryker & Serpe, 1982).

Personal identity

An individual's attributes and traits, values, beliefs and bodily attributes, and in some considerations, interests and competencies, are the core components of a personal identity (Ashforth & Mael, 1989). While it would seem that the personal at this level would be the starting point for an identity, it can also be considered as more of an end, or integrative mechanism, coalescing aspects of group memberships and/or roles (Markus & Nurius, 1986). Personal identity is also described as under-researched and, we propose more specifically, under-theorized in entrepreneurship (Greene & Brush, 2017).

Social Identity Theory

Social Identity Theory (SIT), however, moves beyond the individual to emphasize the social, reflecting on "the group in the individual" (Hogg & Abrams, 1988, p. 3), and applying a social-psychological perspective to focus on social categories. The resultant categorization schemas are defined through the "prototypical characteristics" of the group (Ashford & Mael, 1989; Turner, 1985) and may be based on demographic characteristics such as race, gender, or age. However, they may also be based on affiliations such as political parties or religious denominations. These affiliation categories may be perceived positively or negatively in relation to another group (Tajfel, 1982; Hogg et al., 1995). Notably, SIT emphasizes the dynamic nature of an identity, acknowledging that while demographics may be consistent, the affiliation groups are open to change, again, in either positive or negative directions (Hogg et al., 1995). Overall, the purpose of the classifications is to provide the ability to cognitively segment and provide order to a social environment, leading to the means of defining one's self as well as others (Ashforth & Mael, 1989).

Identity Theory

Identity Theory is considered even more amenable to changes in identities (manager or student to entrepreneur, single to married) because it is predicated upon the relevance of roles (parent, architect, entrepreneur, etc.) (Hogg et al., 1995; Stryker, 1987; Brush & Gale, 2014). Identity Theory explicitly recognizes that individuals will change personal identity characteristics (such as competencies) and will also make decisions about the important aspects of their lives, such as relationships and occupations (Greene & Brush, 2017). After all, we all hold numerous roles, belonging to a variety of groups, and therefore each of us has multiple and potentially overlapping identities (Meister et al., 2014; Burke & Reitzes, 1991). As with SIT, this approach presents identities as cognitive schemas, built from comparisons with the expectations the individual holds for each role (Stryker & Burke, 2000) and recognizing that people will hold different values in different contexts for different roles (Schneider et al., 1971; Brush & Gale, 2014).

Notably, especially for the purposes of our argument, the importance of saliency or centrality runs across each of these approaches to identity. Given multiple inputs into the development and maintenance of an identity, regardless of theoretical approach, different inputs will have different degrees of importance at any particular time, thereby impacting the overall personal identity.

Defining and constructing entrepreneurial identity

The pathway for this paper starts with a recognition that every individual has an identity that, while held by the individual, is a result of a social process of comparison with others. The question of the contribution and impact of role helps us transition to think about how an identity of an entrepreneur is developed.

Early work in entrepreneurship included a great deal of research in the area of attributes and traits, although mostly limited to descriptive studies of white males and rooted heavily in trait psychology (McClelland, 1961; Brush, 1992). The late 1980s saw a shift in focus from the study of "who the entrepreneur is", based on characteristics and types, to what the entrepreneur does, focusing more on entrepreneurial behaviors in the new venture creation process (Gartner, 1988; Katz & Gartner, 1988; Bird, 1989).

The later introduction of cognitive studies into the field of entrepreneurship was explicitly an approach to reconsider the person (Mitchell et al., 2002), and entrepreneurial identity obviously benefits greatly from those efforts. Much of the work on entrepreneurial identity builds on SIT, and therefore we recognize the necessity of an individual being able to identify the group "entrepreneur" in order to compare and shape expectations. This opting for an entrepreneurial self-definition is actually inherently challenging given the extent of the territory that falls under conceptual usages of entrepreneurship, summarized over the years in a variety of

Table 9.1 Typology of entrepreneurs and entrepreneurial activities

Name/type	Entrepreneurial activity
Starter	Enters an independent business by creating a new one
Acquirer	Enters an independent business by acquiring an ongoing concern
Runner	Manages a small to medium business beyond start-up
Take-off artist	Steers a company into a high-growth trajectory
Turnaround artist	Saves a failing company
Innovator	Makes something new happen that is not a company
Champion	Supports innovator
Intrepreneur	Takes initiative for business unit creation inside an established business
Industry captain	Runs a big business
Mumpreneur	A woman running a business and caring for children simultaneously, balancing work and life
Social entrepreneur	An entrepreneur with innovative solutions to society's most pressing problems

Source: Adapted from Vesper in Verheul et al., 2005; Neck et al., 2009; Nel et al., 2010. Original usage in Greene and Brush (2017).

entrepreneurial roles and proposed typologies (see Table 9.1; Stanworth & Curran, 1976; Woo et al., 1991; Westhead & Wright, 1998; Vesalainen & Pihkala, 2000; Fauchart & Gruber, 2011; Crosina, 2017).

These academic conceptualizations of who is an entrepreneur, or what it means to be entrepreneurial, are helpful in laying out the field; however; they are generally assigned to an individual post hoc. As such they may be less helpful to practitioners who are in a process of self-determination and entrepreneurial identity construction. That construction process occurs through a contextualized and complicated interplay of cognitive, affective, and social interactions (Markova, 1987). We suggest anecdotally that two main identities permeate the field. The "ENTREPRENEUR" is most frequently found and fostered in business schools as one with a technological innovation, seeking equity types of capital, in order to capture a substantial market and, in fairly short order, seeking a liquidity exit through either an acquisition or (although more rarely) an IPO (Neck et al., 2009). "Entrepreneur" is also considered in a quite different context by those working from an economic development perspective study who teach, or train from a more basic approach, often illustrating their work as subsistence types of businesses with a mission of contributing to the economic health of a geographic region (Kelley et al., 2016).

The first connection in our pathway is thus between the personal identity and the entrepreneurial identity. Given that the entrepreneurial identity is only one aspect of an overall individual identity, other identity inputs need come into play. Robust research findings over many decades illustrate differences in process and outcomes for members of different demographic groups (race, ethnicity, gender, age, religion, etc.), human capital attributes (education and experience with the resultant networks), affiliations (e.g. around social and sustainability issues), and family stage of life (parenthood, elder care) are only select examples of group categorizations that will interplay with the development of an entrepreneurial identity. Who you are in reference to the rest of your life (the roles you play) will impact who you are, or are trying to be, as an entrepreneur.

Which comes first: organizational identity or organizational culture?

Gartner et al.'s (1992) prescient consideration of organization theory and entrepreneurship is critical to the next part of our discussion. With very few exceptions (most especially Schein, 1983), organization theories such as organizational identity, image, and culture start with an existing organization. Gartner et al. (1992) appropriately fixated on the emerging organization, recognizing Weick's (1979) definition of an organization as "...an on-going process of interactions among individuals..." and drawing from Katz and Kahn (1966) and Weick (1979) to conclude that "Organizations are simultaneous individual and social phenomena" (Gartner et al., 1992, p. 14). Despite a later conclusion that "Individuals and organizations are said to be better understood in terms of becoming than being" (Sveningsson & Alvesson, 2003, p. 1164; Ashforth, 1998), people/participants/actors are almost always taken as a given.

Organizational identity is commonly defined as "who we are as an organization, and reflects the insiders' perceptions and beliefs about what distinguishes their organization from others" (Corley, 2004, p. 1145; Goia, 1998). However, like individuals, organizations can have multiple identities, some construed by actors outside the organization in addition to those from more internal stakeholders. And identities may be stable or unstable. An organizational identity may have a different degree of identity saliency to members of different groups depending on their level or placement in the hierarchy (e.g. doctors and nurses) (Corley, 2004). Indeed, organizational identity construction is argued to be a process of "institutional bricolage, where organizational actors incorporate different cultural meanings, sentiments, rules, and material artifacts into their identity claims and displays" (Christiansen & Lounsbury, 2013, p. 202; Glynn, 2008). Varying combinations of cultural elements also are seen to result in different identities, but these are assembled differently depending on the context as well as the different institutional logics actors may mobilize for their own purposes (Corley, 2004). As per usual in the existing research, the identity and culture are both assumed to already exist.

While their interest lies in a related but somewhat different question, Ravasi and Schultz (2006) provide us with useful starting points to consider our chicken-and-egg question. From a social actor perspective based in institutional theory, identity self-definitions are [*consciously*] proposed by organizational leaders in order to provide their members with the information needed to construct their collective self. As such, this is sense-giving. From a sense-making perspective grounded in social constructivism, the organizational identity lies in the shared beliefs and understandings of the members of the collective (see Ravasi and Schultz for review of supporting literature.) Fittingly, Ravasi and Schultz (2006, p. 437) conclude that "...while organizational culture tends to be mostly tacit and autonomous and rooted in shared practices, organizational identity is inherently relational (in that it requires external terms of comparison) and consciously self-reflexive".

One additional connective point to be made is the relevance of the difference between organizational identity and organizational identification. "Organizational identification is the degree to which a member defines him- or herself by the same attributes that he or she believes define the organization" (Dutton et al., 1994, p. 239). This indeed may be the needed linchpin between the individual-level personal and entrepreneurial identities and the organizational identity. For entrepreneurs the arrow points both ways: the founder is defining and subsequently identifies with the organization by their own personal attributes. And we suggest that the saliency of the entrepreneurial role will have particular import in this process.

Although Ravasi and Schultz's approach once again assumes a collective exists, the sense-giving and sense-making dichotomy is useful when thinking about the concepts of the organizational identity of a new venture and the development of the organizational culture. For the purposes of the introduction of our cognitive pathway, we put a stake in the ground that the development of the organizational identity comes first. Drawing from a sense of individual (or founding team) identity, which is becoming integrated with an entrepreneurial identity, the person generally has decided on their product or service and soon after determines the appropriate business model. This largely defines the nascent business in suggesting the type of opportunity being pursued, the resources needed – type and quantity (particularly people, capital, and possibly space), and therefore the expected sources for each. The founder(s) now not only has a story to tell about the venture, but in comparisons to those who have founded businesses with similar identities, a story to tell about him or herself as part of their evolving entrepreneurial identity. While this certainly includes some internal (to the individual) sense-giving, overall it is a sense-giving message to the external audiences.

At this point, although anecdotally based, our complementary conclusion on culture is that the amount of sense-giving provided by the founder(s) for the organizational culture of an emerging venture is minimal and quite secondary to the identification of the organization being created. However, the contribution of the founder to the development of that culture remains critical. To revisit, the culture of an organization is generally described as a social construction based on shared beliefs that emerge from a basic pattern of assumptions—a pattern of assumptions behind which there are values that guide structure, relationships, hierarchy, and policies (Schein, 1983). Schein (1983), uniquely for his time, further argues that a culture does not exist in an organization until a founder(s) intentionally creates a group to carry out the work that cannot otherwise be done by a single individual.

Like identity, culture has been studied in a variety of disciplines and thus through a diverse set of lenses. Schein grounds the systematic aspects of organizational culture as a "pattern of norms and attitudes that cut across a whole social unit" as described in a host of classic earlier works in organizational theory (Jacques, 1951; Likert, 1961, 1967; McGregor, 1960; Katz & Kahn, 1966). Smircich (1983) goes further to include aspects of symbolism and symbolic activities, including ceremonies, and legends and myths (Pfeffer, 1981; Dandridge et al., 1980). Smircich's approach is rooted in a broader array of literatures and synthesizes disciplinary concepts of "culture" and "organization" to suggest "themes" of organizational culture approaches, including (1) cross-cultural or comparative management, (2) corporate culture, (3) organizational cognition, (4) organizational symbolism, and, intriguingly for our purposes, (5) unconscious processes and organization (Smircich, 1983). Traditional organizational theory hinges much of the development of organizational culture on history (Hannan & Freeman, 1977; Lawrence, 1984; Zald, 1988), some on "early political and social processes" (from Selznick in Boeker, 1989), or events (from Stinchcombe in Boeker, 1989). Notably for our interest in entrepreneurship, Kimberly (1975, p. 438 in Boeker, 1989, p. 490) provides that "just as for a child, the conditions under which an organization is born and the course of its development in infancy have important consequences for its later life".

Organizational culture in an emerging organization

One of the primary differences in the existing approaches to organizational theory lies in Smircich's (1983, p. 342) conclusions built from the structuralist approach of Levi-Strauss: "Culture is a projection of mind's universal unconscious infrastructure". For Schein, culture had a more instrumental element; including:

> 1) A pattern of basic assumptions, 2) invented, discovered, or developed by a given group, 3) as it learns to cope with its problems of external adaption and internal integration, 4) that has worked well enough to be considered valid and, therefore, 5) is to be taught to new members as the 6) correct way to perceive, think, and feel in relation to those problems. (Schein, 1988, p. 7)

This approach suggests an intentionality that seems in contrast to that "unconscious process" (Levi-Strauss).

Bird's early work on entrepreneurial behavior comes down on the side of intentionality, proposing not only that entrepreneurs create their organizations intentionally, but also that the values added by the organization tend to be consciously chosen (Bird, 1989). She argues that the selection of particular individuals reinforces certain principles, assumptions, values, and rules, thereby shaping the organization. Because founders start with their own "theories" about business, they make choices that reflect these. Day-to-day activities, relationships, and work norms are reflected in the choice made by founders. This is similar to Boeker's (1988) consideration of the imprinting of the founder on the early organization and certainly connects aspects of identity with culture.

Pettigrew (1979) may be even more accurate when addressing the context of organizational emergence, placing the development of organizational culture as the way in which "purpose, commitment, and order are generated in an organization both through the feelings and actions of its founder and through the amalgam of beliefs, ideology, language, ritual and myth. . ." (p. 572). Pettigrew positions the overall argument by stating: "the essential problem of entrepreneurship is the translation of individual drive into collective purpose and commitment (p. 573).

In his early work Schein (1983) argued that the individual entrepreneur determined goals for the new venture that were rooted in his/her personality. As a result, the culture of the organization (the ways in which the values/assumptions behind patterns of work) was intentionally created by the individual entrepreneurs. This assumption of intentionality may not completely hold true for all ventures for a number of reasons. First of all, we know that many ventures are started by teams and that teams may often be more successful in the start-up process (Forster, 2009). This suggests that the values/assumptions would be negotiated by the founding team rather than directed by and reflective of a single individual.

Second, similarly to the development of the organizational identity, the direct influence of the founder(s) on the goals/work of the organization may be diluted depending on the sources of capital, a board of directors or others who have a strong stake in the organization. In these cases, the emergent culture may well be a reflection of the values/assumptions of others rather than of the founding entrepreneurs. For example, ventures that are launched in accelerators may take on the values and assumptions (culture) of the incubating organization, while ventures that receive angel financing, and therefore have angels or other experienced founders/investors as stakeholders, may take on the culture prescribed by these stakeholders.

Third, there is also the possibility that the entrepreneur's strategy and/or goals are uncertain or unclear in the early stages. Founders may try something, fail, pivot then try something else (trial and error). These trials may be sets of activities carried out by volunteers, students, contract workers or others who are not distinctly tied to the organization. This would suggest that the cultural components are not strongly imprinted but rather they emerge gradually, and possibly unintentionally.

Finally, and in our argument the most relevant point for the largest number of businesses, given the current climate for some businesses of acting quickly by starting a website, generating sales swiftly, and taking action, the reality is that by the time most venture enterprise founders start thinking about ensuring a distinctive culture in their business, it is usually too late. The culture has already emerged and some rudiments of norms and assumptions, generally unconsciously based on the values and beliefs of the founders, are guiding the behaviors and actions of the firm. From a resource perspective, a lack of attention to culture early in organizational founding may not be healthy for the founder, employees, or the future of the business itself. In sum, this culture of the enterprise emerges from the mind, values, and practices of the founder(s) (Boeker, 1988; Bird, 1989) while the business is being created—a time when the founder generally places more priority on the creation of value than the creation of culture. Looking at this work together suggests a dichotomy, although admittedly more likely a continuum, of conscious and intentional creation of the organizational culture, particularly by the founder(s) versus organic development of organizational culture in new ventures.

To summarize our proposed cognitive pathway, we suggest the following relationships (Figure 9.1) as an illustrative guide.

The mapping of this pathway is at yet tentative and is presented for initial discussion. In sum, the (1) personal identity aspects of the founder (demographics, affiliations, etc.) have an interactive relationship with the (2) emerging entrepreneurial identity, one that then interacts with the (3) organizational identity of the business under development, and (4) the continued interaction of the individual, entrepreneurial, and organizational identity is ultimately manifested in the organizational culture. (Beyond the scope of this paper is a recognition of feedback loops from the organizational culture to each of the other types of identity).

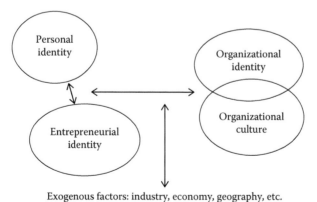

Exogenous factors: industry, economy, geography, etc.

Figure 9.1   Proposed cognitive cultural creation pathway

Proposed pathways linkages

Three particular concepts have been proposed to link entrepreneurial identity and organizational identity: distinctiveness, centrality, and endurance (Kreiner et al., 2015). We suggest that these concepts can be extended further to span each of the concepts addressed in this chapter, building a platform for further understanding.

A sense of, or even a need for, *distinctiveness* has been a frequent theme in the entrepreneurship literature (Baker & Nelson, 2005; Shepherd & Haynie, 2009). Social Identity Theory (SIT) is built on commitments to belonging, with memberships, or even perceived memberships, framing and shaping identities and ultimately behaviors. While traditional SIT regarding work roles refers to potential memberships such as "work group, department, union, lunch group, age cohort, fast-track group, and so on" (Ashforth & Macl, 1989, p. 22), none of these exist within the organization for a nascent entrepreneur (Greene & Brush, 2017). Indeed, the entrepreneur is simultaneously creating both a personal identity as an entrepreneur and an organizational identity as a business (Gartner & Brush, 2007; Greene & Brush, 2017). As we mentioned earlier, organizational identity depends a great deal on the type of business being pursued, as well as the entrepreneur's previous experience; cognitive aspects such as motivation and aspirations or goals; role models; resources (especially capital); sources; and planned uses, networks, etc. (Greene & Brush, 2017). We posit that each of these will then also impact the type of organizational culture that ensues, with differences also determined by the culture construction process, be it intentional or organic.

Centrality, considered here as similar to salience, is another crucial concept for each of our concepts as it helps us recognize that individuals have multiple, overlapping, and interacting group memberships that contribute toward an identity (Meister et al., 2014). Centrality is an indicator of which of those social memberships take precedence. Thus, centrality also relates to learning about entrepreneurs/entrepreneurship, finding the appropriate role models, and modeling in the creation of one's entrepreneurial identity. Given the quite robust findings to date of the importance of values in venture creation, centrality also helps us deliberate about the elements considered most important within an organizational culture. One current example is the debate on competing values in ventures with a social mission—how does one balance the desires for a social outcome with coinciding needs for commercial success (Zhu et al., 2016)? What impact does this then have on the culture the entrepreneur desires?

The third concept is *endurance*, which we connect with construction—how one builds something that will be durable and last, or in more recent parlance, be sustainable (Kreiner et al., 2015). Again, the integration of all aspects under discussion come into consideration, although how they do so is part of our pursuit. It is generally accepted that the entrepreneurial behaviors necessary to start and begin to grow the business are not necessarily those that are needed to support larger scale and durable growth. As these needs change, theoretically the cognitive schemas will change as the entrepreneur must also adapt and, as we here posit, change their entrepreneurial identity. We further consider that the organizational identity and the culture of the organization will therefore also change, with the ideal situation being that these types of personal and organizational changes can again be conducted in an intentional manner. The recognition of changes in organizational roles is crucial. To date the entrepreneurship research has been more careful about when someone becomes an entrepreneur, as in defining the role of a nascent entrepreneur (Shaver et al., 2001), than when someone is no longer an entrepreneur, particularly when in the business s/he founded (Greene & Brush, 2017).

In sum, personal identity, entrepreneurial identity, and organizational identity should indeed answer the questions of who we are as a group and what we stand for. Organizational culture guides the how—the means through which these identities are enacted.

From identity to organizational culture: a pathway test

We propose one final way to examine the pathway, a model built from an integration and amendment of Schein's (1988) work and the Competing Values Framework (CVF) to further illustrate the connections between the values the entrepreneur brings to the creation of the organizational culture. The CVF was developed as a tool for analyzing organizational cultural traits—and their centrality—in order to identity a cultural profile (see Table 9.2). CVF has a history of extensive application across many types of organizational settings and questions (Cameron & Quinn, 1999; Buenger et al., 1996; Goodman et al., 2001; Hooijberg & Petrock, 1993). Our approach is to use this adaptation of the key dimensions and attributes to suggest some of the underlying assumptions, dimensions, concepts, etc., in order to illustrate the connection between the individual, entrepreneurial, and organizational identities and organizational culture.

The purpose of this initial framework is to identify and track the effects and interactions between each type of identity and culture. For instance, if sense is to be made of a fundamental value held by a founder that people are inherently good, how does this track across how an entrepreneur will value people, the organizational identity this prompts externally and internally, and how this is manifested inside the organization to guide structure and functions? In sum, this work provides a direct link between individual identity, entrepreneurial identity, organizational identity and the organizational culture created as a result of those identities. Our conclusion is that this can then also lead to a diagnostic when used for the intentional creation of organizational culture in a new venture.

Table 9.2 Identity pathways to organizational culture

Key dimensions	Values and attributes			
	Individual personal identity	Entrepreneurial identity	Organizational identity	Organizational culture
Sense of being	Humans essentially good, neutral or evil	Kind of value to be created from the business Human capital approach	Type of place to work Type of place to do business with	Degree of emphasis on human development Degree of trust and openness Rigidity of work structures Authority systems as autocratic/paternalistic vs. collegial/participative? Reward systems
Sense of relationships	Leadership style Solo vs. team work Importance of loyalty and trust	Entrepreneurial leadership style (development and communication of vision) Solo vs. team work	Competitive vs. collaborative Type of place to work Community leader (or not)	Degree of internal competitiveness Distribution of power Competition vs. cooperation? Individualism vs. groupism? Importance of mentoring, facilitating, or nurturing Visionary Level of focus on teamwork, building consensus, and being concerned about people
Sense of activity	Proactive, reactive, passive Risk taking	Proactive, reactive, passive Innovative or risk taking	No-nonsense, aggressive, results oriented Having the most unique and newest products and services	Importance of organizing Degree of efficiency orientation and urgency

Dimension				
Sense of time	Desired pace of work and play	Emphasis on achievement and goals	Winning in the marketplace and outpacing the competition Dependable, efficient, and low cost	Founder's extent of engagement with employees Importance of face time Ability to work remotely
Sense of reality and truth	Definition of truth Preference for formal/informal approach to rules and policies	Use of role models and advisors Going beyond a sense of what is "right", do I accept all the research that shows diversity is a productivity resource?	Place in product/service markets Expectations of employees Trustworthiness Degree of honesty Self-awareness	How storytelling occurs internally and externally Existence of formal mission/vision statements What is the role of evidence, data, proof? What is stated and not stated? Shared sense of organizational success
Sense of place	Attachment to locations/communities Awareness and importance of design aesthetics	What kind of place do I want to spend all my time? What kind of place do I need to attract the people I need – and have them stay? How different do I want to (must I) be?	Home town heroes Move to attain resources Valued enough to receive resources for moving Willing and able to spend money on aesthetics	Consideration for comfort of employees Participation in external community Competitive and achievement oriented Controlled and structured

Source: Adapted from Schein, 1988; Cameron & Quinn, 1999.

Conclusion

The objective of this chapter was to review a set of concepts related to identity and connect them in a proposed cognitive pathway to the creation of culture as a resource in a new venture. Next steps in this project are to more completely articulate and ultimately test the framework for its theoretical and practical value. Future research also includes the impact of endogenous factors, such as the gender of the owner, and exogenous influences, such as external cultural and economic environment. The desired outcome is to provide a foundation of knowledge for the development of entrepreneurship education materials leading to the sustainability of healthy organizational cultures.

When it comes to entrepreneurship education, as a field we do a far better job working on start-up processes and entrepreneurial behaviors than we do on organizational design, particularly around components such as organizational culture. Even in the field of organization theory, theory and application on emerging organizations is rare and courses on how to plan your new organization are unicorns. Education and training in this area too often depend simply on the replication of existing (and very dated) models. If one accepts that organizational culture is an entrepreneurial resource that is dependent on the founder and founding team, ergo we should actually spend time and energy learning more about how to teach this as an entrepreneurial skill.

Also, entrepreneurship education and training, as well as entrepreneurship related policies, are most often evaluated by the expectation of the creation of an economic return. In particular, in these discussions the approach to launching an organization is about the outcome, the creation of revenues, jobs, or even social good; however, the findings that people are most often motivated to start businesses by their desire to be independent, to do things their way, are quite robust. Despite this, we rarely explicitly consider the start of a new business as a statement on how someone wants to live their life. And it is even rarer that we teach and train about how to create an organizational culture that supports a life style statement. In this case, by "life style" we resoundingly do not mean a limited business size, but instead recognize the pursuit of various types of life style as a personal choice based on the values of the founder or founding team.

References

Ashforth, B. E. (1998). Epilogue: What have we learned, and where do we go from here? In D. Whetten & P. Godfrey (Eds), *Identity in Organizations*. London: SAGE, pp. 269–71.

Ashforth, B. E. & Mael, F. (1989). Social identity theory and the organization. *Academy of Management Review*, 4(1), 20–39.

Baker, T. & Nelson, R. E. (2005). Creating something from nothing: Resource construction through entrepreneurial bricolage. *Administrative Science Quarterly*, 50(3), 329–66.

Barney, J. B. (1991). Firm resources and sustained competitive advantage. *Journal of Management*, 17(1), 91–120.

Bird, B. (1989). *Entrepreneurial Behavior*. Glenview, IL: Scot Foresman.

Boeker, W. (1988). Organizational origins: Entrepreneurial and environmental imprinting at the time of founding. In G. Carroll (Ed.), *Ecological Models of Organizations*. Cambridge, MA: Ballinger Publishing, pp. 33–51.

Boeker, W. (1989). Strategic change: The effects of founding and history. *Academy of Management Journal*, 32(3), 489–515.

Brush, C. G. (1992). Research on women business owners: Past trends, a new perspective and future directions. *Entrepreneurship: Theory & Practice*, 16(4), 5–31.

Brush, C. G. & Gale, M. 2014. Becoming entrepreneurial: Constructing an entrepreneurial identity in an elective entrepreneurship course. In V. Crittenden, K. Esper, N. Karst, & R. Slegers (Eds), *Evolving Entrepreneurial Education: Innovation in the Babson Classroom*. London: Emerald Publishing, pp. 305–22.

Brush, C. G., Greene, P. G. and Hart, M. M. (2001). From initial idea to unique advantage: The entrepreneurial challenge of constructing a resource base. *Academy of Management Executive*, 15(1), 64–78.

Buenger, V., Daft, R. L., Conlon, E. J. & Austin, J. (1996). Competing values in organizations: Contextual influences and structural consequences. *Organization Science*, 7(5), 557–76.

Burke, P. J. & Reitzes, D. C. (1991). An identity theory approach to commitment. *Social Psychology Quarterly*, 239–51.

Cameron, K. S. & Quinn, R. E. (1999). *Diagnosing and Changing Organizational Culture: Based on the Competing Values Framework*. Reading, MA: Addison-Wesley.

Christiansen, L. H. & Lounsbury, M. (2013). Strange brew: Bridging logics via institutional bricolage and the reconstitution of organizational identity. In M. Lounsbury & E. Boxenbaum (Eds), *Institutional Logics in Action, Part B*. Bingley, UK: Emerald, pp. 199–232.

Corley, K. G. (2004). Defined by our strategy or our culture? Hierarchical differences in perceptions of organizational identity and change. *Human Relations*, 57(9), 1145–77.

Crosina, L. (2017). On becoming an entrepreneur: Unpacking entrepreneurial identity. In P. G. Greene & C. G. Brush (Eds), *The Construction of Social Identity: The Case of Women Entrepreneurs*. Cheltenham, UK: Edward Elgar.

Dandridge, T. C., Mitroff, I. & Joyce, W. F. (1980). Organizational symbolism: A topic to expand organizational analysis. *Academy of Management Review*, 5(1), 77–82.

Dutton, J. E., Dukerich, J. M. & Harquail, C. V. (1994). Organizational images and member identification. *Administrative Science Quarterly*, 239–63.

Fauchart, E. & Gruber, M. (2011). Darwinians, communitarians, and missionaries: The role of founder identity in entrepreneurship. *Academy of Management Journal*, 54(5), 935–57.

Forster, W. (2009). *When a Second Person Enters the Scene: Of Founding Partnerships, Firm Creation and Profitability*. Charlottesville, VA: University of Virginia.

Gartner, W. B. (1988). "Who is an entrepreneur?" is the wrong question. *American Journal of Small Business*, 12(4), 11–32.

Gartner, W. B. & Brush, C. G. (2007). Entrepreneurship as organizing: Emergence, newness and transformation. In M. Minitt (Ed.), *Entrepreneurship: Place*. Santa Barbara, CA: Praeger Publishing, pp. 1–20.

Gartner, W. B., Bird, B. J. & Starr, J. A. (1992). Acting as if: Differentiating entrepreneurial from organizational behavior. *Entrepreneurship Theory & Practice*, 16(3), 13–31.

Gioia, D. A. (1998). From individual to organizational identity. In A. D. Whetten & P. C. Godfrey (Eds), *Identity in Organizations: Building Theory through Conversations*. Thousand Oaks, CA: SAGE, pp. 17–32.

Glynn, M. A. (2008). Beyond constraint: How institutions enable identities. In R. Greenwood, C. Oliver, R. Suddaby, & K. Sahlin-Andersson (Eds), *The SAGE Handbook of Organizational Institutionalism*. Thousand Oaks, CA: SAGE, pp. 413–30.

Goodman, E. A., Zammuto, R. F. & Gifford, B. D. (2001). The competing values framework: Understanding the impact of organizational culture on the quality of work life. *Organization Development Journal*, 19(3), 58–68.

Greene, P. G. & Brush, C. G. (2017). *The Construction of Social Identity: The Case of Women Entrepreneurs*. Cheltenham, UK: Edward Elgar.

Hannan, M. T. & Freeman, J. (1977). The population ecology of organizations. *American Journal of Sociology*, 82(5), 929–64.

Hessels, J., Van Gelderen, M. & Thurik, R. (2008). Entrepreneurial aspirations, motivations, and their drivers. *Small Business Economics*, 31(3), 323–39.

Hogg, M. A. & Abrams, D. (1988). *Social Identification: A Social Psychology of Intergroup Relations and Group Processes*. London: Routledge.

Hogg, M. A., Terry, D. J. & White, K. M. (1995). A tale of two theories: A critical comparison of identity theory with social identity theory. *Social Psychology Quarterly*, 255–69.

Hooijberg, R. & Petrock, F. (1993). On cultural change: Using the competing values framework to help leaders execute a transformational strategy. *Human Resource Management*, 32(1), 29–51. [Special issue on the competing values framework].

Jacques, E. (1951). *The Changing Culture of a Factory*. London: Tavistock.

Katz, D. & Kahn, R. L. (1966). *The Social Psychology of Organizations*. New York, NY: Wiley.

Katz, J. & Gartner, W. B. (1988). Properties of emerging organizations. *Academy of Management Review*, 13(3), 429–41.

Kelley, D., Singer, S. & Harrington, M. (2016). *Global Entrepreneurship Monitor. 2015/16 Global Report*. Wellesley, MA: Babson College.

Kimberly, J. (1975). Environmental constraints and organizational structure: A comparative analysis of rehabilitation organizations. *Administrative Science Quarterly*, 20, 1–9.

Kreiner, G. E., Hollensbe, E., Sheep, M. L., Smith, B. R. & Kataria, N. (2015). Elasticity and the dialectic tensions of organizational identity: How can we hold together while we are pulling apart? *Academy of Management Journal*, 58(4), 981–1011.

Krueger, N. F. & Carsrud, A. L. (1993). Entrepreneurs intentions: Applying the theory of planned behavior. *Entrepreneurship and Regional Development*, 5(4), 315–30.

Krueger, N. F. & Dickson, P. R. (1994). How believing in ourselves increases risk taking: Perceived self-efficacy and opportunity recognition. *Decision Sciences*, 25(3), 385–400.

Krueger, N. F., Reilly, M. D. & Carsrud, A. L. (2000). Competing models of entrepreneurial intentions. *Journal of Business Venturing*, 15(5), 411–32.

Lawrence, B. S. (1984). Historical perspective: Using the past to study the present. *Academy of Management Review*, 9(2), 307–12.

Likert, R. (1961). *New Patterns of Management*. New York, NY: McGraw-Hill.

Likert, R. (1967). *The Human Organization*. New York, NY: McGraw-Hill.

Manolova, T., Brush, C., Edelman, L. & Shaver, K. (2012). Once size does not fit all: Entrepreneurial expectancies and growth intentions of US women and men nascent entrepreneurs. *Entrepreneurship Theory & Practice*, 24(1–2), 7–27.

Markova, I. (1987). Knowledge of the self through interaction. In K. Yardley and T. Honess (Eds), *Self and Identity: Psychosocial Perspectives*. Oxford: John Wiley & Sons, pp. 65–80.

Markus, H. & Nurius, P. (1986). Possible selves. *American Psychologist*, 41(9), 954.

McClelland, D. C. (1961). *The Achievement Society*. Princeton, NJ: Von Nostrand.

McGregor, D. (1960). Theory X and theory Y. *Organization Theory*, 358–74.

Meister, A., Jehn, K. A. & Thatcher, S. M. B. (2014). Feeling misidentified: The consequences of internal identity asymmetries for individuals at work. *Academy of Management Review*, 39(4), 488–512.

Mitchell, R. K., Busenitz, L., Lant, T., McDougall, P. P., Morse, E. A. & Smith, J. B. (2002). Toward a theory of entrepreneurial cognition: Rethinking the people side of entrepreneurship research. *Entrepreneurship Theory & Practice*, 27(2), 93–104.

Neck, H., Brush, C. & Allen, E. (2009). The landscape of social entrepreneurship. *Business Horizons*, 52(1), 13–19.

Nel, P., Maritz, A. & Thongprovati, O. (2010). Motherhood and entrepreneurship: The Mumpreneur phenomenon. *International Journal of Organizational Innovation (Online)*, 3(1), 6.

Pettigrew, A. M. (1979). On studying organizational cultures. *Administrative Science Quarterly*, 24, 570–81.

Pfeffer, J. (1981). *Power in Organizations*. Marshfield, MA: Pitman.

Ravasi, D. & Schultz, M. (2006). Responding to organizational identity threats: Exploring the role of organizational culture. *Academy of Management Journal*, 49(3), 433–58.

Shaver, K. G., Carter, N. M., Gartner, W. B. & Reynolds, P. D. (2001). Who is a nascent entrepreneur? Decision rules for identifying and selecting entrepreneurs in the Panel Study of Entrepreneurial Dynamics (PSED). *Frontiers of Entrepreneurship Research*, 122.

Schein, E. H. (1983). The role of the founder in creating organizational culture. *Organizational Dynamics*, 12(1), 13–28.

Schein, E. H. (1988). Organizational culture. WP# 2088-88. December, MIT Press.

Schneider, B., Hall, D. T. & Nygren, H. T. (1971). Self image and job characteristics as correlates of changing organizational identification. *Human Relations*, 24(5), 397–416.

Shepherd, D. A. & Haynie, J. M. (2009). Birds of a feather don't always flock together: Identity management in entrepreneurship. *Journal of Business Venturing*, 24, 316–37.

Shepherd, D. A., Patzelt, H. & Haynie, J. M. (2010). Entrepreneurial spirals: Deviation-amplifying loops of an entrepreneurial mindset and organizational culture. *Entrepreneurship Theory & Practice*, 34(1), 59–82.

Smircich, L. (1983). Concepts of culture and organizational analysis. *Administrative Analysis Quarterly*, 28, 339–58.

Stanworth, M. J. K. & Curran, J. (1976). Growth and the small firm—an alternative view. *Journal of Management Studies*, 13(2), 95–110.

Stryker, S. (1987). Identity theory: Developments and extensions. In K. Yardley & T. Honess (Eds), *Self and Identity: Psychosocial Perspectives*. New York, NY: Wiley, pp.89–103.

Stryker, S. & Burke, P. J. (2000). The past, present, and future of an identity theory. *Social Psychology Quarterly*, 64(4), 284–97.

Stryker, S. & Serpe, R. T. (1982). Commitment, identity salience, and role behavior: Theory and research example. *Personality, Roles, and Social Behavior*, 119, 218.

Sveningsson, S. & Alvesson, M. (2003). Managing managerial identities: Organizational fragmentation, discourse and identity struggle. *Human Relations*, 56, 1163–93.

Tajfel, H. (1982). Social psychology of intergroup relations. *Annual Review of Psychology*, 33(1), 1–39.

Turner, J. C. (1985). Social categorization and the self-concept: A social cognitive theory of group behavior. *Advances in Group Processes*, 2, 77–122.

Verheul, I., Uhlaner, L. & Thurik, R. (2005). Business accomplishments, gender and entrepreneurial self-image. *Journal of Business Venturing*, 20(4), 483–518.

Vesalainen, J. & Pihkala, T. (2000). Entrepreneurial identity, intentions and the effect of the push-factor. *International Journal of Entrepreneurship*, 4, 105.

Weick, K. E. (1979). *The Social Psychology of Organizing* (2nd edn.). New York, NY: Random House.

Westhead, P. & Wright, M. (1998). Novice, portfolio, and serial founders: are they different? *Journal of Business Venturing*, 13(3), 173–204.

Woo, C. Y., Cooper, A. C. & Dunkelberg, W. C. (1991). The development and interpretation of entrepreneurial typologies. *Journal of Business Venturing*, 6(2), 93–114.

Zald, M. (1988). History, sociology and theories of organization. CSSTS Working Paper #6. CRSO Working Paper #357. July.

Zhu, Y., Rooney, D. & Phillips, N. (2016). Practice-based wisdom theory for integrating institutional logics: A new model for social entrepreneurship learning and education. *Academy of Management Learning & Education*, 15(3), 607–25.

10 The co-development process of new venture ideas and entrepreneurs' learning

Tadeu F. Nogueira and Gry A. Alsos

Introduction

Entrepreneurship research seeks to explain the generation of new economic activity through new venture creation or through the renewal of established organizations (Wiklund et al., 2011). Such processes are directed by the agency of entrepreneurs as they are situated in a broader context, which has, in itself, characteristics that influence the scope of entrepreneurs' action. Interested in this dual-development process, we examine the interplays between opportunity development and the learning processes of entrepreneurs. In this effort, we build on and extend the literature on entrepreneurial learning, which is concerned with the process by which entrepreneurs, teams, and organizations develop knowledge and skills to perform entrepreneurial actions (Rae and Wang, 2015). We also partake in the discussion about entrepreneurial opportunities, following a recent conceptualization by Davidsson (2015) which distinguishes new venture ideas (NVI) from external enablers and opportunity beliefs—all parts of the opportunity concept. Hence, with the intent to develop theorizing on the nexus between entrepreneurs and the artifacts they act upon, we conceptualize entrepreneurial learning as a key part of the opportunity development process.

Entrepreneurial experience can be treated as a *stock*, i.e. a quality of the entrepreneur based on their cumulative experiences, or as a *flow*, i.e. events that occur over time, which the entrepreneur learns from (Reuber and Fischer, 1999). Entrepreneurial learning (EL) literature has particularly dealt with the role of entrepreneurs' stock of pre-entry experiences and knowledge in a number of different outcomes. For instance, in regard to opportunity-level outcomes, Gruber et al. (2008) found that teams with prior entrepreneurial experience identify more market opportunities than teams lacking this experience. In regard to individual-level outcomes, Lee and Jones (2008) concluded that human and social capital facilitate learning in the post-start-up process. In regard to firm-level outcomes, Dencker et al. (2009) found that founders' pre-entry knowledge and management experience increase new firm survival. Consequently, there is widespread support for the important role that pre-entry experiences and knowledge play in entrepreneurship.

To a lesser extent, EL literature has considered the experiences of entrepreneurs as a flow of events involving learning. Treating experiences as a flow means being closer to the learning phenomenon because learning is better described as a process rather than an outcome (Kolb, 2014). Even though Experiential Learning Theory (ELT) depicts individuals' learning as a dynamic and continuous process, this perspective has scarcely been used in the scholarly discussion of entrepreneurial learning. In this chapter, we address this gap by giving more emphasis to learning as a process/flow, taking place over time during the NVI development.

Research on the connection between entrepreneurial learning and opportunity development has been limited so far. While acknowledging the important role of learning in entrepreneurial activities in general, extant research has focused more on the role of entrepreneurs' pre-entry experiences and knowledge in the discovery of opportunities (e.g. Shane, 2000; Gruber et al., 2013). Taking a process perspective to entrepreneurial learning, we ask *how does the development of a NVI interplay with the entrepreneur's learning processes?*

In addressing this question, we see NVI as developed over time, from starting in a rough form as a vague idea and undergoing changes and refinement during the process before they can be commercially exploited. Learning plays a crucial role in this process, given the high levels of uncertainty and ambiguity involved. However, the mechanisms of how entrepreneurs learn in interaction with the idea development are still unclear.

Addressing these issues, we aim to contribute to the literature in three ways. First, we conceptualize NVI development as a learning process, thereby adding to the vivid discussions on entrepreneurial opportunities. Second, through case studies of technology entrepreneurs, we show how the process of developing NVI triggers entrepreneurs' learning, as well as how the resulting learning influences its further development. Third, we contribute to the literature on entrepreneurial learning by emphasizing the learning related to NVI development, attempting to distinguish entrepreneurial learning from other types of learning of entrepreneurs.

Theoretical framework

Entrepreneurial learning

Entrepreneurial learning (EL) has received increased attention in the past decades, fueled by the synergies between the fields of individual/organizational learning and entrepreneurship (Wang and Chugh, 2014). The study of entrepreneurial learning was inspired by human capital research, which, among others, explores the role of entrepreneurs' stock of pre-entry experiences in firms' performance (Lamont, 1972; Box et al., 1993; Cooper et al., 1994). However, by recognizing that a direct relationship between entrepreneurs' pre-entry experiences and firm performance is problematic (Politis, 2005), EL research has focused on the relationship between entrepreneurs' stock of pre-entry experiences and outcomes at the individual level, as well as on the underlying transformation process of experiences into knowledge.

For instance, entrepreneurs' stock of pre-entry experiences has been linked with the generation of new business ideas by entrepreneurs (Gabrielsson and Politis, 2012), entrepreneurs' amount of learning (Sardana and Scott-Kemmis, 2010), entrepreneurs' attitudes towards failure (Politis and Gabrielsson, 2009), the ability to manage several firms simultaneously (Huovinen and Tihula, 2008), skills for coping with the liabilities of newness and preference for effectual reasoning (Politis, 2008), and entrepreneurs' performance and aspirations (Westhead et al., 2005). Overall, EL research has sought to explain how differences in entrepreneurs' stock of pre-entry experiences result in different levels of entrepreneurial knowledge and skills. One common proposition in EL literature is that experienced entrepreneurs are more knowledgeable and skilled than novice entrepreneurs and, thus, are better able to capitalize on such knowledge and skills (Politis and Gabrielsson, 2009). In turn, this is argued to contribute to superior performance at the firm-level (Delmar and Shane, 2006).

The literature on EL has largely relied on Kolb's ELT (Kolb, 2014). Even though Kolb's ELT focuses on the transformation process of experiences into knowledge, the learning of entrepreneurs has still been depicted in quite a static way by EL literature, largely seen as the result of differences in stocks of pre-entry experiences. Further, research has included examinations of individuals' learning styles, which are seen as stable states. The issue that arises from this static view of learning is that it focuses on the results of learning or its antecedents, and does not reflect the phenomenon of learning in itself (Corbett, 2005). Despite the overall static orientation of EL research, there are also examples of studies that treat entrepreneurs' experiences as a flow. For instance, Rae and Carswell (2001) conducted life-story interviews with people who had shown a disposition to become an entrepreneur, highlighting learning as a life-long process. Such studies show the value of looking more closely into the process of learning in entrepreneurial activities.

Learning can be explored from many different perspectives, including behaviorism, cognitivism, constructivism, and social learning (Merriam and Bierema, 2013). The behaviorist approach stresses individuals' actions and stimulus-responses mechanisms; the cognitivist approach highlights the internal mental processes in individuals' cognitive structures; the constructivist approach places the locus of learning in the construction of meaning by the individual; and the social learning perspective advances that learning has its locus in socialization/interaction activities. While particular perspectives may have gained momentum for a period of time, none of them has come to full prominence. Each approach has distinct contributions to provide, given the complex and multi-faceted nature of learning. As such, learning has been approached from a plurality of perspectives in entrepreneurship literature.

Following this plurality of perspectives to learning, the concept of EL has been defined as: (1) learning how to recognize and act on opportunities (e.g. Franco and Haase, 2009); (2) learning how to initiate, organize and manage ventures (e.g. Cope, 2005; Rae, 2005; Rae, 2006; Berglund et al., 2007; Huovinen and Tihula, 2008; Voudouris et al., 2011; Miller, 2012; McCann and Vroom, 2015); (3) learning how to work in entrepreneurial ways (e.g. Rae, 2000); (4) learning how to accumulate and update knowledge (e.g. Minniti and Bygrave, 2001; Ravasi and Turati, 2005); (5) the construction of meaning in the process of entrepreneurship (e.g. Rae and Carswell, 2001; Thorpe et al., 2006; Kauppinen and Juho, 2012); (6) a process where entrepreneurs transform direct and indirect experiences into knowledge in disparate ways (e.g. Young and Sexton, 2003; Politis, 2005; Holcomb et al., 2009; Sardana and Scott-Kemmis, 2010; Westhead and Wright, 2011); (7) a cognitive and social process through which knowledge is generated, articulated and distributed (e.g. Fang et al., 2010; Cope, 2011); (8) the development of entrepreneurial skills and entrepreneurship-specific behaviors (e.g. Matlay et al., 2012); and (9) the development of attitudinal competencies such as resilience and self-efficacy (e.g. Becot et al., 2015).

On the one side, EL is seen as the learning of the entrepreneur during creation and organizing a new firm. Emphasis is thus given to new firm creation. On the other side, EL refers to the learning processes in the recognition, evaluation, exploitation, and/or creation of opportunities. Emphasis is thus given to entrepreneurial opportunities, regardless of whether they involve the creation of a new firm. In line with the latter, this chapter advances that learning associated with the pursuit of opportunities is what defines the boundaries of entrepreneurial learning.

Experiential Learning Theory

Although EL literature has borrowed from several theoretical perspectives, Experiential Learning Theory (ELT) is frequently used as the theoretical foundation in this field of research (Wang and Chugh, 2014). ELT consists of a comprehensive, holistic, and appealing set of explanations about how individuals learn. The theory posits that the acquisition and transformation of experiences into knowledge are central to the learning process and defines learning as "the process whereby knowledge is created through the transformation of experience" (Kolb, 2014, p. 49). ELT stresses learning as a continuous process; it emphasizes individuals' experiences from where knowledge is derived and tested out in; it highlights two opposed modes of adaptation to the world, namely by observing and acting; it acknowledges the transactions between the individual and the environment; it acknowledges that learning encompasses multiple interactions between the subject and object; and it distinguishes between different kinds of knowledge, namely personal and social knowledge. ELT is thus a holistic cognitive learning theory that assimilates the external environment in its explanation, suiting the entrepreneurship context well.

ELT emphasizes that individuals develop knowledge from a continuous flow of experiences. Knowledge is developed both by integrating new experiences into existing systems of beliefs and ideas, as well as by substituting old beliefs and ideas by new ones, when faced with confusing, disruptive situations. As ELT portrays learning as a process and not as an outcome, the knowledge that is developed in the process is constantly shaped and reshaped, never achieving an ultimate state.

Aligned with this dynamic view, the experiential learning cycle illustrates two dialectic ways through which individuals grasp experiences (through abstract conceptualizations or concrete experiences) and transform experiences (through reflection or action) (Kolb, 2014). In regard to the first dialectic (abstract/concrete), individuals grasp experiences by relying on mentalistic/symbolic representations, i.e. *comprehension*, or by relying on the tangibility of the immediate experience, i.e. *apprehension*. In regard to the second dialectic (reflection/action), individuals transform experiences through internal reflection, i.e. *intention*, or through experimentation with the external world, i.e. *extension*.

ELT acknowledges the importance of the environment for the learning of individuals. However, it still focuses more on the individual at the expense of contextual conditions. Although ELT does not advance that types and forms represent the ultimate reality, it still advances that individuals learn in preferred ways (learning styles)—this is because the learner cannot process all the information from the environment, only a portion of the received information.

While behavioral theories of learning bring in the environment more emphatically, they see learning as a one-sided activity—the environment triggers responses from the individual, but the individual does not have any influence on the environment (Merriam and Bierema, 2013). The feedback from the individual to the environment is thus largely ignored by behavioral theories of learning. ELT addresses this issue by placing emphasis on experiences, which represent an important transaction between the individual and the environment.

In this study, we emphasize the interaction between the entrepreneur and the environment in the learning process. In the process of developing an NVI, the entrepreneur interacts with the environment (Dimov, 2007) in a process that is likely to trigger learning. However, importantly, the entrepreneur also actively takes part in the process of developing the opportunity (Dimov, 2011; Snihur et al., 2017) and, hence, influences the environment.

Entrepreneurial opportunities

Entrepreneurial opportunities have become a key concept in entrepreneurship research. Shane and Venkataraman (2000) emphasized the importance of the concept by arguing that the field should move beyond the study of individual characteristics that supposedly differentiate entrepreneurs from non-entrepreneurs, to the study of the nexus between individuals and entrepreneurial opportunities. The introduction of this concept reconnected entrepreneurship research with economics, and had the intention of establishing theoretical boundaries for the field. Since Shane and Venkataraman (2000), much effort has been given to defining opportunities, and to discussing whether or not they are objective and independent of the perception and actions of entrepreneurs (e.g. Alvarez and Barney, 2007; Sarasvathy et al., 2010; Shane, 2012).

The discovery and creation views are the most prevalent approaches to opportunities in entrepreneurship literature. One key distinction between them is whether or not opportunities exist objectively without the action of entrepreneurs, as the definitions below clearly illustrate:

> Entrepreneurial opportunities are those situations in which new goods, services, raw materials, and organizing methods can be introduced and sold at greater than their cost of production. (Shane and Venkataraman, 2000, p. 220)

> Opportunities are created, endogenously, by the actions, reactions, and enactment of entrepreneurs exploring ways to produce new products or services. (Alvarez and Barney, 2007, p. 15)

More recently, the dichotomy between discovered and created opportunities has started to lose traction, given the realization that opportunities reflect the interaction between entrepreneurs' action and structural conditions that can be conducive for entrepreneurship. Among the researchers that support this view, Garud and Giuliani (2013) argue that both agency and entrepreneurial opportunities are distributed and emergent, and thus discovery and creation interact dynamically during the entrepreneurial process. That is, entrepreneurial opportunities can be both made and found (Venkataraman et al., 2012).

Moreover, opportunities, seen as means–ends relationships (Eckhardt and Shane, 2003), can involve elements of both the discovery and creation views, depending on conditions of uncertainty (Sarasvathy et al., 2010, p. 82): (1) opportunities are discovered when there is the "possibility of correcting errors in the system and creating new ways of achieving given ends", which assumes that only supply or demand is known, given information asymmetries among individuals; and (2) opportunities are created when there is the "possibility of creating new means as well as new ends", which assumes that neither supply nor demand exists. Applying this means–ends perspective to technology-related opportunities, two situations are derived: (1) the source of the opportunity can either be the technology itself, or, alternatively, a market demand (this resembles Sarasvathy et al.'s (2010) "discovery" view in that only one side of the means–ends relationship is known); and (2) both the technology and the market are unknown and consequently developed simultaneously (this resembles Sarasvathy et al.'s (2010) "creative" view).

Another issue in the opportunity discussion is the lack of construct clarity. Despite the acknowledgement of the difference between business ideas and opportunities (Shane and Venkataraman, 2000; Eckhardt and Shane, 2013), current depictions of how opportunities come into existence rarely take this into account. One of the exceptions is Vogel (2016), who defines a venture idea as a preliminary and mostly incomplete mental representation of the concept for a potential future venture, whereas a venture opportunity is a favorable combination of endogenously shaped and exogenously given circumstances. Vogel suggests a chronological order to these constructs, advancing that a venture idea is followed by a venture concept, which is finally followed by the venture opportunity.

Despite this important step in further delineating the differences between a venture idea and an opportunity, Vogel's conceptualization does not acknowledge that a venture idea is not just the preliminary and mostly incomplete mental representation of the concept for a new venture, but it is something that entrepreneurs work with throughout the process of creating a new venture. Entrepreneurs constantly make mental representations of anything that is pertinent to their ventures, and the venture idea is one of the most important artifacts entrepreneurs act upon during their entrepreneurial journeys. Moreover, current depictions of how opportunities come into existence often suggest linearity. Either the opportunity is the starting point for entrepreneurial efforts or it is the final destination. This does not seem to apply to real-life situations where venture ideas are constantly tried out, refined, discarded, and replaced by new ones in interaction with changing structural conditions, in a co-evolution process. As such, the acknowledgement that the opportunity construct encompasses both external factors and venture ideas allows the accommodation of the apparently contrasting views between discovered and created opportunities because it recognizes that there are situations that may be conducive for entrepreneurship, and it also grants that the creative work of entrepreneurs plays a role in transforming environmental conditions.

This is aligned with a recent call for more clarity for the opportunity construct. Davidsson (2015) argues that because too many different concepts have been discussed under the label 'opportunities', such construct is surrounded by problems. Especially problematic, in Davidsson's view, is the application of this construct at the micro level in a prospective context because it does not represent very well the non-actor nexus component, i.e. the entity acted upon by entrepreneurs. Consequently, he has suggested for the opportunity construct to be divided into three sub-constructs: (1) *external enablers* to represent aggregate-level conditions, such as changes in regulation and demography; (2) *opportunity confidence* to represent entrepreneurs' subjective evaluation of the desirability of a situation; and (3) *NVI* to represent the non-actor nexus component.

Entrepreneurial learning and opportunities

Extant research provides different theoretical frameworks with regard to the relationships between learning and entrepreneurial opportunities. For instance, Corbett (2005), following ELT, suggested a creativity-based model for the opportunity recognition process; Dutta and Crossan (2005) proposed a reconciliation between the discovery and creation view on entrepreneurial opportunities by applying the 4I organizational learning framework; Lumpkin and Lichtenstein (2005) advanced that the opportunity recognition process is comprised of two phases (discovery and formation), and each phase requires the engagement in different learning activities (cognitive, behavioral, action learning) by entrepreneurial firms; Politis (2005) offered a conceptual framework depicting entrepreneurial learning as an experiential learning process, which plays an important role in the recognition of entrepreneurial opportunities; and Dimov (2007), building on insights from creativity research, proposed that, instead of being the result of a single insight from a single entrepreneur, opportunities emerge through continuous shaping and development of an initial idea, through social learning processes.

Empirical research on the relationship between learning and entrepreneurial opportunities has been scarce. Existing studies focus mostly on the link between different types of pre-entry experiences and the recognition of entrepreneurial opportunities. Examples include Gruber et al. (2008), who examined the connection between prior entrepreneurial experience among teams of entrepreneurs and the number of market opportunities identified; Gruber et al. (2013), who found that industry experience and external knowledge sourcing contributes to a higher number and variety of opportunities identified; Hajizadeh and Zali (2016), who investigated the role of prior knowledge, entrepreneurial alertness, and entrepreneurial learning in opportunity recognition; and Mueller and Shepherd (2016), who examined how entrepreneurs' business failures influence the identification of entrepreneurial opportunities.

From a cognitive learning perspective, extant literature has focused on the role individuals' cognitive processes play in opportunity recognition. For instance, Gaglio (2004) explored how mental simulations (e.g. rehearsing a sales pitch) and counterfactual thinking (thinking in a way that is contrary to facts) influence opportunity identification; Bingham et al. (2007) discussed the role of experience and heuristics in the capturing of opportunities; and Corbett (2007), building upon ELT, found that individuals with preference for acquiring new information through comprehension identify more opportunities than individuals with preference for acquiring new information through apprehension. While such studies have increased our understanding of opportunities under the discovery view, the mutual interactions between actor and non-actor components, i.e. the individual–opportunity nexus, have been largely overlooked, partly because of the lack of clarity for the opportunity construct, as previously discussed.

Given the overemphasis on a static representation of entrepreneurial learning, the uneven weight given to the individual entrepreneur at the expense of the individual–opportunity nexus, and the focus on opportunities as discovered, we need more theorizing on the nexus between actor and non-actor components taking a dynamic perspective, i.e. seeing opportunities as developed and individuals as changing their knowledge in relation to the opportunity over time. This chapter, in particular, explores the interplays between the entrepreneurial learning processes (as an actor component) and the NVI development (as a non-actor component).

Method

As there is limited theory on the interplays between the NVI development process and the learning of the entrepreneur, we conducted a multiple-case study with the aim to develop theoretical understanding about such relationships, with an overall inductive approach (Eisenhardt, 1989). Even though our research process was characterized by constant interactions between theory and data (Dubois and Gadde, 2002), we focused more on the development of theory from empirical data. The research setting was entrepreneurs in Norway involved with a technology-related NVI. These entrepreneurs were embedded in situations where their learning was heightened by the higher degree of newness, ambiguity, and uncertainty associated with technology-related ideas.

Case selection

The cases were sampled using the following criteria: (1) entrepreneurs had to be working with a technology-related NVI; (2) they had to be the founders of the firm or in the founding team; (3) they had to be the lead entrepreneur in the new firm; (4) and the firms had to be located in Norway. Additionally, the six cases were selected in such a way that firms were diverse in relation to their industry and the entrepreneurs diverse in relation to their pre-entry start-up experiences. Lastly, we also sought variation in relation to the presence of a founding team. Table 10.1 summarizes the cases in this study. This is followed by a brief presentation of each case, with background information of the firm, the NVI, and the entrepreneurs.

Table 10.1   Characteristics of cases

Cases	Firm		Entrepreneur		Team of founders
	Founded in	Industry	Habitual or novice	Role	
PharmaX	2008	Bio-technology	Novice	Co-founder and CEO	Yes
LaKs	2009	Bio-technology	Habitual	Founders	Yes
iTech	2012	IT; Programming services	Habitual	Founder and CEO	No
LibrT	2013	IT; Programming services	Novice	Co-founder	Yes
Msport	2013	Sports, Physical training	Habitual	Co-founder and CEO	Yes
SolEn	2016	Leasing of solar panel systems	Novice	Founder and CEO	No

Source: Author's own composition.

PharmaX

This case consists of a biotechnology firm. The firm has very close relations to a Norwegian university, where basic research on how to synthesize proteins from bacteria started in the early 1990s. The firm was started to explore this technology, after it was found to be useful for industrial application.

The entrepreneur joined the research team in 2003, when the commercial potential of the technology had already been realized. He then engaged in several industry–university collaboration projects, which helped verify that the technology worked and could be applied commercially. The entrepreneur subsequently started leading the venture.

LaKs

This case consists of a biotechnology firm. The firm has close connections with different universities in Norway. The NVI combines research from different academic fields and is aimed at the fish farming industry in Norway.

The firm has two co-founders, who are the key people ahead of its development. Each is responsible for different aspects of the business. One is a researcher in biotechnology and in charge of the technological aspect of the business, and the other is an experienced entrepreneur within the fish farming industry, responsible for the administrative and financial aspects of the business. The entrepreneurial team therefore started with a high level of pre-entry knowledge and experience.

iTech

This case involves a software firm. The NVI consists of the development of a software for improved Customer Relationship Management (CRM), an idea heavily based upon the entrepreneur's pre-entry knowledge and experiences. After the realization that the processes of management were slow and complex, the entrepreneur decided to start the firm to make a better use of the vast amount of data available to companies, and transform it into inputs for good decision making.

He is a portfolio entrepreneur with substantive experience as a manager within CRM. One of his other enterprises consists of a consultancy-based firm that invests in technology-based companies. As a general manager, he had worked with the development of applications for management systems, such as Enterprise Resource Planning and Customer Information Systems.

LibrT

This is a software firm, with close connections with a Norwegian university. The firm, through this university, has access to valuable resources such as collaboration partners. The NVI consists of a digital library software based on an open-source software for management of digital, electronic resources. This technology (digital library software) can be applied in different industries.

The entrepreneur, without pre-entry start-up experiences, relied more on his educational background, which combined engineering and business studies. During the start-up of the firm, the entrepreneur was following a master program in entrepreneurship in the same university. This program gives incentives for students to start a new firm, and provides guidance throughout the start-up process.

Msport

The firm was started with the intent to help solve the problem of widespread physical inactivity. It has close links to one university in Norway, through which the firm has access to research, potential customers, and new team members. Despite having more than one NVI, the main idea consists of a web application that provides research-based physical training programs and innovative health indicators, such as the user's biological age.

The firm explores knowledge from three main areas: medical research, market research, and software development. The entrepreneur, through pre-entry start-up experiences, is skilled in the second knowledge area (market research). He follows a master program in entrepreneurship, in the same university with which the firm has close links (this program gives incentives for students to start a new firm – same as LibrT).

SolEn

This firm works with the leasing of solar panel systems to international organizations. The firm started with the intent to solve the problem of unreliable electrical grids in Africa, where diesel generators are the main alternative to such problem. The NVI consists of providing solar power technology to such organizations, offering a leasing model so they can pay per month and avoid upfront costs.

The entrepreneur relied on his educational background in economics and political economy, as well as on his previous work experiences in international organizations. His background contributed a great extent to the formation of this NVI.

Data collection

Interviews were the main source of data for this study. Prior to the conduction of the interviews, we developed a case study protocol, an interview guide, and carried out a pilot study with one entrepreneur (Yin, 2013). Once we tested the interview guide, we refined our questions in such a way that it was relatable to respondents, while still appropriate for our topics of interest.

All interviews were conducted in the English language and lasted, on average, one hour. Following a semi-structured format, informants were asked, for instance, about their prior work experiences and educational background, about the emergence of their venture ideas, and whether their ideas had changed over time, and how. They were also asked about challenging situations during the development of their ideas, and how they dealt with these. The interviews provided us with rich accounts of how their venture ideas emerged and changed over time, as well as allowing us to identify the learning situations throughout this process.

The interview data was combined with registry data on firms, the new ventures' websites, and LinkedIn information on entrepreneurs. Such alternative sources of data served the purpose of validating the interviews. The interviews were subsequently transcribed in Nvivo v.11 software, which was used for the analysis of the data, in combination with Excel 2013.

Data analysis

The cases have been analyzed by the coding of data into categories—each individual case was analyzed separately, and this was followed by a cross-case analysis. The data was organized in a "case-ordered descriptive meta-matrix" (Miles et al., 2013), which consists of the ordering of cases according to selected criteria to compare common variables. The analytical focus was on the interplays between the learning of the entrepreneurs and the NVI development. This analysis sought to unravel the mutual interactions between the learning of entrepreneurs (actor components) and the NVI (non-actor component). While this analytical focus stemmed from entrepreneurial learning literature, as well as from recent theorizing on entrepreneurial opportunities, the relationships between *learning→NVI development→learning→NVI development* were achieved by an inductive approach to the data (Eisenhardt, 1989).

For building the data matrix, we identified, from the interview data, the events with relevance to both the learning of the entrepreneur and the NVI development. Thereafter, we coded the type of learning involved in these instances, as well as the implication for the NVI as a means–ends relationship. After carrying this out for each individual case, we proceeded to a cross-case analysis. At this point, we could identify significant characteristics of the NVI development as well as of the learning processes of the entrepreneurs. Having identified such characteristics, interplays between them were explored.

Results and discussions

New venture ideas

The NVI in our sample were different in relation to how specified they were at the beginning of their development. There was a difference between the NVI with initially well-specified means from the ones with well-specified ends. Some cases had an initial NVI that was well-formulated on the supply-side (or means-side), but largely unspecified on the demand-side (or ends-side), whereas other cases had an initial NVI that was well-formulated on the demand-side, but unspecified on the supply-side.

The NVI for PharmaX, LaKs, and LibrT contained a high level of specialized knowledge about their respective technologies. As such, they were specified on the means-side, to a large extent, from the very beginning. As an example, the technology being explored by PharmaX consisted of a method for producing proteins from bacteria. This technology, originally developed as a research tool, was found to have potential commercial application, hence the initial NVI consisted of an existing, well-established technology with promising, yet vague market applications. The following quotation illustrates this:

> It started out as basic research with no intention of getting commercialization or generating anything of commercial value. It started as pure basic research to understand how bacteria synthetize proteins. To aid this research, this technology was developed, not to be used commercially but just as a research tool and it turned out that this technology could also be used at industrial levels and hence it had a commercial value, but that was completely unintentional, but when it was discovered that this tool could also be used commercially, the research became more applied. (VT, PharmaX)

The other NVI with well-specified means also contained a high-level of specialized knowledge about existing technologies. Additionally, they were shared by different actors, and this knowledge was codified to a larger extent. In the PharmaX example, other researchers working with the same technology could have conceived of similar or even the same NVI. These NVI were therefore already largely independent from the entrepreneurs from the very beginning of the process.

In contrast, the NVI for iTech, Msport, and SolEn contained extensive knowledge about customer problems. As such, they were specified on the ends-side, to a large extent, from the start. As an example, the customer problem being addressed by SolEn stemmed from the entrepreneur's work experiences in international organizations such as the United Nations. Through such experiences, the entrepreneur realized that these organizations could benefit from alternative sources of electricity, given the lack of reliable electrical grids in the places where they operated. The initial NVI was therefore largely shaped by the entrepreneur's pre-entry experiences, and hence it consisted of a well-specified customer problem with a vague solution to such problem:

> After I worked for the Norwegian ministry of foreign affairs, I started working for the UN first in Sudan and later on in New York at their headquarters there. That brought me to September when I started (the firm) with a colleague from the World Bank. The idea around (the firm) was something that evolved over the years, it was something that I had thought of when I was in Sudan in 2013, where diesel generators were widely used, so organizations that require electricity, they use diesel generators to compensate for the lack of reliable electrical grids. These generators require a lot of resources from the organization both because they require constant diesel, but also because they require

maintenance and service, so with the development of solar systems or solar technology, our idea is that it is a cheaper and more reliable option compared to diesel. . . (KE, SolEn)

The other NVI with well-specified ends were also more intertwined with the pre-entry knowledge and experiences of the entrepreneurs in the beginning of their development. In the SolEn example, as the knowledge involved in the NVI was for the most part tacit and difficult to share with others, it was more dependent on the entrepreneur at the beginning of the process. However, even for these NVI, other individuals with similar work experiences could have conceived of similar ideas.

Despite how they started, it was possible to see a distinction between the entrepreneurs' learning (actor component) and the NVI (non-actor component) in all six cases. Moreover, the NVI were not contingent on the outcome of the entrepreneurial process. The ideas were still under development and the outcome of such process was unknown. Theorizing on the interplays between the entrepreneurs and NVI was thus possible. This would not have been possible with the opportunity construct because it requires success. As such, we argue that it is much preferable to adopt the sub-construct of NVI, in prospective studies, to represent one important artifact acted upon by entrepreneurs, instead of the opportunity construct, as the latter inherently carries the notion of favorability.

Consequently, the cases provide support for a recent view of the 'opportunity' construct, as advanced by Davidsson (2015). In this view, the 'opportunity' construct is divided into three sub-constructs: external enablers, the NVI, and opportunity confidence. The cases explored in this chapter illustrated the nexus between one actor and one non-actor component, namely the interplays between entrepreneurs' learning and the NVI. The NVI refers to an imagined future venture, cognized by the individual entrepreneur and/or by the entrepreneurial team (Davidsson, 2015). Even though NVI are, for the most part, in the realm of cognition, all the NVI being developed by the entrepreneurs in our sample had been tested in practice. These NVI therefore represented the actual development of the idea over time, in interaction with stakeholders.

NVI development process

The six NVI were developed from a rudimentary means–ends relationship to a more specified one. In line with Dimov (2007) and Sarason et al. (2006), results showed that the NVI, instead of being the result of a single insight from the entrepreneurs, actually emerged over time through the continuous shaping of a rudimentary initial idea into a more developed one. In this process, the NVI were also shaped from contextual influences, where entrepreneurs interacted with different stakeholders and had to deal with contingencies.

The initial specification of either the means or ends-side of the NVI divided their development process into two distinctive paths: (1) the search for potential market applications, for the NVI building upon existing technology; or (2) the development of solutions to customers' problems, for the NVI building upon entrepreneurs' pre-entry knowledge and experiences. For PharmaX, LaKs, and LibrT, the development started with creation processes (technology), and this was followed by discovery processes (searching for market applications). For iTech, Msport, and SolEn, the development started with discovery processes (customers' problems), and this was followed by creation processes (development of solutions).

Consequently, the cases provide support for the view of opportunities as both discovered and created (Garud and Giuliani, 2013; Venkataraman et al., 2012), and help dissolve the dichotomy between the two predominant views on entrepreneurial opportunities. Rather than being opposites, the discovery and the creation views, having very different definitions over the opportunity concept, engage in different discussions. While the discovery view defines opportunities as objective external conditions, the creation view defines them as the process or result of entrepreneurs' action. These two definitions, however, do not exclude each other. They are complementary in that individual action and external conditions are always present in the entrepreneurship process.

At the same time, there were instances when both sides of the NVI underwent changes as a result of new knowledge being acquired during their development process. Taking LaKs as an example, the NVI was also changed on the means-side due to the need of co-development of the technology (despite the fact that its NVI started with well-defined means). LaKs operates within the salmon farming industry, and its NVI consists of a platform that can run different types of tests with salmon fish. As the platform had not been applied in this industry before, the NVI required not only the identification of specific customers' problems, but also the co-development of the technology. Technical complexity increased as entrepreneurs aimed to achieve higher commercial value. At the same time, however, they needed to ensure technical feasibility, which required further work with the technology. Both sides of this NVI, as a means–ends relationship, were therefore developed, at times.

New venture idea development as a learning process

The six NVI were poorly defined and in a rough form in the beginning of the process. Similarly, entrepreneurs' initial knowledge-base and set of experiences, while important for triggering the start of the entrepreneurial process, were not sufficient for dealing with all the events that unfolded thereafter. This dual development process was noticeable for all cases. The NVI were modified, changed, and refined during such process. Likewise, the entrepreneurs' knowledge base was improved upon, refined, combined with complementary knowledge and skills, and replaced by newly created knowledge.

Entrepreneurs frequently described the development of their NVI as a learning process: "every step you take gets you into a new area of knowledge" (DG, iTech). They often described the different stages or events in the development process as triggers for learning. As such, the progress of the NVI development required learning from the entrepreneur, and this learning fed back into the NVI development, pushing the process forward. Both the NVI and the knowledge-base of the entrepreneur were developed over time and in interaction with each other. The NVI triggered the learning of the entrepreneurs at several occasions, and the learning of the entrepreneurs contributed to their further development.

The entrepreneurs learned continuously throughout the NVI development. Entrepreneurs' knowledge was derived from their pre-entry experiences and they were also tested and reshaped in post-entry experiences. At the same time that entrepreneurs' pre-entry experiences facilitated learning, they were unreliable at times. This is because many new events unfolded during the new venture creation process—some of these events fell within entrepreneurs' initial pool of experiences and knowledge, while others fell close to the borderline, and others completely outside of this pool. Therefore, entrepreneurs' learning was not always a linear, neat, cohesive, cumulative process where they ended up with more usable knowledge and better prepared for subsequent challenges. This is aligned with ELT, which advances that learning occurs precisely at the intersection between expectation and experience. That is, individuals always carry pre-formed knowledge and expectations to new situations, which means that all adult learning is essentially re-learning in the form of validation, refinement, or replacement of old beliefs (Kolb, 2014).

This chapter, by acknowledging that learning is non-cumulative at times, calls attention to the problem of adopting a static view to entrepreneurs' learning. ELT has been applied in entrepreneurship literature mainly in a static way. The problem with this is the underlying assumption that learning is cumulative, i.e. the more knowledge and experiences accumulated, the better the performance of the entrepreneur in a number of different activities. In contrast, the process view allows the possibility for learning to result in non-usable knowledge, and it also acknowledges that experiences can be confusing and ambiguous. As such, we argue for a more nuanced application of ELT in entrepreneurship—one that recognizes the importance of ongoing experiences in the new venture creation process and the possibility of experiences leading to non-useful knowledge.

The social context in NVI development

The social context within which the NVI development took place influenced the learning processes of the entrepreneurs to a large extent. Not only did the entrepreneurs engage in individual learning, transforming experiences into knowledge throughout the process (Kolb, 2014), but they also learned in interaction with others.

One predominant social context for PharmaX and LaKs was the academic research community. In the former case, the entrepreneur started to develop the NVI while undertaking a PhD in biotechnology. In the latter case, the firm had two lead entrepreneurs. One of them was a researcher within biosciences and aquaculture, and the other had extensive work experience in the salmon farming industry. In both cases, such an environment contributed to a dynamic and interactive learning process. Looking at this environment from a community of practice perspective (Klein et al., 2005), the academic environment is generally characterized by a high degree of knowledge-sharing activities and an egalitarian distribution of power among its members. As such, the learning processes of the entrepreneur were characterized by multiple, dynamic interactions with the members of this community. At the same time, both cases interacted with other people outside academia, e.g. potential customers, investors, and other stakeholders. PharmaX had loose ties to several potential customers, whereas LaKs had strong ties with one trusted customer. For PharmaX, however, these other interactions were not as important in the NVI development process as the interactions within academia. In contrast, for LaKs, the interactions with the one trusted customer were very important.

Similarly, the NVI development process for LibrT and Msport was embedded in an educational setting. In both cases, the entrepreneurs were part of an entrepreneurship master program, in which students are encouraged to start new firms. This master program is also characterized by a high-level of knowledge-sharing activities. However, the distribution of power within such context was slightly different than that of the last two cases. As students, these entrepreneurs experienced a higher level of power imbalance. Of course, knowledge was exchanged in many directions (students–professors; professors–students; students–students, etc.), but still the distribution of power in this setting was not perfectly egalitarian. In that respect, the learning process of these two entrepreneurs was interactive, but more rigid than the first two cases. Through the university LibrT had access to one important partner, which was the developer of the technology being explored by the firm. Similarly, Msport had access to valuable research-based knowledge—for instance, access to the university's research on the habits of Norwegians in regard to physical activity, as well as research on particular physical exercises and their health benefits.

On the other hand, for iTech and SolEn the development of the NVI was not strongly embedded in any particular social context. Despite multiple interactions with potential customers and technology stakeholders, these NVI were, to a large extent, developed internally in these ventures. This contributed to a more individualistic learning process for these two entrepreneurs.

Social learning was more often than not a pervasive process for the entrepreneurs. This not only helped them cope with ambiguity, but it also helped them develop their entrepreneurial identities (especially the novice). When entrepreneurs interacted with others, their learning shifted away from their minds into the arena of social relations, where conflicts take place and power relations matter (Blackler and McDonald, 2000). Consequently their learning not only consisted of acquiring/processing knowledge, but it also consisted of becoming part of a social system (Cook and Brown, 1999). As such, their knowledge was often distributed and negotiated with others in the larger environment.

By recognizing the importance of social learning activities for entrepreneurs, this chapter contributes to the discussion about the locus of learning. Entrepreneurial learning (EL) literature usually works under the assumption that the locus of learning lies either on individuals or on organizations. When borrowing from individual learning theories, EL literature emphasizes changes in behavior and/or entrepreneurs' cognitive processes (e.g. Matlay et al., 2012, Holcomb et al., 2009). In contrast, when borrowing from organizational learning theories, EL literature highlights that individuals do not learn in a vacuum; rather, they learn within organizational contexts, in which the individual learns from the organization and the organization learns from the individual (e.g. March, 1991).

This chapter, by illustrating the presence of both individual and social learning activities within the new venture creation process, shows that learning can be both an individual as well as a supra-individual activity taking place in a social context. This is compatible with ELT because the incorporation of social, cultural, historical, and political factors in its discourse about how individuals learn actually enhances the understanding of experiential learning (Kolb, 2014). As such, we argue that the field of EL would benefit from a stronger combination of individual and social learning theories.

Interplays between the new venture idea development and learning

A noticeable characteristic of the NVI development was how the missing side of the NVI was developed. This process was either open or focused. It was open during the search for market applications and also when the development of solutions to customers' problems was carried out in an exploratory way. Figure 10.1 illustrates such interplays.

PharmaX and LibrT, with NVI well-specified on the means-side, were very open in relation to which industries (and customers within a given industry) could become the target for their offerings:

> . . .so we started the company but were not sure exactly what was our target market because there was so many [. . .] so the big question then was which segments to target, should we target pharmaceutical sector? Or production of drugs? Or should we target the production of enzymes industry? And this is something that we weren't really sure, and I think we went out pretty broad at the beginning, in the sense that okay let's see where we could get some traction and then we can narrow down the focus. (VT, PharmaX)

Likewise, Msport, with a NVI well-specified on the ends-side, was quite open in how to address customers' problems:

> . . .we gave them a task, it was 137 students gathered from the middle of Norway and Sweden to work in 24 hours, and it was to solve the inactivity problem for 16-year-old Norwegians because they are 2nd place in the world in sitting still, they are almost world leader in inactivity so the trend is like this, so we ask them, find a solution for this and they

196

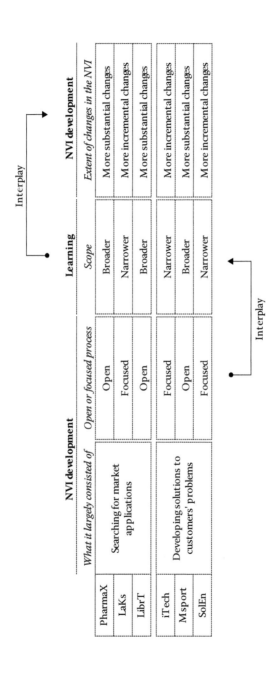

Source: Author's own composition.

Figure 10.1 Interplays between the NVI development and learning

came up with a lot of ideas [. . .] so they presented 37 different commercial solutions and three of the ideas were so good that we think we want to take them and put them in our concept, and this is an example of how we work. . . (MW, Msport)

On the other hand, this process was focused when market applications as well as solutions to customer problems were sought in a directed way. LaKs, with a NVI well-specified on the means-side, was very focused in relation to its targeted industry and customers, and one important reason for this was the work experiences of one of the entrepreneurs within the targeted industry:

> I have worked in the salmon farming industry and my business partner has been a lecturer for 18 years now, and a lot of his students are now in leadership positions. It is easier to get out to them if you know them in advance. That is how we have our first customer, it is a company I used to work for before I was a student, so they are really helping us but it is because they know us from before. (BV, LaKs)

iTech and SolEn, with a NVI well-specified on the ends-side, were also focused in developing solutions to their customers' problems. What influenced their focused efforts was the presence of pre-entry knowledge and experiences on a preferred solution. The following quotation illustrates this:

> . . .so in my case it's a lot about the combination of my background having 25–30 years as a manager, being a process control engineer [. . .] I had the technological knowledge as I was educated in engineering and process control [. . .] and also having worked with analytic tools and making those kind of tools, and then you combine things from different areas. . . (DG, iTech)

In turn, this characteristic of the NVI development (open or focused process) influenced the scope of learning of the entrepreneurs. When the process was open, the scope of their learning was broader. Taking LibrT as an example, by searching broadly for market applications, the entrepreneur's learning involved testing the technology in different industries. By interacting with potential customers in different industries, the entrepreneur developed knowledge about customers' problems on a broader level:

> . . .it is hard to learn from your. . .on the sales side, I think we have done quite good, it took much more time to get the first customers than we believed and now it is much faster, and the customer did not necessarily come from where we thought it would come from. . . (TD, LibrT)

On the other hand, when the process was focused, the scope of entrepreneurs' learning was narrower. Taking LaKs as an example, by searching narrowly for market applications the entrepreneurs' learning involved testing the technology with one trusted customer in one single industry where one of the entrepreneurs had previously worked. By doing so, the entrepreneurs developed knowledge about customers' problems on a specific level:

> ...we had just one trusted customer and we have a signed agreement with him [...] we have done a project testing if this could actually be done. We made a system and tested it in a farm, very simple system, and we have access to the lab in the salmon farm and we put some cheap equipment [...] we put it there and run tests in the lab there. (BV, LaKs)

Consequently, this characteristic of the learning of the entrepreneurs (scope) fed back to the development process of their NVI, influencing the extent of changes in their ideas (magnitude). A broader scope of learning resulted in more substantial changes in the NVI. For instance, PharmaX had a major change to the NVI when the ends-side of the idea was specified:

> The original idea was to build the company to out license this technology. The aspect that has changed is who we are targeting, we started out with this broad... going out and targeting all companies and seeing where we could get deals and then focusing on those, and now we have become a very targeted pharmaceutical supplier... (VT, PharmaX)

On the other hand, a narrower scope of learning resulted in more incremental changes to the NVI. As an example, SolEn modified the ends-side of the NVI slightly (choice to focus on international organizations with less bureaucratic procedures), and refined how the solution would be delivered to customers (by opting for a collaboration with a technical partner to procure and design the solar panel systems instead of doing this internally):

> I think it became much more nuanced overtime, so our initial idea was fairly vague [...] so what we've done is we focus on the clients that have less bureaucratic procurement procedures [...] we have adjusted our business plan a little bit in terms of how much of the responsibility we take on as a company and how much we partner with other organizations, so initially we thought we would do all the procurement and design of the systems ourselves and do all these installations or be responsible for the installations and where we have moved into is that we want to have local partners that do the installation for us... (KE, SolEn)

In sum, the NVI, being initially well-specified either on the means- or on the ends-side, triggered the search for market applications or the development of solutions to customers' problems, respectively. This process was either open or focused, which determined the scope of learning for the entrepreneurs (broader or narrower). By learning broadly, the entrepreneurs implemented more substantial changes to the NVI (as a means–ends relationship). In contrast, when they learned in a narrower way, entrepreneurs implemented more incremental changes to the NVI.

These interplays between the NVI development and entrepreneurs' learning is, admittedly, a simplification of such process. The authors acknowledge that the linearity implied in Figure 10.1. is likely to be more complex and intertwined in reality. Moreover, the causal direction between *NVI development→learning→NVI development* needs testing and further refinement. In addition, the authors acknowledge that other factors may influence the scope of learning for entrepreneurs, as well as the extent of changes in the NVI. In regard to the former, entrepreneurs' individual preference for a generalist vs. specialist learning style may have played a role in their scope of learning, for instance. In regard to the latter, regulatory changes, for example, may have influenced the triggering of more substantial changes to the NVI. Lastly, the temporal boundaries of the NVI have been assumed as quite open. Different from existing conceptualizations that treat them as the most incomplete mental representation of a new venture, our interpretation is that NVI includes well-developed business ideas, as well as ideas that have been tested out in practice.

Conclusion

This chapter has worked with a more precise definition for EL, as extant literature usually defines the concept too broadly and inconsistently. We propose that "entrepreneurial learning" should be conceptualized as the learning of entrepreneurs in relation to an opportunity development process. Concurrently, we have adopted a definition for the opportunity construct that recognizes its objective and subjective sides—the objective side consists of non-actor components, e.g. external situations and NVI; the subjective side refers to actor components, e.g. entrepreneurs' actions (Davidsson, 2015). In particular, we have highlighted the interplays between one non-actor component (the NVI) and one actor-component (entrepreneurs' learning).

We have looked at such interplays in an exploratory way. As such, they are to be seen as potential relationships to be further developed in future studies. Despite the entangled nature of entrepreneurs' learning and the NVI development process, we argue that it is still possible to conceptually separate them and to theorize on how they are co-developed over time. Moreover, we encourage theorizing on the interplays between other actor and non-actor components, e.g. between external situations (such as technological changes) and the decision-making processes of entrepreneurs.

This study is not without limitations. As a first step into analyzing the mutual interplays between the opportunity development and the learning of the entrepreneur, this chapter has built on retrospective data and one informant per case. Future studies should validate these findings using longitudinal approaches and more detailed case studies. Particularly, as a large share of new technology based ventures are started by entrepreneurial teams, it will be particularly interesting to examine how the learning of several team members in interaction influences and is influenced by the opportunity development process. An entrepreneurial team does not only represent a social context of the individual members for learning, but because they work jointly on the development of an NVI, there is likely to also be learning at the team level. Extending the concept of entrepreneurial learning to account for how entrepreneurial teams learn seems to be a potentially fruitful direction of future research. This raises questions such as: what is the relationship between individual learning and team learning? How is team learning triggered in the process of NVI development? How is the NVI influenced by individual as well as team learning during the development process?

This study has shown that entrepreneurs learn in interaction with the development of an NVI. This interaction process does not take place in a vacuum. It is influenced by the social context in which the entrepreneur(s) are embedded. Our findings indicate that learning can both be an individual and a supra-individual activity taking place in a social context. Hence, we call for integration of individual and social learning theories. Relevant questions for future research include: when does the NVI development process facilitate entrepreneurial learning, and when is learning hampered? Are there some ways of approaching NVI development that better facilitate learning of the entrepreneur? When does the learning of the entrepreneur contribute substantially to NVI development, and when is the transfer of learning into a changed NVI hampered? We encourage further research on the mechanisms of learning and idea development.

To conclude, this chapter contributes to EL literature and to the discussion about opportunities by exploring the mutual relationships between entrepreneurs' learning and one important artifact they act upon (NVI). The authors advocate for a closer connection between the learning of entrepreneurial individuals and the artifacts they act upon, as well as the larger environment.

References

Alvarez, S. A. and Barney, J. B. 2007. Discovery and creation: Alternative theories of entrepreneurial action. *Strategic Entrepreneurship Journal*, 1, 11–26.

Becot, F., Conner, D. and Kolodinsky, J. 2015. Where do agri-food entrepreneurs learn their job and are there skills they wished they had learned? *International Journal of Entrepreneurship and Innovation*, 16, 207–15.

Berglund, H., Hellström, T. and Sjölander, S. 2007. Entrepreneurial learning and the role of venture capitalists. *Venture Capital*, 9, 165–81.

Bingham, C. B., Eisenhardt, K. M. and Furr, N. R. 2007. What makes a process a capability? Heuristics, strategy, and effective capture of opportunities. *Strategic Entrepreneurship Journal*, 1, 27–47.

Blackler, F. and McDonald, S. 2000. Power, mastery and organizational learning. *Journal of Management Studies*, 37, 833–52.

Box, T. M., White, M. A. and Barr, S. H. 1993. A contingency model of new manufacturing firm performance. *Entrepreneurship Theory & Practice*, 18, 31.

Cook, S. D. and Brown, J. S. 1999. Bridging epistemologies: The generative dance between organizational knowledge and organizational knowing. *Organization Science*, 10, 381–400.

Cooper, A. C., Gimeno-Gascon, F. J. and Woo, C. Y. 1994. Initial human and financial capital as predictors of new venture performance. *Journal of Business Venturing*, 9, 371–95.

Cope, J. 2005. Toward a dynamic learning perspective of entrepreneurship. *Entrepreneurship Theory & Practice*, 29, 373–97.

Cope, J. 2011. Entrepreneurial learning from failure: An interpretative phenomenological analysis. *Journal of Business Venturing*, 26, 604–23.

Corbett, A. C. 2005. Experiential learning within the process of opportunity identification and exploitation. *Entrepreneurship Theory & Practice*, 29, 473–91.

Corbett, A. C. 2007. Learning asymmetries and the discovery of entrepreneurial opportunities. *Journal of Business Venturing*, 22, 97–118.

Davidsson, P. 2015. Entrepreneurial opportunities and the entrepreneurship nexus: A re-conceptualization. *Journal of Business Venturing*, 30, 674–95.

Delmar, F. and Shane, S. 2006. Does experience matter? The effect of founding team experience on the survival and sales of newly founded ventures. *Strategic Organization*, 4, 215–47.

Dencker, J. C., Gruber, M. and Shah, S. K. 2009. Pre-entry knowledge, learning, and the survival of new firms. *Organization Science*, 20, 516–37.

Dimov, D. 2007. Beyond the single-person, single-insight attribution in understanding entrepreneurial opportunities. *Entrepreneurship Theory & Practice*, 31, 713–31.

Dimov, D. 2011. Grappling with the unbearable elusiveness of entrepreneurial opportunities. *Entrepreneurship Theory & Practice*, 35, 57–81.

Dubois, A. and Gadde, L.-E. 2002. Systematic combining: An abductive approach to case research. *Journal of Business Research*, 55, 553–60.

Dutta, D. K. and Crossan, M. M. 2005. The nature of entrepreneurial opportunities: Understanding the process using the 4I organizational learning framework. *Entrepreneurship Theory & Practice*, 29, 425–49.

Eckhardt, J. T. and Shane, S. A. 2003. Opportunities and entrepreneurship. *Journal of Management*, 29, 333–49.

Eckhardt, J. T. and Shane, S. A. 2013. Response to the commentaries: The individual–opportunity (IO) nexus integrates objective and subjective aspects of entrepreneurship. *Academy of Management Review*, 38, 160–63.

Eisenhardt, K. M. 1989. Building theories from case study research. *Academy of Management Review*, 14, 532–50.

Fang, S.-C., Tsai, F.-S. and Lin, J. L. 2010. Leveraging tenant-incubator social capital for organizational learning and performance in incubation programme. *International Small Business Journal*, 28, 90–113.

Franco, M. and Haase, H. 2009. Entrepreneurship: An organisational learning approach. *Journal of Small Business and Enterprise Development*, 16, 628–41.

Gabrielsson, J. and Politis, D. 2012. Work experience and the generation of new business ideas among entrepreneurs: An integrated learning framework. *International Journal of Entrepreneurial Behavior & Research*, 18, 48–74.

Gaglio, C. M. 2004. The role of mental simulations and counterfactual thinking in the opportunity identification process. *Entrepreneurship Theory & Practice*, 28, 533–52.

Garud, R. and Giuliani, A. P. 2013. A narrative perspective on entrepreneurial opportunities. *Academy of Management Review*, 38, 157–60.

Gruber, M., Macmillan, I. C. and Thompson, J. D. 2008. Look before you leap: Market opportunity identification in emerging technology firms. *Management Science*, 54, 1652–65.

Gruber, M., Macmillan, I. C. and Thompson, J. D. 2013. Escaping the prior knowledge corridor: What shapes the number and variety of market opportunities identified before market entry of technology start-ups? *Organization Science*, 24, 280–300.

Hajizadeh, A. and Zali, M. 2016. Prior knowledge, cognitive characteristics and opportunity recognition. *International Journal of Entrepreneurial Behavior & Research*, 22, 63–83.

Holcomb, T. R., Ireland, R. D., Holmes Jr, R. M. and Hitt, M. A. 2009. Architecture of entrepreneurial learning: Exploring the link among heuristics, knowledge, and action. *Entrepreneurship Theory & Practice*, 33, 167–92.

Huovinen, J. and Tihula, S. 2008. Entrepreneurial learning in the context of portfolio entrepreneurship. *International Journal of Entrepreneurial Behavior & Research*, 14, 152–71.

Kauppinen, A. and Juho, A. 2012. Internationalisation of SMEs from the perspective of social learning theory. *Journal of International Entrepreneurship*, 10, 200–31.

Klein, J. H., Connell, N. and Meyer, E. 2005. Knowledge characteristics of communities of practice. *Knowledge Management Research & Practice*, 3, 106–14.

Kolb, D. A. 2014. *Experiential Learning: Experience as the Source of Learning and Development*. London: Pearson Education.

Lamont, L. M. 1972. What entrepreneurs learn from experience. *Journal of Small Business Management (pre-1986)*, 10, 36.

Lee, R. and Jones, O. 2008. Networks, communication and learning during business start-up: The creation of cognitive social capital. *International Small Business Journal*, 26, 559–94.

Lumpkin, G. T. and Lichtenstein, B. B. 2005. The role of organizational learning in the opportunity-recognition process. *Entrepreneurship Theory & Practice*, 29, 451–72.

March, J. G. 1991. Exploration and exploitation in organizational learning. *Organization Science*, 2, 71–87.

Matlay, H., Rae, D. and Wing Yan Man, T. 2012. Developing a behaviour-centred model of entrepreneurial learning. *Journal of Small Business and Enterprise Development*, 19, 549–66.

McCann, B. T. and Vroom, G. 2015. Opportunity evaluation and changing beliefs during the nascent entrepreneurial process. *International Small Business Journal*, 33, 612–37.

Merriam, S. B. and Bierema, L. L. 2013. *Adult Learning: Linking Theory and Practice*. New York, NY: John Wiley & Sons.

Miles, M. B., Huberman, A. M. and Saldaña, J. 2013. *Qualitative Data Analysis*. Thousand Oaks, CA: SAGE.

Miller, J. I. 2012. The mortality problem of learning and mimetic practice in emerging industries: Dying to be legitimate. *Strategic Entrepreneurship Journal*, 6, 59–88.

Minniti, M. and Bygrave, W. 2001. A dynamic model of entrepreneurial learning. *Entrepreneurship Theory & Practice*, 25, 5–16.

Mueller, B. A. and Shepherd, D. A. 2016. Making the most of failure experiences: Exploring the relationship between business failure and the identification of business opportunities. *Entrepreneurship Theory & Practice*, 40, 457–87.

Politis, D. 2005. The process of entrepreneurial learning: A conceptual framework. *Entrepreneurship Theory & Practice*, 29, 399–424.

Politis, D. 2008. Does prior start-up experience matter for entrepreneurs' learning? A comparison between novice and habitual entrepreneurs. *Journal of Small Business and Enterprise Development*, 15, 472–89.

Politis, D. and Gabrielsson, J. 2009. Entrepreneurs' attitudes towards failure: An experiential learning approach. *International Journal of Entrepreneurial Behavior & Research*, 15, 364–83.

Rae, D. 2000. Understanding entrepreneurial learning: A question of how? *International Journal of Entrepreneurial Behavior & Research*, 6, 145–59.

Rae, D. 2005. Entrepreneurial learning: A narrative-based conceptual model. *Journal of Small Business and Enterprise Development*, 12, 323–35.

Rae, D. 2006. Entrepreneurial learning: A conceptual framework for technology-based enterprise. *Technology Analysis & Strategic Management*, 18, 39–56.

Rae, D. and Carswell, M. 2001. Towards a conceptual understanding of entrepreneurial learning. *Journal of Small Business and Enterprise Development*, 8, 150–58.

Rae, D. and Wang, C. L. 2015. *Entrepreneurial Learning: New Perspectives in Research, Education and Practice*. Abingdon, UK: Taylor & Francis.

Ravasi, D. and Turati, C. 2005. Exploring entrepreneurial learning: A comparative study of technology development projects. *Journal of Business Venturing*, 20, 137–64.

Reuber, A. R. and Fischer, E. 1999. Understanding the consequences of founders' experience. *Journal of Small Business Management*, 37, 30–45.

Sarason, Y., Dean, T. and Dillard, J. F. 2006. Entrepreneurship as the nexus of individual and opportunity: A structuration view. *Journal of Business Venturing*, 21, 286–305.

Sarasvathy, S. D., Dew, N., Velamuri, S. R. and Venkataraman, S. 2010. Three views of entrepreneurial opportunity. In Z. J. Acs and D. B. Audretsch (Eds), *Handbook of Entrepreneurship Research*. New York: Springer, pp. 77–96.

Sardana, D. and Scott-Kemmis, D. 2010. Who learns what? A study based on entrepreneurs from bio-technology new ventures. *Journal of Small Business Management*, 48, 441–68.

Shane, S. 2000. Prior knowledge and the discovery of entrepreneurial opportunities. *Organization Science*, 11, 448–69.

Shane, S. 2012. Reflections on the 2010 AMR decade award: Delivering on the promise of entrepreneurship as a field of research. *Academy of Management Review*, 37, 10–20.

Shane, S. and Venkataraman, S. 2000. The promise of entrepreneurship as a field of research. *Academy of Management Review*, 25, 217–26.

Snihur, Y., Reiche, B. S. and Quintane, E. 2017. Sustaining actor engagement during the opportunity development process. *Strategic Entrepreneurship Journal*, 11, 1–17.

Thorpe, R., Gold, J., Holt, R. and Clarke, J. 2006. Immaturity: The constraining of entrepreneurship. *International Small Business Journal*, 24, 232–50.

Venkataraman, S., Sarasvathy, S. D., Dew, N. and Forster, W. R. 2012. Reflections on the 2010 AMR decade award: Whither the promise? Moving forward with entrepreneurship as a science of the artificial. *Academy of Management Review*, 37, 21–33.

Vogel, P. 2016. From venture idea to venture opportunity. *Entrepreneurship Theory & Practice*. doi:10.1111/etap.12234.

Voudouris, I., Dimitratos, P. and Salavou, H. 2011. Entrepreneurial learning in the international new high-technology venture. *International Small Business Journal*, doi:0266242610369739.

Wang, C. L. and Chugh, H. 2014. Entrepreneurial learning: Past research and future challenges. *International Journal of Management Reviews*, 16, 24–61.

Westhead, P., Ucbasaran, D. and Wright, M. 2005. Decisions, actions, and performance: Do novice, serial, and portfolio entrepreneurs differ? *Journal of Small Business Management*, 43, 393–417.

Westhead, P. and Wright, M. 2011. David Storey's optimism and chance perspective: A case of the emperor's new clothes? *International Small Business Journal*, doi:0266242611424552.

Wiklund, J., Davidsson, P., Audretsch, D. B. and Karlsson, C. 2011. The future of entrepreneurship research. *Entrepreneurship Theory & Practice*, 35, 1–9.

Yin, R. K. 2013. *Case Study Research: Design and Methods*. Thousand Oaks, CA: SAGE.

Young, J. E. and Sexton, D. L. 2003. What makes entrepreneurs learn and how do they do it? *Journal of Entrepreneurship*, 12, 155–82.

11 Entrepreneurial language through a linguistic lens: emerging opportunities

Diana M. Hechavarría and Amy Ingram

Introduction

A breadth of studies in entrepreneurship has highlighted the importance of narratives and discourse as a window into the thoughts and actions of the entrepreneur (e.g. Gartner, 2007, 2010; Garud and Giuliani, 2013; Hjorth and Steyaert, 2004; Venkataraman et al., 2013). This rich strand of research has led to greater insights about the entrepreneurial process, including how entrepreneurs think. These studies showcase the importance of the entrepreneurial language because the words individuals speak are proxies of their thoughts that guide their behaviors. Moreover, entrepreneurial narratives and discourses are how "entrepreneurs communicate their theories of practices to others" (Gartner and Ingram, 2013), and thus help researchers glean practical insight into the entrepreneurs' world. Naturally, the words and language used by entrepreneurs can therefore be examined to glean insights about underlying cognitive factors which drive entrepreneurial intention and action during the complex process of new venture creation. More recently, work in entrepreneurship, although rare, has begun to lever linguistic lenses to understand how language influences entrepreneurial behavior. Linguistic theories and analysis build upon and extend the discursive and narrative analysis, stemming from the "linguistic turn" in organizational and entrepreneurship studies (Ruebottom, 2013; Pollach, 2012). Linguistics differs from narratives and discourse analysis, and is the scientific study of language, focusing on the actual structure of language, patterns, word grouping, among other areas, to demonstrate how the language an actor uses can impact many decisions including economic decisions, and it is an important influential intuitional force (Terjesen et al., 2016). Indeed, North (2005, p. 39) emphasizes "the fundamental building blocks of a culture begin with the languages whose categories and vocabulary reflect the cumulative experience of society and thus, via culture, it is likely that language influences entrepreneurial activity." Reinforcing this, Boroditsky and Gaby (2010) find that language structure influences socio-economic outcomes and choices and because entrepreneurs strive to create certain socio-economic outcomes via new ventures, it is important to explore the words entrepreneurs use. As such, because language is central to human interaction, shaping thoughts and behaviors, it is surprising that limited focus has been given to the interplay among linguistics and entrepreneurship.

Language via a linguistic lens

Language is a complex sign structure, created by humans, of words or signs that are combined into a meaning for the interpreter (Saussure, 1970). In order to deal with the fact that words may have different meanings not just across cultures but also within cultures, some help may be found in the area of linguistics. Linguistics is the scientific study of language, ranging from the structure of words, sentences and discourse (involving more than one sentence), patterns, syntax structure, and meaning. There are a variety of linguistic disciplines ranging from sociolinguistics, dialectology, psycholinguistics, and applied linguistics that apply a host of methods, with the majority focusing on empirical quantitative analysis of words at various levels of analysis. Accordingly, if language shapes thoughts and action, it is important to understand the impact of different grammatical structures such as phonetics, phonology, morphology, syntax, semantics and pragmatics. Linguistic frames and analysis can help us gain richer insight into the entrepreneur's internal and external worlds because languages are embedded in different cultures that draw upon and use different grammatical resources and structures based upon the dominant language and forms that shape how individuals think (Lucy, 1997).

Extending this, linguists use Linguistic Relativity theory to gain insight into the differential impacts of language as a result of the variety of cultures, societies, and institutions that individuals are embedded in, which impacts the language structure used and how individuals interpret and behave based on these macro structures. Linguistic Relativity theory (Sapir, 1921, 1951; Whorf, 1956; Lucy, 1997) highlights how structural differences in language systems influence how an actor's thoughts and thus actions are a byproduct of their culture. Individuals therefore adopt the language structure of the culture they are embedded in, which also recursively influences the culture. Indeed, this recursive relationship occurs because language influences the way actors interpret and make sense of information in order to make decisions (Boroditsky, 2010, 2011)—because language functions as an institution.

Institutional scholars Richard Scott and Douglass North support the notion of culture as an institution; however, extant research has treated language and culture equally, despite considerable literature outlining clear distinctions (e.g. Kramsch, 1998; for exceptions see Brannen, 2004; West and Graham, 2004). Linguistic Relativity theory emphasizes the distinct role of language structure in interpreting experience and influencing thought, and is different from cultural relativity "which encompasses the full range of patterned, historically transmitted differences among communities" (Lucy, 1997, p. 295). The notion of linguistic structure as a primary institution is supported by Slobin (2001, p. 159): "Communication is embedded in culture, and much of culture is carried—indeed, constructed—by language," and by Levinson and Wilkins (2006, p. 1): "where we have cultural divergences, language may not so much reflect underlying cognition, as actively drive it." North (2005, p. 39) cites work by cognitive neuroscientist Merlin Donald in articulating institutional theory:

The fundamental building blocks of a culture begin with language whose categories and vocabulary reflect the cumulative experience of a society. Merlin Donald asserts that "Other species start at basically the same level with each new generation; not so humans. Semantic content and even the cultural algorithms that support certain kinds of thinking can accumulate, and the symbolic environment can affect the way individual brains deploy their resources. The process of enculturation must have started very slowly, presumably with very gradual increments to a primate knowledge-base, but has evidently accelerated in an exponential manner in the modern period." (Donald, 1991, p. 12)

In the field of linguistics, language is increasingly recognized as an institution. Port (2010, p. 313) argues that "a language is a kind of social institution, that is, a partially structured system of conventions created by a community of speakers and refined over generations. It is a technology developed by a community for coordination of behavior." In economics, Rubinstein (2000) illustrates how formal language shapes economic theories. Taken together, contributions from psychology, sociology, economics, and linguistics suggest that language, specifically the linguistic structure of grammar, is a formative institution that endures and shapes semantics, cognition, and discourse. Political, economic, and other cultural regimes change more frequently and are secondary to the linguistic regime. Language understanding is present from birth—one-year-olds are able to internalize language (Cutler, 2012). Language categorization by lexicon and grammar, as well as by speech gestures and sounds, is shaped over generations (Hock and Joseph, 1996).

Linguistic relativity has been extensively tested in linguistics, with recent reviews (Boroditsky, 2010, 2011; Kay and Kempton, 1984; Gumperz and Levinson, 1996) noting that these studies strongly indicate that languages shape the thoughts we wish to express and that human nature varies tremendously based on language. Although linguistic relativity is extensively debated, even a harsh critic, such as Pinker, acknowledges that "one's language does determine how one must conceptualize reality when one has to talk about it" (Pinker, 1989, p. 360).

For entrepreneurs, therefore, the language they use will ultimately impact the decisions they make surrounding entering entrepreneurship and the management of their ventures. More importantly, research shows variance in entrepreneurship stemming from various cultural, societal, and institutional beliefs, and therefore the language that is dependent upon the culture a person is embedded in will impact how that person thinks about entrepreneurship and their subsequent actions. Linguistics therefore provides opportunities to unpack entrepreneurs' mental lexicons and subsequent actions.

Linguistics and entrepreneurship

There is anecdotal evidence of the importance of linguistics to management practice. Johansson and Strømnes (1995) document that due to the Finnish linguistic structure in which prepositions are represented in two-dimension space with a third dimension of time, Finnish organizations are structured around the worker rather than the overall temporal organization. The structure results in a limited ability to communicate certain processes on the factory floor and thus higher error rates compared to Swedish-speaking counterparts who can use prepositions in three dimensions to represent space. Other studies indicate that certain linguistic structures can impact product experience (Lucy and Gaskins, 2001; Fenko et al., 2010). There are emerging explorations in consumer (Puntoni et al., 2008) and economic (Chen, 2013; Givati and Troiano, 2012) behavior which indicate that grammatical structure is an important consideration.

Linguistic Relativity theory may provide insight into the phenomenon of entre-preneurship. A large body of entrepreneurship indicates the strong presence of a cognitive phenomenon, which is not shared across countries (Mitchell, 2000). Furthermore, an emerging literature in entrepreneurship examines linguistics; however, the focus is on narratives and metaphors, as well as analyses of text, dram-aturgy, and discourse (Hjorth and Steyaert, 2004). Although limited, recent work has pointed out the importance of exploring the language structure to examine how language can either hinder or promote entrepreneurship in various cultures and regions. Studies drawing on Linguistic Relativity in the domain of entrepre-neurship are limited. Recently, work by Hechavarría et al. (2017) found that gen-dered linguistic structures reinforce gender stereotypes and discourage women's entry into entrepreneurship. Specifically, in countries where the dominant lan-guage's structure incorporates sex-based systems and gender-differentiated pro-nouns, there is a greater gender gap in entrepreneurial activity. Additional research by Hechavarría and Ingram (2016) found that language influences behavior among entrepreneurs. They argue normative language that is used to discuss commercial entrepreneurship and social entrepreneurship impacts the kind of entrepreneurs selecting into that organizational form. Specifically, their study found that in socie-ties with strong normative gender stereotypes in language, male entrepreneurs tend to select into commercial entrepreneurship and female entrepreneurs tend to select into social entrepreneurship. Indeed, Linguistic Relativity theory (Sapir, 1921, 1951; Whorf, 1956; Lucy, 1997) highlights how structural differences in lan-guage systems influence how an actor's thoughts and thus language are a useful paradigm to understand the entrepreneurial phenomenon.

Linguistic methods

Linguistics is concerned with the nature of language and, therefore, linguis-tic analysis examines the syntactical, semantic, and morphological structures of langue. Syntax surrounds how words are juxtaposed to form sentences, semantics examines the meaning of words in context, and morphology concerns the actual structure of words. Contrastingly, most discourse and narrative analysis is qualita-tive and concerned with larger units than the sentence and structure of the sen-tence. However, in linguistic analysis there are a variety of quantitative approaches and mixed, quantitative, and qualitative methods used to examine language.

Computational linguistics levers statistical methods to examine insights from large amounts of texts that cannot be hand coded (McEnery and Hardie, 2011; O'Keeffe and McCarthy, 2010; Baker, 2012).

One method that garners great insight into individual use of language and the underlying meaning is computational linguistics, which is the juxtaposition of linguistics and computer and uses computer aided technology to explore various types of linguistic information ranging from the word, sentence, to entire corpora level of analysis. Specifically, linguistic phenomena are explored via computer analysis to investigate formal correctness, language structure, and computational integration, and to examine the specific grammatical structures of language. One specific promising avenue of computational linguistics to garner greater insight into what language represents and the meaning attached is corpus linguistics. Corpus linguistics explores aspects of grammar and langue such as word parsing, lexigraphy, collocation, parts of speech tagging, and terminology extraction and thus can break down language at the grammatical and syntactical level or the larger discourse level to statistically analyse langue.

Corpus linguistics is a set of methods for exploring a language in a corpus, text, or a body of texts that allows for a rich depiction of meaning, patterns, and impacts of words embedded in a context (Biber and Reppen, 2012) both qualitatively and quantitatively (Biber et al., 1998). This multi-method approach aids in the understanding of patterns of words and meanings, moving beyond just decontextualized frequency to infer meaning, a large deviation from standard computer aided content analysis (Pollach, 2012) or a bibliometric study. Moreover, Pollach (2012) argues that corpus linguist methods can be more useful and lead to deeper insights than content analysis by moving beyond the "surface features" of a text, instead determining patterns that can be quantified in a large corpus. With this method, normalized keyword frequencies, dispersions, collocations for both words and phrases (phraseology), concordancing or keywords in context (KWIC), among other suggested analytical techniques, are emphasized. Keywords are significant words that when investigated in context reveal patterns of meanings. Further, phraseology examines idioms and phrases to help represent the true meaning of a document. This is important because context-specific domains use a myriad of unique phrases, such as resource base view, that are captured in phrase searches but missed in single word searches. In addition to descriptive statistics, such as dispersion and normalized frequency or keywords and phrases, words are used with one another via collocation analysis with hierarchical clustering, correspondence analysis, and multidimensional scaling. Stubbs (1995) describes collocation as a relationship of habitual co-occurrence between words, which according to Chen (2013, p.167) creates "higher level structures from word-occurrence patterns in text." Collocation analysis is important because it makes salient patterns in language and meanings evident which would not be possible to infer from just frequency alone (Pollach, 2012). There are two assumptions about the function and importance of co-occurrence analysis. First, when two words or phrases co-occur in the same document, there is an association between the words (Cambrosio et al.,

1993), and second, the co-occurrence is correlated with patterns, shared interests/ language, and different research problems and themes (Braam et al., 1991). Further, concordancing examines the KWIC to explore the context within which words/ phrases are embedded to ensure appropriate contextualization of all analysis. Examining the word in context both quantitatively and qualitatively is vital because words have a myriad of meanings and can change dependent on the context they are used in, and thus we investigate word and phrase usage in context.

Applying linguistics to the entrepreneurial process: new directions

This chapter adds to the ongoing debate regarding the power of Linguistic Relativity (see Gumperz and Levinson, 1996). After reviewing prior studies, we suggest several promising directions for future research on linguistics institutions in entrepreneurship. First, current research at the intersection of entrepreneurship and linguistics focuses on the foundational linguistic structure element of grammar, complementing extant work at higher levels (e.g. semantics, metaphors). This work could be extended to look at cross-linguistic differences in semantics and context. Future research can examine future tense and verb or satellite-framing as aspects of semantic structure that could also influence entrepreneurial behavior. At the most basic level, entrepreneurship has varying meanings across languages, which may be due to historical and linguistic differences. French scholars such as Cantillon (1755) argued that entrepreneurs engaged in exchanges for profit and exercised business judgment in the face of uncertainty; as did English scholars (e.g., Marshall, 1890; Mill, 1848) who used terms such as "adventurer." These strong future tense definitions that highlight uncertainty are in contrast to weak future tense definitions that focus on "undertaking," as in German, Danish, Norwegian, and Swedish. Furthermore, around the world, the term "entrepreneur" has a male, rather than gender neutral or female connotation (Ahl, 2006; De Bruin et al., 2007), which may be a semantic outcome of linguistic structure. As another example, the concept of entrepreneurial "passion" motivates English-speaking employees (Cardon, 2008), but may not translate into another language. For instance, the Finnish term for passion has an entirely different connotation around high levels of emotion and a lack of rationality and seriousness. Enquiries about passion will be offensive to some Finnish entrepreneurs (Brännback, Lång, Carsrud, and Terjesen, 2014:10). These examples illustrate the imperative to test established and emerging entrepreneurship scales in different language settings because linguistic structure may impact semantics and cognition.

Second, prior studies indicate significant patterns in terms of authors' geographical bases and corresponding preferences for certain topics, worldviews, and methodologies in entrepreneurship research (Brush, Manolova, and Edelman, 2008; Davidsson, 2013), which might be explained by researchers' linguistic structures. For example, research on metaphors, including in entrepreneurship, is predominantly conducted by individuals whose native languages are satellite-framed and naturally characterized by metaphors, i.e. English, Dutch, Finnish, and Swedish.

Future work should examine how researchers' native language structure influences research preferences, processes, and operationalizations. Moreover, bicultural/ bilingual or transnational individuals (that is, individuals who are truly able to equally negotiate two linguistic spaces) may possess a special ability to navigate distinct linguistic structures, and may engage in entrepreneurial behavior differently than monocultural/monolingual individuals.

Third, Linguistic Relativity perspectives hold promise for other investigations in entrepreneurship and management. In entrepreneurship, researchers could examine linguistic differences in discovery, evaluation, or exploitation. In management, there may be applications for interpreting international mergers and acquisitions or alliances that involve companies with varying linguistic structures. As an example, a growing body of international business research illustrates that language has important influences on the structure of organizations, for example in mergers and acquisitions of companies (Tietze and Dick, 2013; Marschan-Piekkari et al., 1999). We could extend this work by examining the structure of entrepreneurial organizations.

Fourth, recent work has highlighted the need for qualitative studies in international business (Birkinshaw et al., 2011) and entrepreneurship (Neergard and Ulhøi, 2007). Qualitative methods such as observing entrepreneurs' interactions, for example transnational entrepreneurs trying to negotiate different boundaries, may be required. Of course, this necessitates the use of researchers whose own bicultural abilities can understand these interactions. Furthermore, within entrepreneurship, there is evidence of cross-cultural variation in cognitive scripts associated with venture-creation decisions (Mitchell, 2000) and in semantic categories of entrepreneurial metaphors (Hyrsky, 1999), which may, in part, reflect underlying linguistic structure. An understanding of the role of linguistic structure may provide insights into the higher levels of language, answering calls for a better understanding of the interrelationships between narration, drama, metaphor, discourse, and deconstruction in entrepreneurship (Hjorth and Steyaert, 2004). In relation to the availability of textual data representing how entrepreneurs talk, there are great opportunities to gain deeper insight into how entrepreneurs think and behave. Unfortunately, conventional qualitative discourse analysis (Leitch and Palmer, 2010) and narrative analysis are limited in empirically exploring large amounts of text.

References

Ahl, H. (2006). Why research on women entrepreneurs needs new directions. *Entrepreneurship Theory & Practice*, 30(5), 595–621.

Baker, P. (2012). Acceptable bias?: Using corpus linguistics methods with critical discourse analysis. *Critical Discourse Studies*, 9(3) 247–56.

Biber, D. & Reppen, R. (2012). Corpus linguistics. In D. Biber & R. Reppen (Eds), *Corpus Linguistics*. London: SAGE, pp. 151–70.

Biber, D., Conrad, S. & Reppen, R. (1998). *Corpus Linguistics: Investigating Language Structure and Use.* Cambridge, UK: Cambridge University Press.

Birkinshaw, J., Brannen, M. Y. & Tung, R. L. (2011). From a distance and generalizable to up close and grounded: Reclaiming a place for qualitative methods in international business research. *Journal of International Business Studies*, 42(5), 573–81.

Boroditsky, L. (2010). How the languages we speak shape the ways we think: The FAQs. In M. J. Spivey, K. McRae & M. Joanisse (Eds), *The Cambridge Handbook of Psycholinguistics*. New York, NY: Cambridge University Press. pp. 615–32.

Boroditsky, L. (2011). How language shapes thought. *Scientific American*, 304(2), 62–5.

Boroditsky, L. & Gaby, A. (2010). Remembrances of times east: Absolute spatial representations of time in an Australian Aboriginal community. *Psychological Science*, 21(11), 1635–9.

Braam, R. R., Moed, H. F. & Van Raan, A. F. (1991). Mapping of science by combined co-citation and word analysis, I. Structural aspects. *Journal of the American Society for Information Science and Technology*, 42(4), 233–51.

Brännback, M., Lång, S., Carsrud, A. L. & Terjesen, S. (2014). Cross-cultural studies in entrepreneurship: A note on culture and language. In A. L. Carsrud & M. Brännback (Eds), *Handbook of Research Methods and Applications in Entrepreneurship and Small Business*. Cheltenham, UK: Edward Elgar, pp. 156–76.

Brannen, M. Y. (2004). When Mickey loses face: Recontextualization, semantic fit, and the semiotics of foreignness. *Academy of Management Review*, 29(4), 593–616.

Brush, C. G., Manolova, T. S. & Edelman, L. F. (2008). Properties of emerging organizations: An empirical test. *Journal of Business Venturing*, 23(5), 547–66.

Cambrosio, A., Limoges, C., Courtial, J. P. & Laville, F. (1993). Historical scientometrics? Mapping over 70 years of biological safety research with co-word analysis. *Scientometrics*, 27(2), 119–43.

Cantillon, R. (1755). Essai sur la nature du commerce en général. *History of Economic Thought Books*. United States: General Books.

Cardon, M. S. (2008). Is passion contagious? The transference of entrepreneurial passion to employees. *Human Resource Management Review*, 18(2), 77–86.

Chen, M. K. (2013). The effect of language on economic behavior: Evidence from savings rates, health behaviors, and retirement assets. *The American Economic Review*, 103(2), 167.

Cutler, A. (2012). *Native Listening: Language Experience and the Recognition of Spoken Words*. Cambridge, MA: MIT Press.

Davidsson, P. (2013). Some reflection on research "schools" and geographies, *Entrepreneurship & Regional Development*, 25, 100–110.

De Bruin, A., Brush, C. G. & Welter, F. (2007). Advancing a framework for coherent research on women's entrepreneurship. *Entrepreneurship Theory & Practice*, 31(3), 323–39.

Fenko, A., Otten, J. J. & Schifferstein, H. N. (2010). Describing product experience in different languages: The role of sensory modalities. *Journal of Pragmatics*, 42(12), 3314–27.

Gartner, W. B. (2007). Entrepreneurial narrative and a science of the imagination. *Journal of Business Venturing*, 22(5), pp. 613–27.

Gartner, W. B. (2010). A new path to the waterfall: A narrative on the use of entrepreneurial narrative. *International Journal of Small Business*, 28 (1), 6–19.

Gartner, W. B. & Ingram, A. (2013). What do entrepreneurs talk about when they talk about failure? The Babson 2013 edition of the *Frontiers of Entrepreneurship Research*.

Garud, R. & Giuliani, A. P. (2013). A narrative perspective on entrepreneurial opportunities. *Academy of Management Review*, 38(1), 157–60.

Givati, Y. & Troiano, U. (2012). Law, economics, and culture: Theory of mandated benefits and evidence from maternity leave policies. *Journal of Law and Economics*, 55(2), 339–64.

Gumperz, J. J. & Levinson, S. C. (1996). Introduction to part I. *Rethinking Linguistic Relativity*, 21–36.

Hechavarría, D. M. & Ingram, A. E. (2016). The entrepreneurial gender divide: Hegemonic masculinity, emphasized femininity and organizational forms. *International Journal of Gender and Entrepreneurship*, 8(3), 242–81.

Hechavarría, D. M., Terjesen, S. A., Stenholm, P., Brännback, M. & Lång, S. (2017). More than words: Do gendered linguistic structures widen the gender gap in entrepreneurial activity? *Entrepreneurship Theory & Practice*, http://dx.doi.org/10.1111/etap.12278.

Hjorth, D. & Steyaert, C. (2004). *Narrative and Discursive Approaches in Entrepreneurship: A Second Movements in Entrepreneurship Book*. Cheltenham, UK: Edward Elgar.

Hock, H. H. & Joseph, B. D. (1996). Language history. *Language Change, and Language Relationship (An Introduction to Historical and Comparative Linguistics)*. Berlin/New York: De Gruyter.

Hyrsky, K. (1999). Entrepreneurial metaphors and concepts: An exploratory study. *International Small Business Journal*, 18(1), 13–34.

Johansson, A. & Strømnes, F. (1995). Cultural differences in occupational accidents. Part I: Theoretical background. In *44th Nordic Meeting on Work Environment, Nantali, Finland*.

Kay, P. & Kempton, W. (1984). What is the Sapir–Whorf hypothesis? *American Anthropologist*, 86(1), 65–79.

Kramsch, C. (1998). *Language and Culture*. Oxford, UK: Oxford University Press.

Leitch, S., & Palmer, I. (2010). Analysing texts in context: Current practices and new protocols for critical discourse analysis in organization studies. *Journal of Management Studies*, 47(6), 1194–212.

Levinson, S. C. & Wilkins, D. P. (Eds). (2006). The background to the study of the language of space. In *Grammars of Space: Explorations in Cognitive Diversity*. Cambridge: Cambridge University Press, pp. 1–23.

Lucy, J. A. (1997). Linguistic relativity. *Annual Review of Anthropology*, 1(1), 291–312.

Lucy, J. A. & Gaskins, S. (2001). Grammatical categories and the development of classification preferences: A comparative approach. In M. Bowerman & S. Levinson (Eds), *Language Acquisition and Conceptual Development*. Cambridge: Cambridge University Press, pp. 257–83.

Marschan-Piekkari, R., Welch, D. & Welch, L. (1999). In the shadow: The impact of language on structure, power and communication in the multinational. *International Business Review*, 8(4), 421–40.

Marshall, A. (1890). *Principles of Economics*. London: Macmillan and Co.

McEnery, T. & Hardie, A. (2011). *Corpus Linguistics: Method, Theory and Practice*. Cambridge: Cambridge University Press.

Mill, J. S. (1848) *Principles of Political Economy with Some of Their Applications to Social Philosophy*. London: John W. Parker.

Mitchell, R. (2000). Anniversary article. Applied linguistics and evidence-based classroom practice: the case of foreign language grammar pedagogy. *Applied Linguistics*, 21(3), 281–303.

Neergaard, H. & Ulhøi, J. P. (Eds). (2007). *Handbook of Qualitative Research Methods in Entrepreneurship*. Cheltenham, UK: Edward Elgar.

North, D. C. (2005). *Understanding the Process of Economic Change*. Princeton, NJ: Princeton University Press.

O'Keeffe, A. & McCarthy, M. (Eds). (2010). *The Routledge Handbook of Corpus Linguistics*. Abingdon, UK: Routledge.

Pinker S. (1989). *Learnability and cognition: The acquisition of argument structure*, Cambridge, MA: MIT Press.

Pollach, I. (2012). Taming textual data: The contribution of corpus linguistics to computer-aided text analysis. *Organizational Research Methods*, 15(2), 263–87.

Port, R. F. (2010). Rich memory and distributed phonology. *Language Sciences*, 32(1), 313.

Puntoni, S., De Langhe, B. & Van Osselaer, S. M. (2008). Bilingualism and the emotional intensity of advertising language. *Journal of Consumer Research*, 35(6), 1012–25.

Rubinstein, A. (2000). *Economics and Language: Five Essays*, The Churchill Lectures in Economic Theory. Cambridge: Cambridge University Press.

Ruebottom, T. (2013). The microstructures of rhetorical strategy in social entrepreneurship: Building legitimacy through heroes and villains. *Journal of Business Venturing*, 28(1), 98–116.

Sapir, E. (1921). *Language*. New York, NY: Harcourt Brace.

Sapir, E. (1951). The status of linguistics as a science. In D. Mandelbaum (Ed.), *Selected Writings*. Berkeley, CA: University of California Press. Originally published in *Language*, 5, 207–14.

Saussure, F. D. (1970). *Curso de Linguistica General*, 8th edn., Buenos Aires: Losada.

Slobin, D. I. (2001). 14 Form-function relations: how do children find out what they are? *Language Acquisition and Conceptual Development*, 3, 159.

Stubbs, M. (1995). Collocations and cultural connotations of common words. *Linguistics and Education*, 7(4), 379–90.

Terjesen, S., Hessels, J. & Li, D. (2016). Comparative international entrepreneurship: A review and research agenda. *Journal of Management*, 42(1), 299–344.

Tietze, S. & Dick, P. (2013). The victorious English language: Hegemonic practices in the management academy. *Journal of Management Inquiry*, 22(1), 122–34.

Venkataraman, S., Sarasvathy, S. D., Dew, N. & Forster, W. R. (2013). Of narratives and artifacts. *Academy of Management Review*, 38(1), 163–6.

West, J. & Graham, J. L. (2004). A linguistic-based measure of cultural distance and its relationship to managerial values. *Management International Review*, 44, 239–60.

Whorf, B. L. (1956). Language, thought, and reality. In J. B. Carroll (Ed.), *Selected writings of Benjamin Lee Whorf*. Cambridge, MA: MIT Press. Originally published in *Technology Review*, 42, 229–31, 247–8.

Index

abstract conceptualizations 182
achievement motivation (NAch) 47–8, 57
achievement values 74, 76
action 8, 10, 182
  attitudes 89–90
  and entrepreneurial intention 10, later
  group 89, 94
  model of 111–12
  predictions of 62
  social 89–90, 93
  transformation of intention to 62
  see also culture; Theory of Reasoned Action
    (TRA); Theory of Trying (ToT)
action control 113
affect-based motivations 128–9, 133, 135
  compassion 126, 131–2, 135
  identity 130–31
  passion 9, 126, 129–30, 135
Agreeableness dimension 55, 56
Ajzen, I. 7–8, 10, 51–2, 88, 90, 107, 108, 109–10,
  115
  see also Theory of Planned Behavior (TPB)
Al-Jubari et al. 9–10
alertness 128
apprehension 182, 185
Ardichvili et al. 123
asymmetric relationships between variables 143,
  146
attitude towards a behavior (ATB) 109
attitude(s) 10, 11, 89–90
autonomy 9–10
average variance extracted (AVE) index 152

Bagozzi, R.P. 89, 94, 94–5, 96, 98–9
Bagozzi, R.P. and Warshaw, P.R. 92
Bandura, A. 52
Barrett, M.A. and Moores, K. 86–7
behavior
  consumer 89
  goal-directed 90
  influence of situations 53–4
  observable 49

  past 92
  prosocial 131
  see also entrepreneurial behavior; Theory of
    Planned Behavior (TPB)
behavioral beliefs 108
beliefs 108–109
belonging 131
bicultural individuals 10
binary classification 149–50, 157
Biraglia, E. and Kadile, V. 9
Bird, B. 9, 167–8
Borodiskty, L. and Gaby, A. 204
business plans 114–15, 116

CANOE 55, 56
Cantillon, R. 209
Cardon et al. 129
Carland et al. 48
Carsrud, A.L. 18, 39
Carsrud, A.L. and Brannback, M. 49, 50, 86
Cassar, G. 10
centrality 170
Chandler, G.N. and Lyon, D.W. 144
classification field 148–50
Classification Trees (CT) 156
clustering algorithms 15–16
co-occurrence analysis 208–209
cognitive-based motivations 125–8, 133, 134
collective intentions 84–5
  see also we-intentions
collectivism 64, 68, 69–72
collocation 208
comparability, principle of 108
compassion 126, 131–2, 135
  self-compassion 131–2
Competing Values Framework (CVF) 171
competitiveness 64, 68, 74
composite reliability (CR) 152
comprehension 182, 185
computational linguistics 208
concordancing 209
concrete experiences 182

configurational analysis 142, 143
  and entrepreneurship research 145–6
  FsQCA *see* FsQCA
confusion matrix of binary classification 149
Conscientiousness dimension 55, 56
consumer behavior 89
contingency matrix of binary classification 149
continuity in family business 87
control beliefs 108, 109
corpus linguistics 208
Coviello, N.E. and Jones, M.V. 144
created opportunities 123, 124
creativity 9
Crisp-Set QCA 146
Cronbach's Alpha 152
cultural relativity 205
culture 9, 62–3, 67–8
  attitude to risk and uncertainty dimension 64,
    68, 74–5
  collectivist 63
  competitiveness and attitude to others
    dimension 64, 68, 74
  definition 63
  economic development and 68, 69, 70, 76
  individualism-collectivism dimension 64, 68,
    69–72
  individualistic 63
  influence of 64–7
  intra-national differences 77
  masculinity 63, 64, 74
  measuring 63
    Hofstede 63
    Schwartz 63–4
    Steenkamp 64
  personal preferences 65, 66, 69
  power and social stratification dimension 64,
    68, 72–3
  social cognition 64–5, 66–7, 69–70, 71, 72–3,
    74, 75, 76
  societal legitimation 65–6, 68–9, 69, 70, 72,
    73, 75
  see also organizational culture
Customer Relationship Management (CRM) 187

Davidsson, P. 184, 191
Dencker et al. 178
developed countries 68, 69, 73
  individualism 72
  social cognition 71
developing countries 68, 69, 70, 73
  collectivism 72
  individualism 70–71

Dheer, R.J.S. and Lenartowicz, T. 9–10
discovered opportunities 123–4
disinclined abstainers 106
disinclined actors 106, 116, 117
distinctiveness 131, 170
Donald, Merlin 205–206
Dutton et al. 131

economic development 67–8, 69, 70, 76
education 144, 174
effectuation theory 87, 144
efficiency-driven economies 53
effortful decision making model 95, 96
egalitarianism 64, 73
emotional motivations 129
Emotionality dimension 56
empathy 9, 132
endurance 170–71
entrepreneurial behavior 9, 47, 48, 49, 50
entrepreneurial cognition 125–8
  definition 161
entrepreneurial identity 125, 129, 130–31
  affiliations 165
  defining and constructing 163–7
  demographic groups 165
  family stage of life 165
  human capital attributes 165
  linkages with organizational identity 170–71
  see also identity
entrepreneurial intention 51
  and action 8, 10
  antecedents 8, 10, 144
  collective 84–5
  concept of 8
  configurational analysis 142, 143
    and entrepreneurship research 145–6 *see
      also* FsQCA
  definitions of 8–9
  intention-behavior relationship 105–106
    empirical support for 109–11
    temporal continuity 108
  literature review of research 143–6
  models of 89–93
  overview of research
    betweenness centrality 15, 20
    closeness centrality 15–16
    co-authorship analysis methodology 13–14,
      17, 18–19, 20, 21, 29–30, 33, 34, 35,
      41–2
    co-authorship graph 16–17
    conclusion 22–3
    data collection 12, 33

double network dimension between
    researchers 20–21
emerging topics 21–2
entity disambiguation 12–13
institutions and collaborations 31
journal sources 12, 16, 27–9
keywords 21, 32
Levenshtein distance 13
methodology of study 11–16
node degree 14–15, 20
results of study 16–22
term analysis over time 17–18, 36–7
thematic blocks 22, 46
topic-author and topic-topic analysis 18–19
Z-score 17, 18, 37
as predictor of behavior 62, 105, 106, 106–7,
    117
research on 88–9
SEE model 8, 11
studies and models of 7–8, 9–10
TPB model 2, 7, 8, 10–11
see also family business; implementation
    intentions; succession intentions; we-
    intentions
entrepreneurial language 204
culture and 205
as an institution 206
via a linguistic lens 205–6
see also linguistics
entrepreneurial learning (EL) 178, 179–81
definitions 181
entrepreneurial opportunities 178, 179, 181,
    182–4
    definitions 183
    relationship with 184–5
entrepreneurs' stock and flow 178, 180
entrepreneurs' stock of pre-entry experiences
    and outcomes 179–80
NVIs case study see NVIs case study
as a process/flow 179, 180
see also Experiential Learning Theory (ELT);
    opportunity development
entrepreneurial motivations 122–3
affect-based motivations 128–9, 133, 135
    compassion 126, 131–2, 135
    identity 130–31
    passion 9, 126, 129–30, 135
cognitive-based motivations 125–8, 133, 134
cognitive processes theories 122, 123
and context 132–3, 135
desire for self-starting 122
as a multidimensional construct 124, 134

compassion 126, 131–2, 135
entrepreneurial identity 125, 126, 129,
    130–31
motivations 125
opportunity recognition (OR) 127
passion 9, 126, 129–30, 135
opportunity recognition (OR) 123–4, 127, 132,
    133, 134, 135
personality and traits theories 122, 123
entrepreneurs
achievement motivation (NAch) 47–8
attributes and traits 163
differences from other people 76–7
entrepreneurial parents 53
individual cognitions 49–50
influence of culture 64
interpersonal competitiveness 48
personality see personality
psychology of 49–50
technological innovation 164
typology 164
unique personality traits 50
see also entrepreneurial identity; identity
entrepreneurship
academic conceptualizations 164
activities 164
borrowing other disciplines' theories 50, 51–2
    liability of oldness 52
cognitive variables 51
as a collective endeavour 70
cross-country differences 53
economic development and 67–8, 76
education and training 174
individualism and collectivism 69–72
local cultural influences 53
pre-entry experiences and knowledge 178, 179,
    179–80
psychological theory 51, 52, 57
relevance of research 2
see also opportunity development
Entrepreneurship and Regional Development 56
Entrepreneurship: Theory & Practice (ET&P) 51,
    56
equifinality, notion of 146
Erdős, Paul 15
expectancy-value conceptualization 108
experiences 181, 182
Experiential Learning Theory (ELT) 179, 180,
    181–2, 193, 195
dialectics 182
environment and 182
Extraversion dimension 55, 56

factor-driven economies 53
family business 84, 86
   background 153
   categorization of 87, 88
   effectuation and succession behaviors 86–7
   shared intentions 93
   social norms 87–8
   stewardship 88, 94
   see also succession intentions; we-intentions
feedback loops 109
formal and informal institutions 65, 69, 70, 71, 74
founders' identity 130, 166
   sense-giving 166
Frieda's Inc. 87, 95
FsQCA 142–3, 146, 157, 158
   binary classification 149–50, 157
   case study 151
      data collection and descriptive analysis
         151–2
      reliability and validity 152
      results 152–5
   complex solutions 148, 154
   core conditions 148
   data calibration 147, 149
   differences with regression analysis 148
   intermediate solutions 148
   parsimonious solutions 148
   prediction based on output configurations
      148–51
   prediction performance 155–7
      classification performance 155–6
      true negative rate (TNR) 156
      true positive rate (TPR) 155, 156
   as a predictive model 146–7
   summary of 147–8
Fuzzy-set Qualitative Comparative Analysis
   (FsQCA) *see* FsQCA

Gartner et al. 165
Gartner, W.B. 48, 52, 88
Garud, R. and Giuliani, A.P. 183
GEM (Global Entrepreneurship Monitor)
   research 53, 93
gender 10, 153, 154, 155, 207
George et al. 123
Gilbert, M. 93–4
Global Entrepreneurship Monitor *see* GEM
   (Global Entrepreneurship Monitor) research
GLOBE project 76
goal desires 91, 95, 97
goal-directed behavior 90
goals 87, 91, 95, 96

Goldberg, L.R. 54
Gollwitzer, P.M. and Sheeran, P. 114, 117–18
Gregoire et al. 123, 128
Gross Domestic Product per capita (GDPpc) 67,
   68
group action 89, 94
Gruber et al. 178, 185

Hansen et al. 123
HEXACO 56
Hofstede, G. 63
Honesty/Humility dimension 56
human capital 73, 128
   research 179

I-intentions 93, 95, 97
identity 125, 126, 129, 130–31
   conflicting identities 131
      belonging 131
      distinctiveness 131
      otherness 131
      sameness 131
   demographic groups 165
   founders' 130
   Identity Theory 163
   organizational identity 165–6
   personal identity 162, 164, 170
   role 130–31
   self-definitions 165–6
   social identity theory (SIT) 87–8, 92, 94, 162,
      163, 170
   see also entrepreneurial identity
Identity Theory 163
if-then intentions *see* implementation intentions
if-then plans 116, 117
implementation intentions 96
   automated processes 113
   business plans 114–15
   cognitive 116
   definition 111
   effect size estimates 114
   empirical support for 113–15
   ideas for future research 115–17
   identifying opportunities to act 112–13, 113
   intention activation 112
   intention elaboration 112–13
   intention variability 112
   intentions-behavior relationship 111–12
      causal factors 115, 117
      quality 114, 117
      self-regulation 114, 117
   model of action phases

action phase 112
    post-action phase 112
    pre-action phase 111–12
    pre-decision phase 111
    poor planners 114, 116
in-group members 94
inclined abstainers 106, 115–16, 116
inclined actors 106, 110, 115, 116
income levels 67, 68, 69
indirect antecedents of intentions 108–109
individualism 63
    and collectivism 64, 68, 69–72
innovation 10, 64
innovation-driven economies 53
institutional theory 165, 205–206
intention *see* entrepreneurial intention
intention activation 112
intention elaboration 112–13
intention variability 112
intentionality 167–8, 171
International Personality Item Pool (IPIP)
    55
iTech 186, 187, 190, 192, 194, 197
Item Response Theory (IRT) 55

Jacoby Construction, Inc. 100
Journal of Business Venturing (JBV) 51, 56
Journal of Small Business Management 56

Kautonen et al. 115, 115–16
Kautonen, Teemu 18, 19
knowledge 128, 181–2, 194
    pre-entry 178, 179, 179–80
    see also prior knowledge
Kolb, D.A. 180
Kolvereid, L. 10
Kolvereid, L. and Isaksen, E. 10
Krueger et al. 9
Krueger, Norris 18, 40, 144

labour 67, 68
labour market 70
LaKs 186, 187, 190, 192, 193, 194, 197, 198
language 56, 57
    see also entrepreneurial language
learning
    behavioral theories of 182
    behaviorist approach 180
    cognitivist approach 180
    constructivist approach 180
    social learning approach 180
    see also entrepreneurial learning (EL)

Lee, R. and Jones, O. 178
Levenshtein distance 13
Lévi-Strauss, Claude 167
liability of oldness 52
LibrT 186, 187–8, 190, 192, 194, 195, 197
Liñán, Francisco 18, 19
Linguistic Relativity theory 205, 206, 207, 210
linguistics
    application to entrepreneurial processes
        209–10
    computational linguistics 208
    corpus linguistics 208
    definition 204, 205
    disciplines 205
    and entrepreneurship 206–207
    gender and 207
    methods 207–209
    see also entrepreneurial language
locus of control 144
Lortie, J. and Castogiovanni, G. 11
Los Angeles Dodgers Major League Baseball
    team 100
low power 73

masculinity 63, 64, 74
mastery values 74
mathematical statistics 145–6
McDougall, P.P. and Oviatt, B.M. 144
metaphors 210
Miller, D. and Le Breton-Miller, I. 87
Mischel, W. 53–4
moral obligation 9
morphology 207
motivation 10, 122
    see also entrepreneurial motivations
Msport 186, 188, 190, 192, 194, 195–7
multi-valued QCA 146
Muñoz, P. and Kibler, E. 146

necessity analysis 155
necessity entrepreneurship 74
Neuroticism dimension 55, 56
new venture ideas (NVIs) *see* NVIs case study
normative beliefs 108, 144
norms and rules 65–6, 69
North, D.C. 204, 205–206
NVIs case study 178, 179, 199–200
    case selection 186–8, 189–91
        iTech 186, 187, 190, 192, 194, 197
        LaKs 186, 187, 190, 192, 193, 194, 197, 198
        LibrT 186, 187–8, 190, 192, 194, 195, 197
        Msport 186, 188, 190, 192, 194, 195–7

PharmaX 186, 187, 190, 192, 193, 194, 195, 198
SolEn 186, 188, 190–91, 192, 194, 197, 198
data analysis 189
data collection 188–9
results 189–99
  development process 191–2, 193
  ends-side (demand-side) 189, 190, 198
  interface between NVI development and learning 195–9
  means-side (supply-side) 189, 190, 192, 198
  new venture ideas 189–91
  NVIs as a learning process 192–5
  social context in NVI development 193–5

Obschonka et al. 10
openness 131
Openness to experience dimension 55, 56
opportunity development 178, 179, 181, 182–4
  definitions 183
  discovery and creation 183, 184, 192
  external enablers 184, 191
  individuals' cognitive processes 185
  means-ends perspective 183
  NVIs see NVIs case study
  opportunity confidence 184, 191
  relationship with learning 184–5
  venture ideas 183–4
  see also entrepreneurial learning (EL)
opportunity recognition (OR) 123–4, 127, 132, 133, 134, 135
  imprinting mechanisms 124, 133
  reflexivity mechanisms 124, 133
optimal distinctiveness 131
organization theory 165
organizational culture 161, 166, 174
  cognitive cultural creation pathway 169
    centrality 170
    distinctiveness 170
    endurance 170–71
    pathway test 171–3
  definition 166–7
  education and training 174
  in an emerging organization 167–9
  founders' identity 166
  founders' influence 168–9
  organic development 169
  recognition of change 171
  themes 167
organizational identification 166

organizational identity 165–6
  linkages with entrepreneurial identity 170–71
other-regarding compassion 131, 132
out-group members 94
outlier individuals 77
Ozer, D.J. 54

Packard Marketing Group case 89, 100
Panel Studies of Entrepreneurial Dynamics (PSED) 55, 93
passion 9, 126, 129–30, 135, 209
past behavior 92
perceived behavioral control (PBC) 90, 109, 144, 153, 154, 155
perceived desirability 11
perceived feasibility 11
personal identity 162, 164, 170
personality
  "Big Five" factors 55, 56
  entrepreneurial 48–9, 49–50
    single 53
  external strategy approach 54
  internal strategy approach 54
  intuitive strategy approach 54
  linguistic issues 56
  observable behaviors 49
  traits and types 54–5
  unique traits 50
Pettigrew, A.M. 168
PharmaX 186, 187, 190, 192, 193, 194, 195, 198
poor planners 114, 116
Port, R.F. 206
power 64, 68, 72–3
power distance 63
practices, cultural 65–6, 68–9, 69, 70, 72, 73, 75
prior knowledge 123, 128, 134, 135, 185
prosocial behavior 131
prospect theory 144
psychological traits approach 65
psychology
  of entrepreneurs 49–50
  entrepreneurship and 51, 52, 57
  situational approach 53–4
  social 51
  see also personality

Qualitative Comparative Analysis 157
  traditional utilization of 146–7
  see also FsQCA
Qualitative Comparative Analysis (QCA) 142, 145–6
Quine–McCluskey minimization procedure 148

Rae, D. and Carswell, M. 180
Ragin, C.C. 142
Ravasi, D. and Schultz, M. 165–6
reflection 182
regression analysis 144, 145, 148
resources 71
Roig-Tierno et al. 146
role identity 130–31

sameness 131
Schein, E.H. 167, 168, 171
Schwartz, S.H. 63–4, 74
Searle, J.R. 84, 85, 93
self-compassion 131–2
self-efficacy 9, 51, 52, 88, 108, 109, 116, 152, 153,
      154, 155
self-employment 144
self-identity 130
semantics 207, 209
sense-giving 166
sense-making 166
Shane et al. 122, 129
Shane, S. and Venkataraman, S. 182, 183
Shapéro Entrepreneurial Event (SEE) model 8, 11
Shaver, K.G. 48–9, 51, 52
Sheeran, P. 105–106, 110
Shepherd, Dean 20, 21, 22
situational approach 53–4
Skinner, B.F. 53
Small Business Economics 56
Smircich, L. 167
Sniehotta et al. 145
social action 89–90, 93
social capital 153, 154, 155
social cognition 64–5, 66–7, 69–70, 71, 72–3, 74,
      75, 76
social–cognitive theory of entrepreneurship 128
social entrepreneurship 9, 21
social groups 94–5
social identity theory (SIT) 87–8, 92, 94, 162,
      163, 170
social learning 194
social norms 11, 152, 153, 154, 155
social psychology 51
social status 72–3
social stratification 64, 68, 72–3
social support 9
societal legitimation 65–6, 68–9, 69, 70, 72, 73, 75
SolEn 186, 188, 190–91, 192, 194, 197, 198
Souitaris et al. 143–4
start-ups 62, 63, 64, 67
   founding teams 168

in-group collectivism 71
in-group relationships 70
   high rates of 63, 69
individualism 72
individualistic cultural practices 71
organic development of culture 169
organizational culture and 168
social legitimacy 66
stakeholders' culture 168
values 166, 168, 169, 170
statistics 145–6
Stavrou, E.T. 84
Steenkamp, J.B. 64
Stevenson, H. and Jarillo, J.C. 123
stewardship 88, 94
subjective norms (SN) 109, 144
succession intentions 84, 85, 99
   control 86
   goals 87, 91, 95
   interpersonal perspective 94–5
   past behavior 92
   plural subject concept 94, 95
   potential for conflict 85, 86, 87
   research on 86
   social norms 85
   see also Theory of Planned Behavior (TPB);
      we-intentions
Suddaby et al. 124
sufficiency analysis 152, 153
supervised learning 149
Support Vector Machines (SVM) 156
Sutton, S. 110
symbolic interactionism 130
symmetrical relationships between variables
      145
syntax 207

Tang et al. 128
Theory of Entrepreneurial Advent 7
Theory of Planned Behavior (TPB) 2, 7, 8, 10–11,
      51–2, 84, 88–9, 90, 92, 105, 115
   imperfect relationships 115
   intention-behavior relationship 109–11
   predicting behavior 107
      assumptions inherent in 107–108
      beliefs 108–109
      evaluations 109
      feedback loops 109
      intentions 109
      intentions to act 109
   variance 110
   weaknesses 142

Theory of Reasoned Action (TRA) 88, 90, 105, 142
Theory of the Entrepreneurial Event model 18
Theory of Trying (ToT) 52, 85, 89, 90–91
  attitudes 91
  desires 91
  goal-directed behavior 92–3
  past behavior 92
  predictors of intention 92
  social norms 91
Thurik, Roy 20
training 174
trait psychology 163
trying *see* Theory of Trying (ToT)
Tuomela, R. 85, 94, 95, 97

uncertainty avoidance 63
unilateral collective intentions 100
unsupervised learning 149

values
  cultural 63, 64–5, 66–7, 69–70, 71, 72–3, 74, 75, 76, 77
  in emerging cultures 168, 169, 170
  of the individual 162, 163
  masculinity/mastery 74
  of the organization 87, 88, 97, 161, 166–7, 168

venture creations 62
venture ideas 183–4
  see also NVIs case study
ventures *see* start-ups
Vogel, P. 183–4

wages 67
Watson, J.B. 53
we-intentions 85, 93, 93–6, 100
  definition 93–4, 94
  measuring 99
  model for 96–9
    collective desire for common goal 96, 97
    collective intentions 98–9
    planning 96
  role of women 87
  shared group-intention 94–5
  social norms 100
  subjective beliefs 95
  unilateral collective intentions 100
  see also succession intentions; Theory of Trying (ToT)
Webb, T.L. and Sheeran, P. 110, 112, 115
Wurthmann, K. 10

Yitshaki, R. and Kropp, F. 132–3

Zhao et al. 10